TO DEFEND THESE RIGHTS

TO DEFEND THESE RIGHTS

Human Rights and the Soviet Union

by Valery Chalidze

Translated from the Russian by Guy Daniels

RANDOM HOUSE NEW YORK

To Andrei Tverdokhlebov,
a founding member of the
Moscow Human Rights Committee

Library of Congress Cataloging in Publication Data
Chalidze, Valerii N   1938–

    To defend these rights.
    Translation of Prava cheloveka i Sovetskii Soiuz.
    Includes bibliographical references.
    I. Civil rights—Russia. I. Title.
Law   342′.47′085   74–9063
ISBN 0–394–48725–7

Manufactured in the United States of America
98765432
First American Edition in the English language

Preface

IN THIS BOOK I survey many of the problems which have concerned participants in the Soviet human rights movement.*

Now Western interest in Soviet human rights problems has increased to the degree that it seems possible to speak of a Western movement to defend human rights in the USSR. This "movement" is expressed in extensive activities in support of the right of Jews to emigrate, in appeals by scientists and writers on behalf of persecuted Soviet colleagues, and the encouraging attention Western psychiatrists have devoted

---

* This book was written in the spring of 1973. Although I have updated the text, I have not commented on some important subsequent events, including *Group 73*, an association formed in Moscow to study the problem of aid to political prisoners and their families; the Yakir-Krasin trial; and the exile of Solzhenitsyn.

For information on these and other recent developments, please consult the *Chronicle of Current Events*, No. 30 et seq. (published in Moscow, samizdat), and the *Chronicle of Human Rights in the USSR*. No. 3 et seq. (published in New York by Khronika Press).

to the misuse of psychiatry in the USSR. Even politicians and businessmen sometimes remember that questions of ethics and human suffering are reasonable issues to raise in connection with the current development of friendly political and trade relations between the USSR and the West.

In addressing those in the West who are interested in this question, I propose that the most important contribution that can be made to the defense of human rights in any country is publicity—making sure that violations of rights and appeals in defense of rights become known to a wide audience. I cannot prove the direct benefit from publicity in every case. But since those who violate human rights strive to prevent any disclosure of their crimes, it is reasonable to suppose that they have studied this matter and understand that publicity restrains their violations of human rights.

And remember, suffering is even more intolerable when a victim knows that he is forgotten, that nobody in the world cares about his pain and destruction.

V. C.

Contents

TO DEFEND THESE RIGHTS

1

The Specifics of Soviet Law.

In this chapter I discuss Communist legal doctrine, the prediction that the state and law will wither away in the bright Communist future, the idea of class discrimination, and the special kind of logic without which Soviet legal doctrine would probably be less workable. This background is vital in order to understand the significance of Soviet legal guarantees of human rights.

Most Soviet lawyers are rather uncultivated people ready to raise the age-old human prejudices typical of the average man to the status of a higher morality. Thus they are guided, in settling the fates of human beings, not only by the ideals of Communist doctrine but by the ideals of the conservative middle classes, who are inclined to reject all free thought and social self-determination. Soviet lawyers (perhaps fortunately) usually perform their duty of regulating legal relations in society without much professional enthusiasm, rather with a feeling of boredom, and in the majority of cases with indifference toward the fate of the irksome

people whose cases they must handle for very slight remuneration. But such matters are properly the object of sociological investigation. I shall not discuss them in detail,
even though it is important to bear in mind the training
and attitudes of the legal profession in assessing the practical functioning of the Soviet legal system. I shall concen-
trate on discussing Soviet legal principles.

THE WITHERING AWAY OF THE STATE AND THE LAW

The Soviet Union has an official ideology, Marxism-Leninism (as interpreted, of course, by the latest Communist
Party congress or plenum of the Central Committee). This
ideology proclaims itself uniquely correct and universal. The
Soviet state system in many respects resembles other states
familiar from history which were also buttressed by uniquely
correct ideologies of different kinds. But in the USSR the
relationship between the state and the individual, based on
the requirements of a uniquely correct ideology, has been
worked out in greater detail, more completely, and with a
greater claim to stability than ever before. The Soviet state
strictly controls much of the socially significant behavior of
its citizens and associations, making certain that this
behavior complies with the requirements of ideological
doctrine. Such control is first of all applied to legal relations
and legal doctrine. In the Soviet Union legal doctrine is
completely subordinated to ideological doctrine.
  Certain consequences of this—in particular, class discrimination—will be discussed here. First, however, I want
to take up the most original aspect of Soviet legal theory,
the thesis that both law and the state will wither away when
communism is built. This thesis was put forward by Communists even before they were in any position to promote
the withering away of law. Immediately after the October
Revolution of 1917 greater hopes were placed in the wither-

ing away of law than turned out to be justified by the future course of events. Some awaited a reign of universal justice, based on the revolutionary legal consciousness of the armed people. Lenin understood the necessity of temporarily employing what he called "bourgeois forms of law," but at the same time he demanded that not the Corpus Juris Civilis but "our revolutionary legal consciousness" be applied to civil legal relations.[1] The courts were instructed, when dealing with both criminal and civil cases, to take as their guide the decrees of the new regime, the policy of the government, and "revolutionary legal consciousness."[2] Certain jurists, getting ahead of themselves, tried to be bolder reformers than Lenin himself. They assumed that law was "the opium of the people" to an even greater extent than religion, and that antilaw propaganda was even more important than antireligious propaganda for the final victory of the Revolution.

In the course of fifty years Soviet law has constantly developed and enriched itself with new precedents, so that today it is a highly regulated system. From this it may seem that the thesis of the withering away of law did not justify itself and has been forgotten, but that is not the case. Great insights are not to be interpreted literally, exactly as they were expressed at some time in the past. Communist theoreticians not only mention this thesis and repeat it in the current Party program[3] but are apparently implementing it gradually. True, this thesis is discussed rather sparingly and not very intelligibly in Soviet legal literature. For example: "Under Communism, law will wither away, but non-juridical normative regulation will remain."[4] It may be, however, that Soviet scholarly literature on the law contains little about this unusual thesis because Soviet jurists do not want to boast of success prematurely.

It is not so simple to trace successes in the withering away of law parallel to the development of Soviet law. This book contains only a few examples illustrating this process. In one sphere, however, the withering away of law in Soviet society has gone rather far. I mean in the interpretation and observance of procedural guarantees.

Lenin believed that "we shall not need a special machine or apparatus for restraint [of individual excesses]: that will be done by the armed people themselves with the same simplicity and ease with which any crowd of civilized people, even in modern society, separates brawlers or prevents the rape of a woman."[5] One may or may not expect such a transformation of legal sanctions, but it is useful to remember that it was planned and is being realized. This transformation, though it may contain much that is attractive, is fraught with potential neglect of procedural safeguards, since it is not clear how to reconcile proper respect for procedural norms with the "simplicity and ease" of action by the public. The Soviet state's achievements in the area of procedural simplification gained lamentable notoriety because of the abuses of the Stalin era.* In many respects the post-Stalin legislative reforms restored respect for procedural norms, but even today the attitude revealed in Soviet legal doctrine and Soviet practice toward the strict observance of these norms justifies speaking of a certain advance in the withering away of law. The main thing here is a disdain—sanctioned by Soviet doctrine—for formalism in legal theory, legislative activity, and juridical practice. Such disdain could be attributed to the very low level of legal training of juridical personnel, but today most Soviet lawyers have some higher legal education, and the disdain for formalism is based on doctrinal and even legislative prescriptions. Thus, in addition to the law, judges are instructed to take socialist legal consciousness as a guide in deciding cases,[9] although there are no legal norms defining this socialist legal consciousness. Again, civil procedural legislation contains a requirement that a decision whose sub-

---

* Certain flagrant procedural simplifications were legalized. I have in mind the simplifications in trying cases of terrorism[6] and sabotage,[7] and also the creation of "special conferences" which in many cases functioned in place of courts.[8]

stance is correct cannot be set aside for formal considerations only.[10]

By way of noting that the withering away of the state is also being realized, we may consider the matter of dualism in Soviet state law—dualism in the sense that the state is governed both on the basis of procedures regulated by laws and by the Constitution, and on the basis of procedures regulated by Party law and not by state legislation. It is known that the Communist Party of the Soviet Union is the ruling party and the only political party, even though the Soviet Constitution does not specifically provide for this monopoly by the Communist Party.* The Constitution states only that this party is the vanguard of the working class and represents the "leading core of all organizations of the working people, both public and state."[12] As for the position of the Communist Party, we learn more details on this from the Party Rules.[13] The Party controls the state. The method for the Party's control of various state organizations, according to the Rules, is to work through Party groups in those organizations.

The exceptional nature of the Party is acknowledged in Article 12 of the Rules, which specifies the possibility of holding former Party members legally responsible for criminal acts: "If a member of the Party has committed acts punishable as crimes, he is expelled from the Party and made answerable in accordance with the law."[14]

The Party program characterizes the process of the withering away of the state as the gradual transformation of socialist statehood into social self-government—as the path to the realization of historical inevitability.

* In general, there is no direct mention of the Communist Party in legislative acts. A rare exception is the decree on the red banner of the police ("militia") which states that the banner is a symbol of their faithful service to the Soviet people and the Communist Party.[11] From judicial practice we learn that the Communist Party and its organs are apparently juridical entities, since it is possible for an employee to bring a suit against a Party institution where he has worked. For example, an employee of a Party district committee can sue the committee.

Insofar as it can be understood, the program means that the functions of the state apparatus will gradually be handed over to social organizations and the people will implement self-government by taking part in the activity of social organizations—led, of course, by the Party through Party groups within these organizations. (There is no provision for the withering away of the Party or the withering away of the Party leadership with the transition to communism.) The withering away of the state is characterized by a shift from the former "bourgeois" state to the present Party-state dualism in law, with a subsequent shift to a purely Party direction of society without any state apparatus. The question of course arises: What, during the withering away of the state and the transition to purely Party direction, will replace such "bourgeois" values as election by popular vote of government leaders? After all, the Party differs from the Soviet Government in that both local and higher organs of state power are, even in the Soviet Union, elective organs. But the Party, so to speak, elects itself, and it is unrealistic to hope that in the future the people will choose Party members by voting. If the question of what will replace the electoral process becomes urgent enough, I believe we will see some thesis to the effect that the value of "bourgeois parliamentarianism" and popular elections is as nothing compared to the fact that the most worthy representatives of the workers are taken into the Party. Naturally, it is impossible to predict how soon the transition from the present dualism in Soviet state law to purely Party direction of society will take place. Communist theoreticians associate this transition with the final building of communism. It is worth noting, however, that this gradual transition has apparently already begun. In recent years the control of Party organizations over state organizations has increased—and, quite recently, not without the participation of the President of the United States. Despite the Soviet Constitution, the General Secretary of the Party has represented the Soviet Union in official international talks and has signed agreements in the name of the Soviet Union,[15] rather than simply controlling the Soviet Union's diplomatic activities through the Party groups in the corresponding state organizations, as provided in the Communist Party Rules.

For that matter, the President's participation is understandable. In view of current world-wide pragmatism, it is natural to strive to negotiate with the real representatives of power and not with people occupying quasi-symbolic posts —even if these are high government posts established by the Constitution.

CLASS DISCRIMINATION IN SOVIET LAW

According to Soviet ideological doctrine, the state is a machine for the oppression of one class by another, a machine whereby one class keeps other, subordinate classes obedient to it. Under this doctrine, law is considered an instrument of class oppression. Since the very inception of the Soviet state, Soviet law has been characterized by class discrimination. By class discrimination I mean the imposition of legislative, administrative, or other limitations on the guarantee of rights or the granting of rights according to criteria which—in the opinion of the authority imposing the limitations—characterize affiliation with a class. Once they had seized power, the Bolsheviks easily divided society into "hostile" classes, "friendly" classes, and classes for which a struggle had to be waged to compel them to be "friendly." To use the Bolsheviks' language, the "exploiter classes" were enemies and in principle the "toiling classes" were friendly, although a struggle had to be waged to win over a certain portion of the toilers. It was considered that the exploiter classes included the bourgeoisie (the owners of any kind of enterprise), the nobility, the clergy, and those members of the intelligentsia who did not make haste to rally to the new regime and who were therefore denounced by the Bolsheviks as supporters of the bourgeoisie. People who, in the opinion of the authorities, belonged to these exploiter classes and who, in the same opinion, lived off unearned income were deprived of voting rights by the Constitution of 1918.[16] Members of these classes were discriminated against in the protection of other rights, including rights to life, freedom, and property, despite temporary concessions to these "nonlaboring" classes during the time of the N.E.P.* As for the peasantry—a class for whose good will it was necessary to struggle—class discrimination was also used in that battle. The peasants were divided into categories: poor peasants, who were assumed to be friendly to the Soviet regime; kulaks (rich peasants), who were assumed to be hostile to the Soviet regime; and middle peasants, whose friendly attitude toward the Soviet regime had to be won. In the late twenties a slogan was advanced calling for the annihilation of the kulaks as a class. It is known that this task was successfully accomplished, so successfully that in the process the "friendship" of the middle peasants was achieved as well—because middle peasants were treated as kulaks unless they hastened to demonstrate their friendship to the authorities, and at that time the demonstration consisted primarily of voluntarily joining a collective farm and transferring most of their property to it. The winning over of the middle peasantry in the process of liquidating the kulaks very vividly demonstrates the application of discrimination based on a vaguely defined criterion. Many historical examples show that a regime can gain political power by declaring a small minority of the population subject to discrimination and then using vaguely defined criteria when applying this discrimination. In regard to the middle peasants, advantage was taken of the fact that "kulak" was not defined in any statute. During the time of the so-called twists in collectivi-

---

* The N.E.P. (New Economic Policy), in effect from 1921 to 1928, represented a partial concession to private enterprise granted by Lenin to rehabilitate the Soviet economy.—Translator's note.

zation policy and the liquidation of the kulaks, the peasants saw that even a middle peasant could be "kulakized" or "dekulakized," and that this did not depend on the amount of his property or his method of farming but instead on his behavior or a denunciation by activists. The persecution of people accused of helping kulaks in various ways was instructive for all strata of the peasantry. Under such conditions each peasant had to give thought to what kind of "class face" he had.

The success of the Soviet regime in realizing its planned changes in the class make-up of society enabled it after some time to renounce legislation embodying the principle of class discrimination. The 1936 Soviet Constitution did not include any restrictions of rights based on class affiliation.[17] By this time the Fundamental Principles of Civil Procedure referred to equality before the law and the courts of all citizens regardless of their social, property, or official status.[18] This does not mean, however, that Soviet law was free of traces of the idea of class discrimination. Discrimination on the basis of vaguely defined criteria related to class affiliation continued.

The discriminatory measures taken against advocates of a "class-alien ideology" are well known. Ideological initiative exceeding the limits dictated by the victorious doctrine is considered unscientific, reactionary, and inimical. The propagation of ideas rejected, or not yet understood, by the representatives of the victorious doctrine is labeled a hostile action or, in liberal times, ideological sabotage. Eliminating such an oppressive approach is hampered by the fact that a society whose thought is guided by belief in a uniquely correct doctrine—a doctrine that has triumphed elsewhere than in academic discussions—becomes isolated from the common evolution of world culture and less open to new ideas. This applies especially to ideas about selecting paths of social development.

Class vigilance, combined with class discrimination, can also be seen in the state's interpretation of public morality.

The notion of class morality determines the character of both censorship and education in the USSR, and may lead to surprising judicial decisions. There is a 1923 case on record in which the Plenum of the Supreme Court of the Russian Soviet Federated Socialist Republic characterized a homicide in a duel as a homicide from vile motives, since dueling was a vestige of feudal nobility traditions, and in Soviet times the motives associated with such traditions must be considered vile.[19] Today there are almost no specific guidelines on class discrimination in Soviet law, or at least they are not viewed as such. For example, it is probably not considered discriminatory that the overwhelming majority of people in white-collar jobs enumerated in a special "list" are not allowed to defend their rights before a court in disputes over their dismissal.[20] This undoubtedly discriminatory proviso concerning procedural rights exists in Soviet law even though the law guarantees equality regardless of social, property, or official status, and even though the USSR has ratified the International Discrimination (Employment and Occupation) Convention.[21]

World revolution, with its anticipated change in the "class make-up" of the community of nations, has not yet taken place; and in Soviet law there are discriminatory regulations with respect to nations that are not considered workers' states. Article 10 of the law on crimes against the state equates a crime committed "against another workers' state" with crimes committed against the Soviet Union. Other states are not protected in this way.[22] Thus the vagueness of the discriminatory criteria does indeed offer a degree of convenience. It is not clear what a workers' state is, and no legislative act defines that concept. The official commentary on this law recommends that one be guided, in determining what states are protected by Article 10, by the following criteria of a "workers' state": "a socialist state, the state of a people's democracy, or another people's state."[23] It can hardly be said that this note makes the criteria for discrimi-

nation more precise. Its vagueness leaves ample latitude for
creative interpretation based on the political requirements
of the moment. Another example of discrimination among
states according to the "class" criterion is furnished by the
1972 decree on "fees for education."[24] Reimbursement of
the cost for higher education provided by the state is
required of citizens leaving the country to live abroad per-
manently, except for those emigrating to socialist countries.
Similarly, the state fee for obtaining a passport for foreign
travel to socialist countries is now one-tenth that of the fee
for a passport valid for capitalist countries.[25]*

As we see, class discrimination in Soviet society and
juridical practice is quite strong even today.

There have even been recent instances in which this idea
influenced the nature of legal pleadings. During a trial in
1972 the judge, apparently acting in accordance with an
unpublished instruction, told one of the defendants, Vladimir Bukovsky, that in a Soviet court it was inadmissible to
compare the policy of foreign capitalist states with the policy of the Soviet Union.[27]†

Along with the formal elimination of class-discriminatory
regulations from Soviet law, a transformation of the concept of the state and law has occurred. From an instrument
of class oppression, the law, as interpreted in Soviet doctrine, has been transformed into an instrument of state policy. From an instrument for assuring the primacy of the

* Fees for renunciation of citizenship have been fixed in the same proportion. For renunciation when emigrating to a capitalist country the fee
is five hundred rubles; when emigrating to a socialist country it is
fifty rubles. Noting that the acquisition of Soviet citizenship by a
political émigré who comes to the USSR involves a fee of fifty kopeks,
the mathematical logician Alexander Volpin, my friend and colleague
in the defense of human rights in the USSR, has written that this
creates the impression that "giving up Soviet citizenship is worth one
thousand times as much as acquiring it."[26]
† This occurred after Bukovsky, a well-known defender of human rights,
had compared the prosecution of himself and his comrades with the
prosecution of demonstrators in Spain.

rights of one class relative to the rights of other classes, Soviet law has become an instrument for assuring the primacy of the rights of the state over the rights of citizens.

THE SUPREMACY OF THE STATE

In many countries the regime tends to identify its own interests as the interests of society. This is the question on which the struggle to establish legal guarantees protecting the interests of the individual and of society has centered for many centuries.

In the Soviet Union the tendency to consider the interests of the state the interests of society has been exaggerated not only in people's consciousness but in the laws and in the aims of state ideologues. Many indications of this are found in Soviet law, but it is most vividly expressed in the following:

Although coming under the indicia of an act specified in criminal law, an act is not criminal if it was committed in a state of extreme necessity; that is, to eliminate a danger threatening the interests of the Soviet state, the public order or the person or rights of a given individual or of other citizens, if that danger under the given circumstances could not have been eliminated by other means, and if the damage caused is less considerable than the damage prevented.[28]

The concept of extreme necessity in protecting the interests of the individual as a circumstance excluding accountability is found in the law of many countries. The extension of this principle to cases of protecting what the legislators called the interests of the Soviet state or the public order fully corresponds to the spirit of Soviet law. Explaining the reason why such a norm is not found in the law of nonsocialist countries, Soviet jurists write:

To protect the interests of the state and the public order is the prerogative of the government itself and its organs; because of the conflict between the interests of the ruling class and those of the working class, the legislator [in nonsocialist states] cannot count on the support of the workers in protecting the bourgeois legal system; and, second, he does not want to entrust such protection to them. Therefore the criminal codes of the bourgeois states allow for the institutions of necessary defense and extreme necessity only with respect to individual and property interests.[29]

Since the concept of the "interests of the state" is very vague, and since it is difficult to compare actual damage to the interests of an individual with the damage to the state which has been prevented, this extension of the concept of necessary defense to the protection of the interests of the state is most convenient in cases when state officials, on grounds of protecting the interests of the state, have violated the rights of an individual. Despite its utility, I believe this article has been applied only rarely in court cases, simply because cases involving violation of the interests of an individual by state officials seldom reach the trial stage.

This norm expresses a principle that has been followed through the entire history of the Soviet state, the principle that for the sake of the interests of the state one should make any sacrifice, *a fortiori* sacrifices associated with the interests of the individual. Here the interests of the individual can be taken to mean everything, including his life or freedom. It is general knowledge that during the half-century since the founding of the Soviet Union many such crimes have been committed in the name of the state. To be more exact, I should speak here of acts formally "coming under the indicia" of a crime and not of crimes, since according to the legal norm such acts are not crimes.

In civil law the supremacy of the interests of the state is expressed in several norms, especially the doctrine that contracts contrary to the interests of the state are invalid.[30] As early as the 1920s the Supreme Court explained that this was applicable even when it was not a question of the interests of the state as a whole but of the interests of any state institution.

The property interests of the state are protected by harsh criminal sanctions. The Constitution declares that those who steal socialist property are enemies of the people. As might be expected of "socialist legislation," socialist (state or public) property is protected to a greater extent than the private property of citizens. In this sphere lamentable notoriety was attained by the law of August 7, 1932,[31] and the decree of July 4, 1947,[32] whose application led to "deprivation of freedom"* for many Soviet citizens, including those accused of petty theft of socialist property. Hungry people who, after the harvest on the collective farms, found scattered ears of grain or a few potatoes in the fields, and took them to feed their families, were sentenced to long terms of deprivation of freedom. The fact that these scanty remnants of the socialist crop would otherwise have been left in the fields to rot was not usually a mitigating circumstance when such cases were tried. Formalism was not entirely alien to Soviet legal proceedings even in those days.

Today, apparently, the authorities are not in as much of a hurry to institute criminal proceedings for petty thefts of socialist property. Although such cases are sometimes brought to trial, especially in instances of systematic theft, this is more often a theme for newspaper criticism of insufficiently vigilant managers who have allowed stealing on their farms. And although criminal legislation still makes it possible to prosecute such thieves quite harshly, the current practice is apparently more liberal in this sphere, even though some experts believe petty thefts of government property are unusually widespread in the Soviet Union.

---

* This phrase goes back to the early days of Soviet law, when it was decided not to use such terms as "imprisonment." Ordinarily it means confinement in a corrective labor camp or in prison, or a sentence to a certain amount of time in each.—Translator's note.

Associated with this liberalism is a special aspect of the relations between the Soviet state and the individual. The authorities, having carefully observed a citizen who commits petty thefts of socialist property where he works—a spool of thread, office supplies, small radio parts, food—can accumulate enough evidence to begin a criminal prosecution against him, but they do not by any means always do it. Thus it is important to note that Soviet legislation provides for much broader punitive possibilities than are used in practice. Prohibitions are rather numerous, and almost all citizens have violated one or another to some extent. A great many of these infractions are recorded, and are available for potential legal prosecution. This offers a very convenient way to regulate the behavior of citizens, especially when their behavior in the ideological sense does not meet the requirements of the authorities. Not only the theft of socialist property but other petty offenses may be used to this end. In Rostov, for example, a man named Lazar Lyubarsky told a fellow worker some of the details of an economic plan that was considered a state secret. This indiscretion became known to the authorities at the time, but it had no serious consequences. Four years later, when Lyubarsky wanted to go to Israel and signed protests against violations of the right of Jews to emigrate there, he was tried and convicted under the article dealing with the divulgence of a state secret.[33]

Such methods are not new; they have been tested by many dictatorships, monarchies, and republics. Keeping each citizen "on the hook" is very useful to a regime. It is also useful, for the instructive intimidation of citizens, occasionally to punish one or two people for what many are guilty of, so that the others will draw the appropriate conclusion. "For spreading rumors," Lenin wrote, "one or two persons should be handed over to justice (as an example)."[34] This prescription is close to Catherine the Great's command to the Moscow authorities to flog "one or two liars" for educational purposes.[35] For that matter, it is a humane policy for those "liars" not flogged. Even though such an approach may be frightful from a legal point of view, millions of people would have been satisfied if one or two kulaks had been exiled as an example rather than all of them.

In speaking of the supremacy of the interests of the state we cannot fail to note the special attention that Soviet legislation devotes to protecting the state against foreign encroachments—all the more so since the Soviet Union is considered to be encircled by predatory enemies. The USSR, which officially favors atheism even in its Constitution, considers the defense of the homeland a sacred duty.[36] Possibly the use of the word "sacred" is necessary to justify the harsh article of the Criminal Code specifying punishment by death or by prolonged deprivation of freedom for surrendering "out of cowardice or faintheartedness," as the lawmakers put it.[37] This article is not the sole example of Soviet legislation requiring a person to disregard his own most natural reactions to defend the interests of the state. Fear and other manifestations of what is called "cowardice" and "faintheartedness" are the natural reaction of the human organism to a threat to life. For the sake of the state, a person must overcome these natural reactions. It is the task of the legislator to specify criminal punishment, but the moral justification of such a law is the task of Communist Party activists, and they will not tell people that fear is a natural reaction. They will say that fear is a reaction unworthy of a Soviet man and that a real man will pay no heed to fear when such an important, sacred obligation as the defense of the homeland is at issue.

Soviet ideologues have been quite effective in morally justifying the supremacy of the interests of the state in social life and in law. Newspapers reporting on workers' meetings often cite testimonials by citizens of their gratitude for the care and concern of the state and the Party. This may well be the result of age-old traditions and not merely of the ideologues' activity, but in any case the ideologues do not inform the population that (for example) the payment of pensions or the allocation of new apartments is not something for which the government should be thanked, but rather something that should be viewed as an obligation of the government under the Soviet economic system. It is always presumed that everything good comes from the state and is a result of the generosity of the state. Even when it is a question of rectifying monstrous violations of human rights, this very rectification is not considered the belated fulfillment by the state of its obligation vis-à-vis the citizen, but a show of kindness, leniency, and concern. As a rule, news of such government actions is formulated in a way that makes it clear there was no compulsion to show such generosity. Here is an example from a former prisoner, Arkady Belinkov:

A few months after the death of Stalin and a few days after the shooting of Beria, we prisoners . . . were herded together for inspection and Captain Vetrov, deputy chief of the camp for political work, shouted: "The Party and the government are complying with requests. We'll see to it that those who work well are buried in coffins." Up to that time [Belinkov explains] people were buried differently: with only a tag on the foot.[38]

It would appear that the Communists do not have enough faith in themselves, and in the people's love for them, to accept the dictum: "For he that is not against us is on our part" (Mark 9:40). On the contrary, they proceed from the presumption that "he who is not with us is against us." To be considered loyal by the authorities, everyone must prove that he is "for." Those who are indifferent, or who do not hurry to prove that they are "for," are viewed as potential enemies. This approach, probably dictated by fear and a lack of confidence, is the basis for many statutes aimed at total control by the state over society, but needless to say, legislative acts do not exhaust the regime's activity in this sphere. Social organizations such as the Communist Party, the Young Communist League, the trade unions, and so on, are responsible for a great deal of the indoctrination that attempts to impose uniformity on the working class. At the same time, any sympathies that might prove to be stronger than love for the state, the regime, and the Communist idea must be suppressed; and any natural regulators of human behavior that historically, physiologically, or psychologically may prove to be stronger than the urge to build communism must be weakened. This is accompanied by a reappraisal of moral values. There are only too many instances of this—for example, the "canonization" of Pavlik Morozov, famous for having informed on his own father, and the general pressure, especially in the nineteen-thirties and -forties, to disown "traitors" even when they were close relatives.

The supremacy of state interests is sharply demonstrated by the fact that the Soviet organs of power, judging from their activity, do not generally consider themselves bound by any legal or moral principles, and disregard them when they consider it necessary. For that matter, they also disregard such principles when they do not remember them in time. This is no joke. In 1964 Khrushchev was dismissed from his posts and the new premier, Kosygin, was appointed by a decree of the Presidium of the Supreme Soviet, even though under the Soviet Constitution this does not fall within the competence of the Presidium: only the Supreme Soviet itself can appoint the chairman of the Council of Ministers.[39] To convene the Supreme Soviet quickly for such an occasion is by no means difficult; this violation of the Constitution was probably not due to tactical considerations; the Presidium simply forgot how the chairman of the Council of Ministers is supposed to be appointed.

The example of higher organs is infectious, and frequently officials of the executive power also do not regard themselves as bound by anything except "the good of the cause." Usually they are convinced that their superiors will not blame them for exceeding their authority so long as no damage is done to "the good of the cause" (as understood by the superiors, of course). I am speaking of all officials, beginning with the premier. For example, marriage formalities do not, in individual cases, come under the jurisdiction of the chairman of the Council of Ministers. Kosygin could hardly have remembered the restrictions on his own authority when he told Stalin's daughter, Svetlana Alliluyeva, "Live however you want, but we're not going to allow your marriage to be registered."[40]

Similarly, the Presidium of the Supreme Soviet did not remember the limitations on its own authority when it adopted unpublished decrees giving retroactive force to increased penalties for certain crimes so that a person could suffer a more severe punishment than the maximum provided by the laws in effect when the crime was committed. (In 1961, as a result of the Presidium's exceeding its authority in this way, Rokotov was sentenced to be shot in a currency speculation case.[41])

THE SUBJECTIVE RIGHTS OF MAN

Returning to the bold predictions of the Communist doctrine on law, I note that in accordance with those predictions, so-called subjective rights will apparently wither away under communism along with law and the state. Commentaries on this topic are not abundant in Communist legal literature, but from the program of the Communist Party of the Soviet Union it seems that in the future we can expect to see all distinctions between man's rights and duties vanish in the Communist society. One commentator assumes that this fusion will result from the fact that under communism no duties will be burdensome, and that all members of society will perform them conscientiously and voluntarily, as willingly as they exercise their rights.[42] This sounds rather strange. And if by rights and duties we understand what is usually meant by these words, the thesis may lead to absurdity. For example, it is difficult to imagine that a person will exercise his right as well as perform his duty to go to prison in accordance with a sentence of "the armed people" (since there will presumably be no courts then).

But apparently we must understand that this is only a seeming absurdity, since under communism the consciousness of the citizens will reach a level difficult for us to imagine, and many concepts will mean something completely different from what they mean now.

I assume that the fusion of rights and duties promised under communism will result not only from the more highly developed consciousness of citizens but also from the transformation of notions about what a right is and what a duty is. To a large extent this transformation is already taking place,* but not sufficiently to merge rights and duties. Presumably the fusion of rights and duties means something more than the fact that legislation simultaneously enunciates the right to do something and the duty to do the same thing—as when Soviet legislation specifies the right of medical care and at the same time stipulates that citizens of the USSR are obligated to take care of their health,[43] or when the Constitution of Panama affirms that "labor is the right and obligation of the individual."[44]

The thesis of the fusion of rights and duties presumably implies something more profound. I illustrate this by citing three possible relationships between the state and the individual. In the first case a person has the right to do whatever is not prohibited. In the second case the person must do only what is specifically required by law. Both these cases

---

* For example, the Constitution guarantees citizens the *right* to vote, but party activists arguing with people who refuse to vote refer to the Constitution and assert that the *right* to vote is the honorable *duty* of a citizen. This perversion of concepts is an instrument for pressuring "recalcitrants." Incidentally, a person's refusal to participate in elections is usually reported to his work supervisor, and such a refusal is of course considered evidence of unreliability.

(they are compatible) presuppose a certain freedom of choice: in the first, the freedom to choose what to do within the limits of the unprohibited; in the second, the freedom to choose what not to do within the limits of what is not prescribed. But a third case is possible: a person must do what is prescribed, and has a right to do only what is prescribed. It is apparently this kind of regime that the futurologists of communism have in mind. They assume that the fusion of rights and duties—and, apparently, the establishment of such a regime—is possible only with a very elevated consciousness among the population.

The level of consciousness undoubtedly depends on the level of information about what a subjective right is. As far as I can judge, Soviet jurists and propagandists have achieved fairly good results in transforming concepts associated with the subjective rights and freedom of man. To cite the words of a Soviet jurist: "To be a free man means to recognize necessity and the limits on one's actions; that is, to act purposefully."[45] It is difficult to imagine what the "conscious" dwellers in the ideal future will mean by freedom and right. Nonetheless, these concepts will no doubt remain. In any case, in discussing the future the Communists' program mentions not only the fusion of rights and duties but also that "communism will bring mankind new, great rights."

Quite possibly this statement is not so much evidence of the planned preservation of the concept of subjective right as a way of getting across the idea in a not very frightening form that communism will bring man new, great duties since it has been stated that rights and duties will merge.

THE EDUCATIONAL ROLE OF LAW

One of the Soviet regime's tasks is the education of the workers. What is involved here is the education of mature people, and we should bear in mind that this is Communist education, whose aim is to infuse citizens with Communist convictions and stimulate them to fulfill, on their own initiative, the requirements of what is called Communist morality. This is also understandable because the withering away of the state and of law has been predicted—and with that, the future inauguration of social self-government, whose realization requires a very high degree of Communist consciousness among the citizens. Naturally, this consciousness must be cultivated.

The methods of inculcating Communist consciousness are extraordinarily diverse. In educating citizens the regime appeals to both their proletarian consciousness and their material interest. It uses social pressure, compulsion, encouragement, and the control of information disseminated among the population.

In this process a very substantial role has been assigned to the law. The basic formulations of legal principles, the character of legal decisions, and judicial procedures must have educational significance. Many works by Soviet jurists are devoted to discussing the educational role of various kinds of juristic activity.

There have even been instances when, in a discussion of what a specific legal norm should be, the argument that this norm should also have educational significance has proved to be the most convincing. For example, there was a discussion about the limits of necessary defense when a person could save himself from attack by flight. It is an interesting question, and one that warrants serious thought. For two Soviet jurists the decisive argument was the following: "What our country needs is not people who flee at a moment of danger but people able, under any circumstances, to defend their country and themselves. And our law should help to form such citizens."[46]

This peculiar use of the law as an instrument of education may also be observed in laws governing public involvement in judicial and police activity. I have in mind the comrades' courts[47] and the people's *druzhiny*,[48]* as well as those citizens who help the organs of state security—in addition to those who, especially in former times, were compulsorily involved in helping the police arrest drunkards and hooligans. (Refusal to perform this civic duty made one criminally liable.) Apparently these various forms of public participation are experiments indispensable to the future realization of what Lenin called the "simplicity and ease" of social influence.

The public's attitude toward the use of private people to perform police and judicial functions is not sharply negative, although of course some reject this way of spending their leisure time. Many people participate in such activity simply because it is the accepted thing or because they are attracted by the privileges proffered for it. Many others apparently consider this their calling, or take satisfaction from the opportunity to participate in something close to purely Communist methods of governing society. Some perhaps take pleasure in joining up with a power surrogate. I don't know how many people enjoy their street duty as people's *druzhinniki*, but certainly the "armchair" form of public participation in the struggle against antisocial elements, class enemies, spies, and saboteurs has had a great vogue, especially in the thirties and forties. Although it is supposed that today there are fewer people who enjoy writing denunciations,† I think such activity could easily be

---

* Comrades' or people's courts are informal tribunals consisting of the litigants' neighbors, fellow workers, etc., which consider minor offenses and can assess fines of up to ten rubles. *Druzhiny* (singular, *druzhina*) are auxiliary voluntary police detachments. A member of such a detachment is called a *druzhinnik*.—Translator's note.

† Judicial proceedings are still sometimes initiated on the basis of "statements" from a director of an institution or a Party organizer, or in accordance with a resolution adopted at a public meeting. In the cases of Vladimir Gomelsky and Genrikh Altunyan such statements played a role in the initiation of proceedings.[49]

revived among some of the population at any moment, since this is perhaps the most nearly perfected means whereby people can with "simplicity and ease" exercise social influence on violators of order or enemies of the people.

I have already said that great prophecies should not be taken literally. Lenin wrote that the armed people would exercise social influence. It is hard to predict what will happen when the consciousness of the people is raised even more, but for the moment it is clear that to arm the people would not be wise from the authorities' viewpoint. To lessen the risk run by unarmed public-spirited citizens defending public order, the authorities have published special decrees guaranteeing the protection of these enthusiasts. As early as the twenties and thirties, when the so-called *rabkory** carried on vigorous activity in writing "exposés," the authorities took care to see that the names of the *rabkory* were not divulged during the investigation of cases brought on the basis of their denunciations, even when they were called as witnesses during the proceedings;[50] that acts of violence against the *rabkory* were punished especially harshly;[51] and that bringing judicial proceedings against *rabkory* for libel on the basis of a private citizen's complaint was obstructed to the maximum.[52]

Now a special decree grants the *druzhinniki* the same protection against interference as that given to police.[53] Disobedience to the orders of a people's *druzhinnik* makes one as liable to criminal proceedings as disobedience to other representatives of the authorities. Moreover, as experience shows, it is by no means obligatory for the *druzhinnik* to wear identifying insignia (they usually wear an arm band) or to present documents identifying him as a *druzhinnik*. Victor Khaustov was convicted of resisting representatives of society during a demonstration in Pushkin

---

* Worker-peasant correspondents; people who as a public service published wall newspapers or informed the local and central press organs of happenings at factories and on collective farms.

Square, although he was not informed that the people who snatched a placard from him were *druzhinniki*.[54]*

Other experiments on the theme of the "simplicity and ease" of social influence, aimed at gradually preparing the population for what is called public self-government, are conducted through discussions at public meetings. In the thirties, meetings would adopt resolutions demanding the death penalty for some enemy of the people who had been named in the newspapers. Today this is a rare thing. Usually the workers assemble to approve actions of the government, criticize production defects, or discuss the "personal affairs" of a member of the collective. Many things may serve as the occasion for this, ranging from pregnancy out of wedlock, or adultery, to poor work, drunkenness, or a politically illiterate act.[55]

THE VOICE OF THE PEOPLE

> We can't judge criminals justly!
> If we did, we'd have to acquit all of them!
> —*the teacher Nozhkina*[56]

If it is planned to have public self-government and amateur participation in police and judicial functions, the interesting question arises whether such self-government will be more liberal in its results than government by means of a state apparatus. By "liberal" I mean having both a greater respect for procedure in the application of punitive sanctions and a greater leniency in those punitive sanctions.

I am convinced that we must not expect liberalism. Although of course judicial and police self-government and amateur participation in them are not what might be termed

---

* It appears that Party officials, even if they never walk a beat as *druzhinniki*, are certified as *druzhinniki* and, when necessary, can perform police functions, including making arrests for "disorderly conduct."

mob law, since they take place under the leadership of the
Party, hopes for leniency and for a more careful observance
of procedural requirements are apparently not well founded.
I have gained the impression that the public, on the average, would prefer harsher punishment for violators of public order than is meted out by the organs of government. Of
course this is not because the organs of government are
kinder than the public, but because the public does not
have adequate experience in judicial and police activity and
is lacking in foresight. The authorities, on the other hand,
understand that for punishments to have any effect, a more
or less proportional scale must be established for them. I
do not believe that what I have said applies only to the
Soviet people, although it is difficult for me to speak of
other peoples, since I am less familiar with them. But I
have read of the so-called Catherine Commission of the
eighteenth century, comprising representatives of various
strata of the Russian population who were to propose to the
Empress what they wanted in the way of new laws. From
reports on this commission's work, it is clear that its proposals concerning the state's punitive functions were often
harsher than the punishments used at the time.

Samizdat* circulated a collection of documents on talks
between the poet and editor Vladimir Lapin and a member
of the Presidium of the Supreme Soviet about Lapin's proposal to abolish capital punishment. The member of the
Presidium told him, "Incidentally, many people write us
about changes in our legislation, but for the most part they
ask that harsher punitive measures be established . . . I
must say that recently you are the only one to write about
abolishing capital punishment."[57]† I am sorry to add that
I place much more credence in this statement by a member

---

* Unofficial literature circulated in typescript (literally: self-publishing).
  —Translator's note.
† This conversation took place before the fall of 1972, when some forty
  Soviet intellectuals submitted a petition to the authorities calling for
  the abolition of capital punishment.

of the Presidium of the Supreme Soviet than in the words of the 1947 decree abolishing capital punishment, which stated that this boon was granted to satisfy the wish expressed by social organizations and trade unions.[58]*

I don't know whether I am right in assuming that the public, on the average, is less humane than the authorities. However, I myself have often heard people express the wish that punishments were harsher, and suggest that one social evil or another (alcoholism, perhaps, or vandalism of pay telephones) was not being rooted out because the punishments for it were too soft. I hope this is not typical of the Russian public, but I have heard perfectly humane-looking elderly women, as they passed by a drunk lying in the street, say very matter-of-factly, "Ugh! How loathsome! Such people should be shot."

Even when the authorities show a certain degree of humanity and proclaim a partial amnesty in connection with some anniversary, many people express their dissatisfaction with this. According to an item in *Kazakhstan pravda*, the editors of that newspaper have received letters expressing the alarm of the public: "Aren't they letting people out before they have learned their lesson?" But that alarm is apparently unfounded. In Soviet practice the concept of amnesty has lost its meaning of "forgetting" and has come to mean a selective pardon as a reward for good behavior at the place of confinement. *Kazakhstan pravda* writes: ". . . we cannot of course free incorrigibles. This would be seen by the Soviet people as an encouragement of evil." Apparently the Kazakh journalist's opinion is that amnesty is not an act of forgetting, that instead it is an act of special trust: "We would like to believe and hope that the persons awarded freedom by amnesty will justify the trust placed in them."[60]

In regard to respect for procedure and such bourgeois values as the presumption of innocence and the right to

---

* Three years later the death penalty was officially restored.[59]

participate in court discussion, I have reason to doubt that
these values will be respected in circumstances of amateur
public activity. This is simply because, to respect procedures, one must know them and have adequate legal training—which even judges often lack.* I am convinced that
the majority of Soviet judges, in hearing, say, a case of mur-
der, fail to understand one thing that is very simple but
very important: that for the court the important question
should not be: Did the defendant kill the victim? but
rather: Has it been proved by admissible evidence and
beyond reasonable doubt that the defendant killed the victim?

Indeed, why talk about respect for procedure when amateur public participation in the judicial and police functions
occurs? It may be that such participation is needed precisely to keep procedure form hampering successful cam-
paigns against violators of the public order and enemies of
the people.

THE LOGIC OF THE END

The background against which we view guarantees of the
rights of man in the Soviet Union would be incomplete if I
did not mention methods of reasoning. It would appear that
the legal system in and of itself is not a sufficiently effective

---

* One can form an idea of the level of legal culture among Soviet judges
from the explanations issued by the Supreme Court of the Russian
Soviet Federated Socialist Republic. In a decision of the plenum of
that court dated December 12, 1964, we read: "We call the attention
of judges to the fact that decisions handed down by them must be
legal and well-grounded. . . ." And in another decision, October 28,
1935, we read: "It is better to decide a case somewhat belatedly than
to make a wrong decision, since the subsequent disaffirmation of an
ill-founded decision by a court of higher instance means that the final
settlement of the case, rather than being speeded up, is greatly de-
layed." (The laws and court decisions of the RSFSR are usually considered models for those of the fourteen other Union republics, including the work of the other republics' supreme courts.)

instrument of state policy unless logic is transformed to make it too an instrument of policy.

Like Soviet law itself, the logic of Soviet juridical reasoning has undergone changes in the past half-century. In the immediate postrevolutionary period, logic in juridical procedures was quite successfully replaced by the revolver and revolutionary legal consciousness. Jurists took pride in the fact that Soviet judicial practice was "created by representatives of the toiling masses unskilled in juridical niceties and scholasticism."[61] As the Soviet regime grew stronger, there was a movement away from purely revolutionary methods in the law. After a time a reference to revolutionary legal consciousness alone was no longer considered adequate grounds for court decisions, for formulating legal doctrine, or for interpreting the statements of jurists. *Reasoning* made its appearance in the works of jurists and in the sentences of courts. This testifies not only to the liberalization of the Soviet system but to the fact that the tasks of courts and jurists were gradually becoming more demanding. Whereas previously the law had been primarily an instrument of class oppression—or, more accurately, of the annihilation of certain classes and of changing the class make-up of society—it was gradually changing into an instrument of state policy with complex goals. It would be a mistake, however, to think that the transition from purely revolutionary methods —appeals to revolutionary legal consciousness or simply the use of force—to basing their actions on *reasoning* means a concession by Soviet jurists to the traditional methods of bourgeois law.

On the contrary, it has turned out that the traditional logic used in bourgeois law is not only imperfect but even harmful, because sometimes reasoning in conformity with this logic leads to undesirable results. Since the law is an instrument of policy, and since the goals of policy are considered definite, the practical application of legal norms and the development of the law must use a kind of reasoning that leads to a previously known result. Classical logic, however, is defective in that, starting from definite premises and reasoning according to definite rules, one may possibly arrive at an unforeseen result. As it has turned out, it is undoubtedly more convenient not to use definite, fixed premises and fixed rules of reasoning but, on the contrary, knowing the result, each time to construct rules of reasoning so that from the given premises, by reasoning according to those rules, one can reach the required result.* In what follows I shall speak mainly of individual practical applications of this interesting system of logic.† It would take a separate book to do justice to a theoretical description of this system.

The advantages of this "logic of the end," as we may call it, have proven so obvious that the study of classical logic has not been encouraged; and the development of the classical science in the form of so-called mathematical logic was quite simply declared to be a bourgeois pseudoscience and to all intents and purposes prohibited. Since logic, like the other social sciences, is of course a class science, the Soviet ideologues understood that the outmoded bourgeoisie have their logic—classical logic—while the victorious proletariat have their own kind of logic—"dialectical" logic, as they call it.

Later, in pure science research, Soviet scientists were allowed to use classical logic, and also to do research in mathematical logic—thanks to the fact that it is essential to the computer industry—but in the sphere of law and juridical practice the methods of reasoning remained as before. It would be unfair, however, not to mention that many legal practitioners try to avoid using the "logic of the end" whenever possible (though usually only to an extent that will not give their superiors grounds for doubting their loyalty and professional fitness). We may also note that

* The premises may also be varied in accordance with the results one needs to obtain.
† By logic I mean here any system that prescribes rules of reasoning.

there are legal scholars who in works published in the USSR try to defend many important legal principles, even when those principles do not fit in too well with Soviet legal doctrine (although they sometimes have to find appropriate quotations from Lenin to justify their point of view).

Let me now illustrate the convenience of the logic of the end. Here is an example of such reasoning in a judicial debate. In trials on political charges the defense lawyers usually ask the court to consider the subjective aspect of the act. For example, did the defendant intend to weaken or overthrow the Soviet state? Or did the defendant actually know that those fabrications he disseminated, and which the court found prejudicial to the Soviet social and state system, were false? During the 1971 appellate hearing in the case of Andrei Amalrik, when Amalrik's lawyer raised this question, the procurator told the court that Amalrik knew he might be arrested, consequently he knew his actions were punishable, consequently he knew he was disseminating palpably false fabrications. Judging from the decision of the appellate collegium, this argument satisfied the judges completely.

Another example shows how the laws are interpreted. Article 190-1 of the RSFSR Criminal Code stipulates punishment for the dissemination of fabrications prejudicial to the Soviet social and state system. The law specifies only the *dissemination of fabrications*. However, examining the decisions in which people are convicted under that article leads to the conclusion that what is punishable extends to prejudicial information, prejudicial moods, prejudicial skepticism, and no doubt prejudicial astonishment and questions. In any event, the verdict in Father Pavel Adelheim's case, in Tashkent, cites as an item in the indictment a witness's testimony that Adelheim "during lunch expressed skepticism toward communism."[62]

In the system of the logic of the end, as in many systems of reasoning, certain statements are considered not to require proof. If you subject one of those statements to doubt and prompt a Soviet legal practitioner to try to substantiate it with only the aid of his own logic, you may hear much that is interesting. Thus for anyone who works in a personnel department, the statement that a person who goes to church and practices religious rituals cannot be a teacher is obvious and does not require proof. If, however, you ask a legal practitioner why such a person cannot be a teacher, he will try to avoid an answer. Or if pressed he will say, "Well, because the students can see that he goes to church." Or he will say the same thing that was said by the rector of the Tbilisi Teachers' Institute: "How can a person who believes in superstitions be a teacher of youth?"[63]

It is characteristic that in this system of reasoning not only "obvious" statements but also those which are not customarily articulated play the role of axioms. In the example cited above, the official, if he was sufficiently aware politically, would try to say nothing that would provide an occasion for bourgeois propaganda to raise a fuss about discrimination in education on the basis of religious convictions. But as a rule, arguments that are not supposed to be articulated are invisibly included in the chain of reasoning (and this is completely correct in the logic of the end), and are understandable to the listeners. Besides, everyone knows that to ask "needless questions" is to show disloyalty.

I have been discussing especially elaborate methods of reasoning to obtain the necessary conclusions. There is, however, one method of obtaining the necessary conclusions and achieving the requisite end that has long since been approved by humanity and does not require special theoretical devices. This method is the lie. Apparently it is used very widely, beginning with the touchingly resourceful tactics of members of the KGB* who, when they knock on the door to conduct a search, say they are from the tele-

* Committee of State Security: secret police.—Translator's note.

phone office,* and ending with lies on an international scale. An article on the right to emigrate written by Professor Alexander Volpin recalls that when that particular right came up during discussion of the Universal Declaration of Human Rights (it was adopted in 1948), the Soviet representative stated that in the USSR there was no one who wished to leave the country but that if such a person should appear he would be able to emigrate, although he would have to comply with a few legal formalities. And Volpin adds, "In the meantime, quite a few people arrested on the border have, because of these few legal formalities, served long terms of imprisonment, sometimes amounting to fifteen or even twenty-five years."[64]

In juridical practice, the lie and other means of deceit would be less dangerous if there were effective procedures for challenging them. For that matter, there exists some opportunity to make such a challenge even now: both plaintiff and defendant participate in court proceedings, and the defendant has the last word; and in administrative proceedings one can enter a written complaint. The question is whether these arguments will be listened to. Ways to ignore arguments that conflict with the necessary conclusion have been well worked out. There is, of course, constant lying in the press and in official public relations, but I would like to call particular attention to those cases where a printed lie touches upon juridical practice and therefore can sometimes be refuted by specific documents. Here is

---

* This tactical resourcefulness is so much a matter of habit with these gentlemen that it seems to me they do not even realize it is a lie—something ethically reprehensible. One personal psychological observation: While my home was being searched, one of the KGB agents, having answered the telephone (in the hall), came into the room and told me, "someone called you, but I said you weren't home so there wouldn't be any interference with our work." I answered, "Ivan Ivanovich, you told a lie." He was astounded. He was probably expecting almost anything—protests, a demand that this event be noted in the record—but certainly not that I would characterize his resourcefulness in a way that was so matter of fact but also so unaccustomed for him.

an example (from earlier times, but typical). A book[65] on the heroic construction of the White Sea–Baltic Canal in 1934 describes the splendid arrangements that exiled former kulaks enjoyed: "The resettled persons—the defeated kulak army—disembark at Medvezhaya Gora with their property, their families, their cows, and their chickens." But we discover a different story in an "interpretation" of the RSFSR Supreme Court during the thirties:

Taking into account the fact that bailiffs, and rural soviets, and police agencies have great difficulty in collecting debts from persons banished during the liquidation of the kulaks, since these persons have no property and the court orders are returned unexecuted, the plenum deems it feasible to consider collections called for by such court orders as completed . . .[66]

In my study of Soviet law I have not totally succeeded in mastering the logic of Soviet juristic practice, but in certain cases I have achieved a few results. Just before President Nixon's arrival in Moscow, in 1972, the physicist Victor Polsky—a Jew who, like a few other Moscow Jews, was protesting restrictions on his right to emigrate to Israel—was picked up by the police one morning and taken to one of the prisons near Moscow. No records of this action were made, and no sentence was pronounced. Polsky was held for ten days and then released. He came to me to draft a complaint about this violation of the law. I told him, "We can draw up any complaint you like, but they will answer that all this simply did not take place." Alas, I proved to be almost right. In answer to his complaint he received a communication from the police precinct where he had been picked up stating that they had no records of the case and knew nothing about it.

By way of a digression, I note that Soviet officials' use of the logic of the end hampers conversation with them if one prefers traditional modes of reasoning. Very often, for example, Westerners trying to defend persecuted Soviet dissenters run up against a stone wall because the officials they talk to are using the logic of the end. And at difficult moments, when an official cannot come up with reasonable arguments he will say anything at all, including lies. In practice this kind of conversation turns out to be one-sided. The Westerner is left with nothing to say in the face of anomalous dialectical statements.

I remember what happened at a Soviet university. During an examination on the history of the Communist Party, the question of Party discussion with the opposition came up. The teacher asked the student what Trotsky said at such-and-such a conference. The student could not answer: there was nothing about that in the textbook. He had to prepare for the examination again, and search for the answer to this tricky question. But he didn't find the answer, and at the second examination he told the teacher he hadn't found out what Trotsky had said at that conference. The smug teacher said, "You didn't find that anywhere because he didn't say anything at that conference. Now tell me why he didn't say anything." Then, not waiting for an answer, he himself triumphantly added, "Because he had nothing to say."

I have recounted this incident to illustrate the fact that among those fond of the logic of the end it is considered a victory when one's opponent has "nothing to say." What actually happens is that the opponent cannot tell his interlocutor "You're lying," because he is well bred. Nor can he say "I agree," when that is not the case.

Of course, having thoroughly studied the problem, one can still try to have a discussion with this kind of thinker, knowing that he will say anything he pleases in response to any argument, and that he may even smile and mention détente. But if this discussion is in public, such an exchange of opinions can be instructive for the audience, and for this reason public exposure is extraordinarily important in a discussion of this kind. This is all the more true because a public discussion restrains the use of lies that, even if not publicly rebutted, can be recognized by the audience.

In many instances Westerners have written to Soviet leaders defending the law and human rights but have not released their statements publicly. I think this is just the sort of gesture in defense of the law that Soviet officials welcome, since they themselves try to avoid any public disclosure of their persecutions.

Of course, even in a public discussion the Soviet participant can say anything at all. But in published form that "anything at all" becomes more interesting.

One method used very frequently and successfully to make sure the opponent has "nothing to say" consists of assuming that the opponent's opinions are not his own, that he is simply a mouthpiece for someone else—presumably someone who has bribed or deceived him. As a recent example, when the German novelist Heinrich Böll protested against the persecution of dissenting intellectuals in the USSR he was answered roughly as follows: "You weren't saying such things before. Isn't this all due to your election as president of the PEN Club and your attempts to meet the demands of certain circles?" (See *Literaturnaya gazeta* for August 8, 1973.) There is no mention, in this answer, of the persecutions Böll had protested, but on the other hand, Böll was expected to have "nothing to say" in reply.

THE INFLUENCE OF SOVIET DOCTRINE ON OTHER COUNTRIES

From the classical works on Communist ideology we know that communism is the bright future of mankind. I don't know to what an extent such a future threatens all mankind, but, a great part of it has already either accepted the Communist ideology as a state ideology or been seriously influenced by some aspects of Communist ideology. This includes Communist ideas in the sphere of law and (perhaps more dangerous to neighboring civilizations) the legal methodology of Communist countries. It would be unjust to attribute this only to the attractiveness of Communist ideas as such. A great many of the principles explicit or implicit in Soviet law and that of other Communist countries have from time immemorial attracted rulers because of their convenience.

Such principles as "with us or against us," "the end justifies the means," and "the interests of the state above all," were used in various state systems long before the arrival of present-day communism. And so long as mankind continues to exist, many other states will probably utilize these principles to their advantage.

These totalitarian principles, as they are called, have not always been applied in pure form. When a society has become accustomed to more human values, it has not always been convenient to proclaim such harsh principles; they have instead been masked with a large number of justifications, appeals to temporary necessity, and other camouflage. At the same time, to make these totalitarian principles the guiding principles of state policy and law, the authorities have used various methods to stir up strong social passions among the population they wanted to win over ideologically. The commonest method for this has always been to preach discrimination against a certain part of the population. The victims may be religious dissenters, foreigners, those who represent a particular political trend, or, as in the Soviet experience, the propertied classes. Many historical examples are available for tracing the development of totalitarian state systems in which the authorities, beginning with discrimination against some specific element of the population, have then expanded the basic criteria and practiced such discrimination on the basis of a vaguely defined standard. This means the victory of the regime over the population, since anyone could become a victim. This has happened many times. But the memory of peoples is short; and when social passions are inflamed, few are capa-

ble of understanding that discriminatory measures against
one group, however small, mean the beginning of total
subjugation.

Although this system of subjugating a population has
been used throughout the history of mankind, and is well
tested, it must not be thought that the Communist subjugation of society has merely followed a beaten path. On the
contrary, the building of communism in the Soviet Union
and other Communist countries has made a valuable new
contribution to that oldest of sciences, the science of con-
quering a human society. We cannot discuss here all the
means involved in incipient Communist conquest of the
world. Some of them, propagandistic or diplomatic, are well
known, even if they have not been studied in sufficient
depth. Of the entire "arsenal of means of struggle for communism," as a Soviet activist would put it, I call attention
here primarily to the means that rely on Soviet legal doctrine.

The past half-century has witnessed in the Soviet Union
the construction of a legal system which is a very convenient
instrument for the political rulers. They have worked out a
legal doctrine and a special logic making it possible to justify every use of this instrument of policy. They have found
ways to compel people to use such logic and propagate this
doctrine. Many people do not understand how one can
propagate such a doctrine and use such logic, but more
significant are the many people who, without compulsion,
find much that is attractive in this political instrument
developed in the Soviet Union—its legal doctrine and its
logic. And there are many states whose rulers, to the extent
of their intellectual refinement, try to master this logic and
this legal doctrine, and try to fashion a similar instrument
to serve their own purposes, the purposes of their political
group or their ideology. In other words, they use principles
similar to the Soviet ones in developing their own legal
system. The present geographical distribution of states
showing a predilection for Soviet legal doctrine should not

promote the illusion that the Western world and the values of Western civilization are immune to the influence of Soviet doctrine. Such hopes might be well founded if the legal values of Western civilization were more deeply assimilated by the people than they actually are. Since the majority of Western people have, to some extent, inherited their social institutions and their freedom as a gift from their fore-fathers, there is a danger that local totalitarianism, subjugating the society gradually, may at first seem attractive to a great part of the population.*

I consider the study of the influence of Soviet legal doctrine on other states very important, not only because of its intrinsic interest but because an up-to-date diagnosis of the success of such influence is vital.

The study of the influence of Soviet doctrine on international law, and in particular on the activity of the United Nations, is also significant. The activity of the Soviet Union in the United Nations, so important for the preservation of peace, is proving to be quite an attractive example for other states—especially in regard to problems of human rights and international protection of human rights. One example is the adoption of the convention abolishing statutory limitations on certain categories of crimes.[67] Another is the fact that representatives of many developing countries, following the Soviet Union's lead, stress the importance of economic and social rights and state that safeguarding civil and political rights is of secondary importance in their countries.

---

* I am speaking of totalitarianism in general, regardless of whether it is "left wing" or "right wing," and I am sometimes distressed by the way these divisions hypnotize the Western public so that it fails to understand that the circle closes—that the basic difference between a "left-wing" and a "right-wing" political trend disappears once the principle that "the end justifies the means" takes hold.

2

The Soviet Union and International Conventions

W<small>E SEE</small> now that the peculiarities of Soviet legal doctrine and Soviet legislation are very marked. Any attempt to begin a dialogue between proponents of the Soviet legal system and of the legal systems of the Western countries might seem to be unproductive, but such is not the case. We know that Soviet jurists, along with jurists from Western countries, have participated in drafting UN agreements on human rights, and this activity may awaken hopes. It is important because, in a very significant sphere of law, representatives of seemingly incompatible legal systems have proved capable of overcoming doctrinal differences and striving for mutual understanding. It is also important because, thanks to these efforts, defenders of human rights can refer to authoritative formulations that guarantee such rights. Although the guarantees may be lacking in domestic Soviet legislation, they are recognized by the Soviet Union both as prevailing international law and also as applicable within the Soviet Union. I mean specifically the guarantees contained in conventions ratified by the Soviet Union.[1] Of course the ideological anomalousness of legal doctrine in the Soviet Union reduces the effectiveness of this collaboration and influences the interpretation of the international-law agreements ratified by the USSR.[2] And although one may welcome the fact that the Soviet Union has ratified many more conventions on human rights than, say, the United States,[3] the problem of securing the rights guaranteed by those conventions is still unresolved. This applies not only to the fulfillment in practice of the terms of the conventions but also to legislative or judicial recognition of the fact that these norms exist and are obligatory for the Soviet Union.

In this respect, there is much that is not clear. It would appear that the basic attitude of Soviet legal doctrine toward the idea of the international legal defense of human rights is as follows. The Soviet Union advocates the principle of the unlimited sovereignty of states vis-à-vis the individual, and considers inadmissible any interference in questions of human rights on its own territory. This basic thesis was expressed by Andrei Vyshinsky in 1947, in the United Nations discussion of the Universal Declaration of Human Rights, when he debated with Professor René Cassin on limiting state sovereignty with respect to matters affecting the defense of human rights. Since that time the Soviet Union has ratified many conventions on human rights, but the thesis Vyshinsky advanced has remained unchanged. Recently the Soviet Ambassador to the United Nations, in a letter to the Secretary General, repeated that thesis in a particular instance: "As regards the departure abroad of citizens of any state, and their return to their own country, these problems fall wholly within the domestic competence of the state in question."[4] I am unable to understand the dialectics of such an approach, when on the one hand a state makes commitments to guarantee human rights on its own territory, while on the other hand it tells those to whom the commitment was made that securing human rights is exclusively its internal affair. I am disturbed by this; but I am nonetheless glad that the Soviet Union has ratified these conventions and, what is especially important, the international covenants on human rights.

It should not be thought that the Soviet Union's attitude toward the international defense of human rights is directly reflected in its legislation. On the contrary, there is a good deal in Soviet domestic legislation that testifies to the USSR's respectful attitude toward its international obligations. For example, the Fundamental Principles of Civil Legislation, the Fundamental Principles of Civil Procedure, and the Fundamental Principles of Legislation on Marriage and the Family contain "collisional" norms affirming the supremacy of international law. True, such norms affect only certain areas of Soviet legislation. Thus the Fundamental Principles of Legislation on Labor[5] lack a norm on the supremacy of international law, and hence lack the guarantees contained in the Discrimination (Employment and Occupation) Convention.[6] Specifically, the guarantee of prohibiting discrimination in employment on the basis of political convictions is virtually disregarded in the Soviet law. There is no need to emphasize the importance for Soviet citizens of protection against discrimination on the basis of political convictions.

However, recognition of the supremacy of international law in any field of legislation can prove rather ineffective, not only in the sense of the practical implementation of the guarantees contained in international conventions but also in the sense of the domestic law's not contravening international obligations. For example, the Fundamental Principles of Legislation on Marriage and the Family, which contain a norm on the supremacy of international law, also contain Article 18, which stipulates: "Parents must rear their children in the spirit of the moral code of the builders of Communism." Meantime, the Convention Against Discrimination in Education affirms the right of parents "to insure . . . the religious and moral education of their children in conformity with their own convictions," without reference to any moral code. Strictly speaking, it cannot be affirmed that we have here a contradiction between domestic and international law, since Soviet legislation has a visible gap in the sphere of "moral" legislation. Soviet legislators have so far refrained from publishing the moral code of the builders of communism. But the Party program—which of course has no juridical force—contains something relevant to this question. It states: ". . . the Party considers that the moral code of the builders of Communism includes . . ." and then gives a list of several qualities—desirable in the eyes of the authorities but not always generally acceptable—including an uncompromising attitude toward the enemies of communism. Although, I repeat, this list has no legal force for Soviet citizens, and parents are not bound by law to be guided by it in bringing up their children, in practice it may—and apparently does —turn out differently. What happens is that the courts and other organs consider the list to be the moral code of the builders of communism, and insist that parents rear their children in the spirit of that moral code. Yet it is obvious that, for example, uncompromising hostility toward the enemies of communism is a quality that may conflict with the ethical system of many people.[7]*

Soviet legislators realize that the USSR will cease being the state of victorious socialism unless they keep the spirit of future generations in thrall. And so the same Fundamental Principles of Legislation on Marriage and the Family provide for the possibility of depriving parents of their parental rights if they fail to fulfill their obligations in bringing up their children. Thus if parents rear their chil-

---

* According to the recently adopted Fundamental Principles of Legislation on National Education, children must be reared in a spirit of respect for their elders. Therefore, parents must, along with an uncompromising attitude toward the enemies of communism, infuse in children a respect for elder enemies of communism. This is nonetheless more humane than pure and simple hostility.

dren in accordance with their own ethical and moral convictions—which is their right under the Convention Against Discrimination in Education—and a Soviet court decides that the children are not being reared in accordance with the moral code of the builders of communism, the parents may be deprived of their parental rights. Information exists that such cases have actually occurred.*

Repudiation of the guarantees of an international convention is not always based on such a clear conflict between the convention and domestic legislation. It may be based on the always available Article 5 of the Fundamental Principles of Civil Legislation. (Civil rights are protected by law except when they are exercised in contradiction to the purpose of those rights in a socialist society during the period of the building of communism.) There is a case on record (*Zuckermann* v. *International Post Office*[9]) in which the court referred to this article, denying the plaintiff his right to a monetary indemnity for the loss of letters mailed to foreign addresses, even though such an indemnity is provided for in the Universal Postal Convention. Of course there is an even simpler possibility: merely to disregard, in practice, both the guarantees and the fact that the conventions exist.† For example, the International Convention on the Elimination of All Forms of Racial Discrimination[11] mentions, among civil rights, the right to leave any country, including one's own. By ratifying this convention the Soviet Union recognized that the right to leave a country

---

* Baptists who wanted to rear their children in the spirit of their faith have been deprived of their parental rights in court cases, and in a recent case Alexander Temkin, who wanted to emigrate to Israel with his daughter, was deprived of parental rights.[8]

† Of course the state has to take care to see that information on its violations of international conventions is not publicized. I know in particular that Glavlit (Main Administration for Literature and Publishing, the censorship agency)[10] prohibits publication of information on the dimensions of the mesh used in Soviet fishing nets, except when the dimensions correspond to those established by international fishing conventions.

is a civil right. And this, by virtue of the Fundamental Principles of Civil Proceedings, enables interested parties to demand that this right be defended by a civil court, since the law indicates no other procedure for defending it.[12] But attempts to defend this right have been fruitless. Soviet courts have simply refused to consider such cases.

In accordance with the position it has taken with respect to the International Court of Justice, the Soviet Union, in ratifying conventions on human rights, has made the reservation that recourse to the International Court, in the event of disagreement over the interpretation or application of a convention, is possible only with the agreement of both parties. No such reservation was made when the Convention on the Nationality of Married Women[13] was ratified, which in principle enabled an interested party to seek to initiate proceedings in the International Court of Justice. I have in mind the case of the lawyer Dora Kolyaditskaya, who requested permission to emigrate to Israel to join her husband, and whose request was rejected on the grounds that she had not been living with her husband for twenty years and that her marriage could not be considered still valid, although it had not been formally dissolved. Kolyaditskaya complained to the court concerning this application of the "principle of the statute of limitations" to a marriage —a principle which, as she knew, does not exist in Soviet marriage and family legislation. After the court had refused to consider the case, Kolyaditskaya appealed to the chiefs of state of Israel and the Soviet Union. She argued that the refusal to allow her to emigrate to Israel prevented her from obtaining the citizenship of her husband; that the grounds for refusal—the long period when she had not lived with her husband—indicated an anomalous interpretation by the Soviet Union of the concept of "a married woman"; and, finally, that this in turn involved a singular interpretation of the Convention on the Nationality of Married Women. Kolyaditskaya asked Chairman Podgorny and Israel's President Shazar to settle the disagreement, and in the event that it could not be settled by means of talks, she asked Shazar to present the case to the International Court. As a procedural experiment this case proved to be a failure, since Kolyaditskaya then received permission to emigrate to Israel, and the interesting possibility of bringing this case before the International Court was lost.[14]

There have been other instances when the Soviet authorities prevented the emigration of wives who wanted to join husbands who were citizens of other countries. It is regrettable that no state which, like the Soviet Union, has ratified the Convention on the Nationality of Married Women, takes a sufficient interest in such cases to ask the International Court of Justice to consider these violations of the convention. Every possibility of utilizing juridical means to defend human rights is very important, from a citizen's appeal to state organs up to the use of procedures for settling disputes among states that involve human rights questions. Most governments show great lack of initiative in the international defense of human rights. It is a fine thing when states develop and adopt conventions on human rights, but it sometimes strikes me as strange that they should do this, since they generally seem so indifferent toward the defense of human rights in the world.

A state's partners in international relations should take a natural interest in its compliance with human rights conventions, simply from the consideration that the contractual capacity of any person, including a state, must be judged from his behavior. It is obvious that if a state neglects its obligations under an international convention on human rights, there is reason to believe that it will neglect its obligations under other international agreements. One might justifiably make the broader assertion that if a state is capable of slighting any of its obligations (whether internal guarantees to its citizens, or external treaty obligations), it is reasonable to consider that state capable of disregarding any obligation—even if it usually fulfills its obligations in certain areas. Thus if a state has enabled its citizens to obtain an education and has declared that education is free, and the same state has later informed some of its citizens that their education was very expensive and must be paid for,[15] it is only sensible for partners of that state in international relations to prick up their ears.

The faith of the Soviet Union's partners in its contractual capacity has undergone many trials, but has apparently remained unshaken. These were very serious trials, ranging from the repudiation of Russian debts in 1917 to the introduction of so-called fees for education, and the movement of armed forces into Czechoslovakia despite the guarantees of the 1955 Warsaw Pact renouncing the use or threat of force and renouncing interference in the internal affairs of signatory states.[16] Even if these discouraging events have not prevented many states from trusting the contractual capacity of the Soviet Union, I dare say that if partners in international relations were to be more exacting toward one another's contractual capacity, it might help to raise the minimum standard of states' compliance with their obligations.

3

The Movement for the Defense of Human Rights in the USSR*

I<small>F</small> WE take into account the specifics of Soviet law discussed in earlier chapters, it is not difficult to understand that a juridical approach to the defense of human rights in the USSR can be made in either of two ways. One can accept Soviet legal doctrine and still take· a stand for human rights, pleading their usefulness for society and for the successful building of communism. Or one can divorce oneself from the legal doctrine and refer only to specific laws, criticizing those laws that seem—like the doctrine—exceptionally anomalous from the standpoint of generally accepted principles of law. Apparently the first approach has proved acceptable to people of a Communist cast of mind, many of whom saw quite enough horrors in Stalin's camps to realize that an unrestrained contempt for human

---

* In this survey of the movement's activities, as throughout the book, I ordinarily mention the names of participants in the movement only in connection with repressions against them. (This restraint does not apply to people who have left the USSR.)

rights was not their dream of a great and well-ordered future. Depending upon how humane or resolute they are, such individuals have criticized Stalin for destroying his own people along with enemies and sometimes they have even criticized him for destroying people generally.* They have also, of course, criticized him for having violated Leninist principles—each critic meaning by "Leninist principles" something very fine from his own viewpoint—which is not difficult, since apparently Lenin by no means took a formal attitude toward his expressions of principle.

It could be said that this Communist movement for human rights was begun by Nikita Khrushchev. Working under very difficult conditions he was still able to do many good things, liberating millions of people from prisons and camps and debunking Stalin, who had taught people to

---

* The official condemnation of Stalinist repressions that began in 1956, after the Twentieth Congress of the CPSU, basically concerned cases of persecution of Communists. Only occasionally was there casual mention of "ordinary Soviet citizens." And yet, among those subjected to repression, the majority had been ordinary Soviet citizens. If their "cases" had been adjudicated justly, these citizens would of course not have been persecuted. As for the Communists persecuted under Stalin, those who had committed crimes together with the Leninist and Stalinist regimes could probably have been convicted for their acts by an impartial court, but under Stalin they had been convicted unjustly: for violations of procedural principles and usually not for those acts they had actually committed. Their subsequent rehabilitation was therefore lawful, since rehabilitation is not the remission of sins but merely the recognition of a person's innocence of charges brought in a specific judicial (or nonjudicial) prosecution.

There are many categories of people falsely convicted under Stalin and not subsequently rehabilitated. Among them are representatives of "alien classes," including a great many peasants; partisans from the Baltic states and the western Ukraine who fought against Soviet occupying troops by right of necessary defense (some are still incarcerated); "basmachis" (members of anti-Soviet bands) from Central Asia who fought for the independence of their countries; and "nationalists" who defended the customs and culture of their peoples, including "Zionists" and many Ukrainians; Orthodox priests, Roman Catholic priests, Uniate priests, mullahs, leaders of numerous sects of various religions, including leaders of Buddhist communes, shamans, and yogis; thousands of simple believers whose religious activity was regarded as politically hostile behavior; and many, many others.

live in constant fear. Yet I have expressed myself inaccurately. He did not do all this alone; those were the days of collective leadership. But thanks to his good will he managed to find among the Stalinist officials some that were rather liberally inclined. The important thing is that it was possible not only to do millions of good deeds but to effect substantial reforms in legislation, including the restoration and improvement of procedural principles, without renouncing Communist doctrine. This inspired many good and critically inclined people who believed in the ideals of Communism, and prompted them to call upon the Party and the government not to stop halfway in their reforms. And although the Party and the government preferred at a certain moment to stop, and even to "correct" some of the reforms, the demonstration of the flexibility of Communist doctrine was convincing enough to give many people hopes for the future. There is no reason not to believe in the practicability of such hopes. The aim of the Communist regime is to survive. This prompts it to be flexible. And it is clear to many people that one cannot always survive with the aid of terror: the N.E.P. period of the twenties and Khrushchev's reforms of the fifties offer examples of flexibility in the direction of liberalism. Of course the lives of many people in the USSR are complicated by uncertainty about what direction the regime's flexibility will take next.

Although the human rights movement in the USSR is usually taken to mean the actions of those who, independently of a belief in communism, are defending rights on the basis of generally accepted principles and not specifically Communist principles, the "Communist movement for human rights" should not be forgotten. It is an integral part of the broader movement. The authorities are very vigilant toward such "Communist liberals," and subject them to more than merely Party repressions. Among those who have defended human rights from a strictly Communist position, Roy Medvedev[1] is widely known. Peter Grigorenko's position also strikes me as an essentially Communist one. The repressions against the former general have been especially harsh: Grigorenko was deprived of freedom for more than five years, three of which he spent in a prison-type psychiatric hospital.

The beginning of the movement for human rights in the USSR is usually associated with the December 5, 1965, demonstration by a group of intellectuals in Moscow's Pushkin Square. The slogans of that demonstration— "Respect the Constitution, the Basic Law of the USSR" and "We Demand That the Sinyavsky-Daniel Trial Be Public"—were typical, in terms of their juridical emphasis, of many subsequent demonstrations. Specifically, defenders of human rights in the USSR are still calling for observance of the constitutional guarantees of rights and for the admission of the public to political trials.

The principle of public disclosure was violated in the February 1966 trial of the writers Andrei Sinyavsky and Yury Daniel, since only people with official invitations could enter the courtroom, while the friends of the defendants were not allowed in and stood on the street. Nonetheless, the court was sufficiently open* for people to learn enough about the trial to criticize the basis of the charges and the justice of the verdict. News of the trial, along with texts of the protests of many intellectuals, was published in samizdat by Alexander Ginzburg,[2] and this, as well as the samizdat activity of Yury Galanskov, provided the occasion for new arrests. Galanskov, Vera Lashkova, and Alexei Dobrovolsky were arrested—which gave rise to the January 22, 1967, protest demonstration in Pushkin Square. The dispersal of this demonstration was accompanied by the arrest of Vladimir Bukovsky and Victor Khaustov. Ginzburg was arrested later.

The situation was alarming. It had become clear that new arrests would provoke new protests and these protests would entail new repressions. And although it was obvious

---

* In the past such trials were as a general rule formally closed.

to many that repression would prevail in this contest, protests became more frequent, and hundreds of people signed a petition against the trial of Alexander Ginzburg and Yuri Galanskov. Prominent Soviet intellectuals took part in these protests, as they had in the protests against the forcible confinement of Professor Volpin in a psychiatric hospital. Dismissals from work, expulsions from the Party, expulsions of students from institutes, and "criticisms" at meetings were soon forthcoming. But despite all this, people realized that something considered impossible was happening. And the realization of this, plus joy at Czechoslovakia's "Prague Spring" of 1968, inspired many intellectuals. It was the time when Anatoly Marchenko, with his book *My Testimony*,[3] called the attention of samizdat readers to the frightful situation of people incarcerated in camps and prisons. It was the time when samizdat expanded, and a group of unknown enthusiasts began to publish the *Chronicle of Current Events*,[4] which was to play a vital role in the further development of the movement. It was the time when Peter Yakir, former General Peter Grigorenko, and several prominent Soviet intellectuals spoke out in opposition to what they called the rebirth of Stalinism.[5]

The movement of Soviet troops into Czechoslovakia had a sobering effect on a good many people. Although the more convinced participants in the movement continued their activity, and seven of them held a demonstration against the intervention in Czechoslovakia,[6] the number of those publicly supporting the movement diminished. Hopes for gathering a hundred signatures on a petition of protest soon faded.

But despite this, and despite the ever more frequent arrests, incarcerations in psychiatric hospitals, dismissals from work, and widespread intimidation, there were enough people to gather information on violations of rights, to protest against those violations, to write articles on social problems, to reproduce samizdat texts, and to provide support to those in trouble.

The movement continued to exist in this "stable" condition until, in 1972, it was weakened by further repressions. I think there were four basic directions in the activity of its members during those years. The gathering and publication, in samizdat, of information on violations of human rights in the USSR was apparently the chief reason for the regime's actions against participants in the movement. The majority of those arrested were charged with the dissemination of information on violations of rights. Although it is difficult to get an accurate picture of the defendants' actions from the indictments brought against them, the charges at least suggest what the authorities fear most. In 1972 the repressions were aimed primarily at stopping publication of the *Chronicle of Current Events,* that calm, objective chronicle of things which, in the course of half a century, the authorities had learned how to conceal from the public. Thanks to the *Chronicle*, we had learned enough over a period of five years to assemble a true picture of the sphere of Soviet life that was supposed to be hidden from everyone except close-mouthed officials and the victims whose voice had not previously reached the outside world —a picture of Soviet political prison camps and political trials.

A second kind of activity has been speaking out in defense of those whose rights are violated. We have the texts of a great many statements and appeals in defense of rights, addressed to individual officials, leading figures of the USSR, international organizations, and world public opinion. Only very rarely have there been direct results from these appeals, but they have reminded the authorities that violations of rights are not always met only with silence. Because of some support from world public opinion, they have also reminded the authorities of the principle of the limited sovereignty of the state vis-à-vis the individual, and that the defense of human rights in any country is everyone's business. Being based, as a rule, on the texts of Soviet laws, these appeals have reminded people that laws can be understood as they are written and not necessarily as they are interpreted by the authorities. And this, under Soviet conditions, is of major importance.

Another activity in the defense of rights has been the study of Soviet laws and international law. Not many have been engaged in this. But since it involves not only research but also the legal education of samizdat readers, the work has had an influence on the whole movement. This is all the more true since, from its inception, the movement has been somewhat law-oriented—in part because of the long-standing program of legal education vigorously carried on by Professor Volpin, which he began even before the movement developed.

And there is one more activity that I would call basic to the movement: the exercise of rights in areas where, although it is not prohibited by law, it is not something the public and the authorities are accustomed to, and even where it may involve unlawful persecution by the authorities. There are many examples of such activity, including exercising freedom of the press by means of typewriters (samizdat), demonstrations, and the founding of associations—the Initiative Group for the Defense of Human Rights and the Moscow Human Rights Committee.[7]*

This survey is brief, since I am concerned with the problems of the movement even more than with its history. Furthermore, I cannot be an objective historian of the move-

---

* This does not apply to Moscow alone. In other cities too there have been actions in defense of rights, samizdat has been distributed, and political trials have been held. In addition to the "general" movement, whose members have usually been interested in defending rights in general, there are movements with specific goals. Among the best known are the activity of the Crimean Tatars demanding their return to the Crimea; the attempts of some Jews to overcome obstacles to emigration to Israel; the Ukrainian movement, whose activity is aimed at the defense of national rights and protests against what they call the forced Russification of culture and education in the Ukraine; the activity of Baptist "initsiativniki," of Catholics in the Baltic area, and of other believers defending the right to profess their faith freely and without interference.

ment. I am a participant in it, even if a rather restrained one because of my role as investigator and observer, and I may not notice aspects of the movement which, subconsciously, I do not want to notice. Such is human nature.

But I can confidently assert that the movement for human rights in the USSR is not a political movement aimed at the overthrow of the existing system or at undermining the Soviet regime, as Soviet officials claim in trying to justify the persecutions, as certain biased well-wishers in the West also claim, and certain arrested participants in the movement may claim after confinement in prison for many months, where they are subject to interrogation and persuasion by the investigating authorities.

Those who defend human rights in the USSR demonstrate their readiness to undergo suffering and show great intellectual boldness, because their principles frequently contradict official doctrine and hence the prejudices the public has become accustomed to over half a century. These people are "caught between three fires." First, they are harshly persecuted by the authorities. Second, they are viewed cautiously and skeptically by the majority of the population, since most people "know it's useless to beat your head against a stone wall." Third, their actions are often distorted by those abroad who label any unorthodox movement in the USSR a struggle against the Soviet system, and thereby make it easier for the authorities to "justify" persecutions. Yet despite the persecutions, the caution of the public, and the tendentious distortions—and despite their limited numbers—these individuals, remaining free from any organization or party discipline, have done a great deal to propagate legal and ethical values common to all mankind.

It is very difficult to speak of all of them at once. They differ greatly from one another: they differ in their world views, in their social ideals, and in their culture. And they have different ways of participating in the defense of human rights, ranging from the natural and simplest human reaction to suffering—the cry of protest—to the realization that merely shouting "Help!" is not productive and that it is desirable to study the problem thoroughly.

Each one has thought and acted in his own way. But it is typical of many that they have recognized the moral principle "I cannot remain silent." Anatoly Yakobson has expressed the opinion of many in his writing about this principle.[8]

Participants in the movement have expressed (rarely, to be sure) hopes that it will be possible to improve the defense of rights by selecting better tactical principles than the principle of almost fatalistic indifference to the question of effectiveness (for that is what the principle "I cannot remain silent" is from the tactical point of view). But the very idea of seeking an optimum tactic is resisted by many who criticize the orthodox idea not because they support another "uniquely correct" idea but because as free spirits they rebel against the very possibility of recognizing any doctrine as uniquely correct. Typical among them is a profound intellectual individualism, a striving to choose for themselves the patterns of their own individual protests, behavior, and a considerable weariness with the external dictates of "optimality" and correctness customarily accepted by most of the population.* It is precisely this individualistic spirit in the movement for human rights which has made possible joint action by people who would never agree to restrict the freedom of their critical thought by subordinating themselves to collective requirements—even those that might promote greater tactical effectiveness.

There is no organization in the movement and no one is under any obligation. Nobody is required to submit to the opinion of the majority; and for that matter the opinion of

---

* This does not of course apply to everyone. In the national and religious movements the national or religious idea is often regarded as a uniquely correct alternative to the official ideology, but more often as (in the opinion of their members) supplementing the official ideology.

the majority is not usually known. Everyone does what he considers acceptable for himself, either on his own or together with others wishing to do the same thing. In saying this I am of course not trying to deny the role of mutual moral influence on the actions of individuals, nor the influence of friendly solidarity. But this is not what is usually called organized behavior, and it does not interfere with individual freedom.

I am familiar with the activity of many participants in the movement and also sometimes sense their attitudes, but I know best my own activity and attitude. And so I shall write about myself.

I was always aware of the underlying principles of my position, but could spare no time to formulate them so long as they were not challenged. Nevertheless, certain basic axioms were clearly defined from the beginning of my involvement, the first being observance of existing laws. This principle requires me to refrain from breaking any laws but does not prevent my criticism of these laws nor disagreement with the official legal and ideological doctrine of communism. One of the first articles I wrote (with Alexander Volpin) after I became involved in 1968 was entitled: "Memorandum on Loyalty." This article defended the right of petition and reminded the authorities that exercise of this right is not by itself evidence of disloyalty.* I had no difficulty in establishing the principle of legality in my work for the defense of rights because this principle was recognized more or less formally by the movement participants with whom I had substantial contacts; but it was also clear that the principle of legality did not at all inhibit my col-

---

* In the USSR collective petitions were forbidden in the army and in places of confinement. Perhaps based on this, some officials preferred not to recognize the right of citizens to petition as a group, not to mention the right of a citizen to draft critical petitions. The wave of petitions toward the end of the nineteen-sixties resulted in reprisals against the "signers" at their places of work. This "blemish" in their personnel files still hinders the professional advancement of many signatories, including even those who offered their repentance.

leagues or me in our criticism or in our noncompliance with unlawful demands by the authorities. The principle of legality was quite natural for me, demanding no special self-restraint, since political struggle and lawbreaking suit neither my temperament nor the nature of my interests in the social sciences.

Another principle also defined at the very beginning of my activity was not as self-evident as the principle of legality. Speaking figuratively, this is the principle of defending political prisoners before they become political prisoners (which does not of course prevent defense of actual political prisoners). In practical terms this means keeping people out of jail. Despite its social significance, the principle of legality does not insure the safety of defenders of rights. I stress the social significance of the legality principle because critical-minded individuals who do not hide their views and who also observe this principle provide society with an unexpected example of legal freedom of thought—and this is vital if we are to encourage the art of thinking in a country that has been subjected for half a century to an ideology pretending to be absolute truth. But as long as people are jailed not only according to laws but also according to KGB interpretation of these laws, abiding by the principle of legality, an unaccustomedly subtle principle for the Soviet authorities, affords no guarantee of safety.

Thus it was important to study court practices and to let people know what acts, even though lawful, might cause their arrest. It was also useful to work out methods of acting that minimize the risk of unlawful repression and to recommend these as substitutes for methods that almost always provoke such repression. Another goal was to persuade well-known individuals who were speaking out for human rights to exercise greater restraint in their statements, since the relative immunity their prestige gave them did not protect others who circulated texts of their statements in samizdat. I rarely succeeded in these various endeavors.

Not that I was exceedingly insistent, since I recognize an individual's right to any action consistent with law as well as the right to self-sacrifice. I objected strenuously only to preaching sacrifice for its own sake, or sacrifice for the great cause of liberty. I recognized an individual's right to sacrifice only himself, and this stand did not satisfy many who were convinced that great causes demand sacrifices. I was often lectured on the grandeur of sacrifice, on the inevitability of many sacrifices for freedom's sake, on sacrifice as an essential quality of the Russian soul. Alas, I could neither accept nor understand these values. I held to my own principle, and I believe I was successful in preventing several demonstrations, the organization of tens of committees, the publication of quite a few sharp protests, and even one self-immolation. Naturally, I prevented these acts solely through discussion with their instigators and only when I was convinced that immediate repression would be the result.

Interestingly enough, people who usually came to me for advice sometimes avoided me when planning a statement that might strike me as sharp. People who knew that I urged restraint on the principle of keeping people out of jail sometimes surprised me by attributing my own restraint to caution, supposing it to be merely a tactical device. But restraint and an inclination to study legal problems are so natural to me that I doubt whether I could have adapted to methods of resounding protest to the authorities instead of simply communicating the distress caused me by violations of rights, even if tactical considerations had warranted a rougher approach.

In the West too I have encountered the opinion that my legalistic approach and my restraint are assumed for tactical reasons, but only rarely, since I have little to do with circles whose views naturally give rise to this thought. Sometimes after a lecture people approach me who understand my ideas better than I do myself and who let me know in one way or another that my stand was an effective tactical device in the Soviet Union, but that now, when I am obliged to remain in the "free world," it is time to move on to the real struggle. I have heard this view of my legalistic position before (although without any hint of approval): KGB investigator E. Fochenkov once informed me that I was engaged in artfully masked anti-Soviet activity. To argue in such cases is senseless. The speakers in both instances are certain that they understand me better than I understand myself. But I will say that my position does not depend on the country where I am living. I will also say that I have never engaged in anti-Soviet activity and that, although I would not recommend the Soviet system to other nations if they were to ask my opinion, I do accept the Soviet system in the USSR as a political reality, and to fight against this system is not among my ambitions. What does interest me is that under any system and in every country human rights should be guaranteed and effective procedures to defend them should exist. And I also want to remind governments of the principle that the sovereignty of the state over the individual is limited and everyone enjoys the right to defend human rights in any country.

My recognition of the existing Soviet state power as legitimate not only *de facto* but *de jure* (within the bounds stipulated by the Constitution of the USSR) surprises many who specialize in criticizing the Soviet regime. They insist that the Bolsheviks usurped power and also that present Soviet elections are falsified. There is no doubt that by dispersing the Constituent Assembly the Bolsheviks usurped power;[9] history has seen many usurpations, and state systems founded by such means are often recognized. With regard to present elections to government bodies in the USSR, while acknowledging their idiosyncrasies, I cannot consider them falsified—a factual basis for that assertion is lacking.* It is, of

---

* I have some doubts, however, as to the observance of the principle of the secret ballot in elections to the USSR Supreme Soviet in territories whose state structure the Soviet Union attended to by way of fulfilling its obligations under the German-Soviet Pact of 1939, "On Friendship

course, strange that ordinarily only one candidate is presented to the voter, but workers may nominate candidates and I know of no case when workers insisted on nominating two candidates and the bosses prevented this.† It is also strange that elections are always practically unanimous, but this is no basis for regarding the elections as falsified. True, in elections with only one candidate it is impossible to vote "against." Printed on the ballot is "Leave the name of the *one* candidate for whom you vote; cross out the other names." This means that a voter who crosses out the name of the sole candidate is violating the electoral rules and apparently his vote is invalid.‡ At least he will not be included with the 99.99 percent (or a bit less) of the population voting "for." So although it is impossible to vote "against," it is possible not to vote "for." But almost everyone votes "for."

Naturally, it would be interesting to know whether people vote from conviction or with indifference.

---

and the Border" (published in the *Record* of the USSR Supreme Soviet for March 29, 1940).

In the elections to the USSR Supreme Soviet in the territories of the western regions of the Ukraine and Bielorussia, Latvia, Lithuania, and Estonia, the voting procedure was simplified as compared with that provided at that time in the "Statute of Elections to the USSR Supreme Soviet," and it was decided that ballots would be handed in without envelopes. (See the *Record* of the USSR Supreme Soviet for February 22, 1940, and November 13, 1940.)

† There was even a case, described by Roy Medvedev, in which the candidate for deputy nominated by the people "was not at all the same person who had been previously selected (behind closed doors) in Tallin. Yet the Central Electoral Commission of the Republic confirmed as candidate the person who had been nominated by the people (the collective of Tartu University in Estonia)."[10]

‡ For that matter, the official statistics show the number of votes cast against the candidate and, separately, the number of ballots ruled void. According to data published by the Presidium of the USSR Supreme Soviet on the results of elections of deputies to local soviets in 1973, in eighty electoral districts (out of a total of 2,193,195) the candidates did not receive an absolute majority of the votes and were not elected. (Out of these eighty electoral districts, seventy-three were districts for elections to rural soviets and seven for elections to urban soviets.)

As the reader may note, I sometimes defend the Soviet regime against unfounded accusations not only because this is a habit acquired in childhood but also because such accusations distract attention from well-founded ones.

I have also defended individual officials as well as the Soviet regime, supposing, perhaps naïvely, that they know not what they do. This may seem strange, but even knowing that an investigator has worked on a case that resulted in a severe, unjust sentence, I would still not treat him as an executioner. For I do not consider him an executioner. The responsibility of each person for all that happens is a complex question. The war crimes tribunal at Nuremberg declared that an order does not free an individual from responsibility. But a Soviet official who violates personal rights and serves as an unjust hangman acts not only in obedience to orders but also in conformity with an ethical value system that was inculcated by force during his childhood, which he assimilated thoroughly and which is reinforced by the congruent behavior of those around him.

I have listened to many discussions of each man's responsibility for every evil act; of, for example, the retribution that will be visited on the whole Russian nation for the deportation of the Crimean Tatars. I have heard the opinion that the man who voted for the death penalty at a public meeting in the thirties, the man who pronounced sentence, and the man who fired the shot are equally executioners. A search for the guilty is natural; it makes life more bearable for people. But I cannot adequately cope with all the needs to defend people and so cannot think about accusations; I must put that question aside. Even when identified officials clearly violate the law, I have never, in defending the law, demanded that they be held to account, although this would be logical from a juridical standpoint.

Perhaps my views are a consequence of my easy life. Perhaps if I had been reduced to despair, like so many martyrs, I would have learned to accuse and to hate. But so far this has not come to pass, and I appeal to people to live without hatred and without preaching hatred for enemies, a precept that long ago alienated me from the Communists' moral system. I believe that even under stress I would maintain this position and would speak of my torturers-by-occupation in words similar to those in Alexander Ginzburg's prison camp letter to Ivan Petrovsky: "This is their job, and they perform their work according to their personality —a humane approach is neither stipulated in the regulations nor, apparently, was it inculcated by their parents."

Many have objected not only to my restraint, not only to my objection on principle to making accusations, but also to the legal position as such (its advocates are called *zakonniki* in the USSR) as artificial and out of touch with social conditions. To the extent that this is a question of world view, discussion is not always fruitful. If for me a state is a legal institution but someone else considers a state "the emanation of the popular soul," a discussion involving such different assumptions is difficult. The situation is similar when someone considers the law a Western import, unnecessary for the USSR, where social relations can be ordered with reliance on the special moral quality of the Russian soul. Partly this attitude toward the *zakonniki*'s point of view results from the evidently inferior level of legal consciousness in Russia. A half-century of "strengthening socialist legality" may have somewhat changed this level, but I recall the words of Kistiakovsky (writing in 1907): ". . . in the minds of Russians insufficient distinction exists between norms of law and norms of ethics; they are mixed together."[11]

This problem is properly a subject for a separate sociological study,* but I should say here that my skepticism about early improvement in the defense of human rights in the

---

* I gave some attention to the problem in my book, *Thoughts on Man*, samizdat, 1971.

USSR stems from my belief that the majority of Russians have a low level of legal culture. This adds to the importance of assisting those minorities in society with a more advanced legal consciousness, although this must certainly not be interpreted as appealing for discrimination in the protection of rights.

4

Freedom of Speech, of the Press, of Assembly, and of Association

> Freedom of speech and of the press is
> primarily freedom to criticize.
> Nobody has ever prohibited praise for
> the government.
>
> —*Vladimir Bukovsky*

SOME PEOPLE in the West have a distorted notion of the extent to which human freedoms are exercised in the Soviet Union. When I said in a lecture that people are not persecuted for their convictions in the USSR, my listeners almost fainted with amazement. They have apparently heard much about the Stalin era, when in fact a person was subjected to repressions even on suspicion of dissent. But things are not the same now. It appears that freedom of thought is not violated today in the Soviet Union. And this shows that a human right can be unviolated in practice even without a legislative guarantee of that right. Of course it would be a fine thing if the Soviet Constitution guaranteed freedom of thought—like the Japanese Constitution of 1947.[1] But let us be content that such freedom is exercised in practice.

It is another matter if a person wants to *express* his

thoughts.* Then it may turn out that from the viewpoint of
the authorities, he said something wrong. This may lead to
difficulties in exercising, in practice, *freedom of speech*,
despite the fact that it is precisely this freedom that is
guaranteed by the Constitution, and not *freedom of correct
speech*. Article 125 of the Constitution of the USSR states:

> In conformity with the interests of the workers and in order to
> strengthen the socialist system, the citizens of the USSR are
> guaranteed by law:
> a) freedom of speech;
> b) freedom of the press;
> c) freedom of assembly and meetings;
> d) freedom of street processions and demonstrations . . .[4]

It is easy to see that the preamble to this article merely
explains that the guarantee of the enumerated rights corresponds to the interests of the workers and the aim of
strengthening the socialist system. But authors of law texts
and legal practitioners interpret this article differently. They
suppose that the enumerated rights are guaranteed with the
proviso that they be exercised in accordance with the inter-

---

* I note here that not only freedom of thought but the freedom to keep
silent is now being manifested in practice. Keeping silent is not of
itself imputable as an antistate crime, except for failure to give information on certain especially dangerous antistate crimes.[2]

   Since I am inclined to seek, in Soviet practice, indications of current liberalism, I note especially that keeping silent is apparently not
imputable as anti-Soviet agitation. By way of contrast I quote the
account of Joseph Berger, a political prisoner during the Stalin era:

> . . . After the murder of Trotsky, Stalin sent *agents-provocateurs* to
> the camps, and they tried to provoke the prisoners into accusing Stalin
> of killing Trotsky or into an expression of regrets at Trotsky's death.
> In the investigation which ended in my second death sentence
> (Norilsk, 1941), an agent's report was used as incriminating evidence.
> The agent wrote: "On the 21st of August *Pravda* announced the
> assassination of Trotsky. I asked Berger, What do you think of it?
> He did not reply." I inquired of my interrogator, "What was wrong
> with that?" He replied: "Why didn't you say, 'A dog deserves a dog's
> death'?"[3]

ests of the working class and with a view to strengthening the socialist system.

This view is also common among jurists: Bukovsky and Pavel Litvinov unsuccessfully protested in court against the distorted interpretation of Article 125.[5]

In the USSR, in accordance with the notion of a uniquely correct state doctrine, information is divided into correct and incorrect. By incorrect information the authorities mean that kind of information which, although not false, is better not mentioned, or information whose mention in the opinion of the authorities, is untimely. Correctness of information is also evaluated by the authorities from the viewpoint of what aim is being served by that information. Thus one propaganda pamphlet states: "Bourgeois propagandists may in certain cases libelously utilize actual facts and reliable statistical data."[6]

So far as I can understand, Soviet juridical practice approaches the question of freedom of informational exchange according to these general principles: Everyone has the right to seek and impart correct information, the correctness of that information to be checked by the appropriate authorized state organs. Of course the possibilities for the state to control everyone's words are limited for the present. The words subject to the strictest and best-organized control are those spoken before a large audience.

Depending upon the general situation and the level of liberalism (the man in the street is very sensitive to fluctuations in that level), people may speak to one another more or less freely. Of course they must bear in mind that in any gathering there may be an activist who by way of his official duties (or motivated by "enthusiasm") will inform the authorities of one's social attitude or whether one is spreading incorrect information. In such cases freedom of speech may have sad consequences for the speaker.

There is reason to believe that there are a good many informers, and also quite a few "seditious" remarks heard by those informers. There is also reason to believe that many reports are kept on file so that, if necessary, they can be used against anyone who has taken the guarantee of free speech too literally. Just as in the case of petty thefts of socialist property, the authorities view indulgently the fact that many people express sharp criticism of the regime's actions, or of living conditions, or even speak disrespectfully of certain Party and government leaders. And if this criticism becomes known to the authorities but is only kept on file and does not provoke repressions, it testifies to a very high level of liberalism in contrast to the Stalin era, when a person might find himself in prison on mere suspicion of dissent, not to mention those instances when there was a report that a person had said something "seditious." However, the authorities are prepared to take an indulgent view of the discontent of individual citizens only so long as their discontent does not go beyond the limits of everyday matters and does not touch upon substantive principles. But if the authorities suspect a person of intending systematically to express his unorthodox, "incorrect" convictions, certain educational measures may be taken. For instance, a "chat" at Party committee headquarters—a chat to which citizens are summoned whether or not they are Party members. If, in the opinion of the authorities, the person's statements are anti-Soviet or slanderous vis-à-vis the Soviet system, prosecution may be instituted. Legal commentators assume that dissemination of such information is subject to criminal punishment even when a person has said something unlawful to only one other person. The same rule applies in the transmission to one other person of manuscript or printed works containing what the authorities consider anti-Soviet propaganda or fabrications libeling the Soviet system.*

---

* But liberalism does exist. In the writings of one jurist I have read that opinions expressed between spouses are not *per se* punishable, since otherwise (so the author feels) the atmosphere of trust in the Soviet family would be undermined. Apparently this does not apply to cases of unregistered marriages. Witness the conviction of the spouses Rumyantsev and Volzhskaya, who were living as man and

As for freedom of speech not among friends but, say, at a factory meeting, people generally express themselves freely about production shortcomings and the local bosses. In deciding to what extent they may speak freely of such things, people must basically take into account the local bosses' possible dissatisfaction with their criticism, rather than fearing persecution from the central authorities. In principle, the regime welcomes criticism from below, and always stresses that this criticism must be encouraged regardless of how high the position of the person subjected to criticism. It is hardly likely, however, that in practice the authorities are ready to put up with criticism if it affects people in very high positions. Persecution for criticism at the local level is in principle prohibited by the authorities, but local authorities can react to systematic criticism either by correcting the defects noted or by trying to get rid of the annoying critic. And since local bosses can hand out various rewards and punishments (whose use, as a rule, it is very difficult to contest), arbitrary criticism by a worker of any superior is considered a bold or senseless act. It is another matter when a person criticizes an individual or shortcomings already criticized by the bosses. In this case the exercise of freedom of critical speech involves no dangers whatsoever. And when it is a question of criticism useful to the bosses, that criticism may be very harsh, following the best models of revolutionary criticism—like the criticism of Lysenko's opponents at the 1948 session of the All-Union Academy of Agricultural Sciences.[7] And sometimes, though rarely, such criticism may affect even high officials of the state, if they have lost their position. This was demonstrated at the Twenty-second Party Congress, when Molotov, Malenkov, Kaganovich, and their ally Shepilov were subjected to very harsh criticism.[8] As a rule

---

wife without having registered their marriage. According to their indictment, they gave each other illicit works to read (for example, Anatoly Marchenko's book, *My Testimony*).

the main speeches at meetings and congresses are planned
in advance* and cleared with the appropriate ideological
authorities. And in these speeches the proportion of attention to successes and to shortcomings is so calculated that
the discussion of shortcomings will not make the listeners
pessimistic but, on the contrary, will inspire them to new
achievements. Of course what Lenin would no doubt have
called the excesses of certain persons can always happen,
even at well-organized meetings. If during the discussion
period a person gets up on the rostrum and starts to say
something completely inadmissible, the audience, guided
by the Party ideologues, will simply prevent him from
speaking. There was, however, one Party conference when
a Soviet general began his speech by politely criticizing the
new Party program because it did not contain guarantees
against the rise of a new cult of personality. The general

---

* Of course there may be exceptions. Thus according to the *Political
Diary* the Twenty-second Party Congress

> . . . followed a different course from what had been planned in ad-
> vance. Attention became focused not on the Party program but on
> the question of Stalin's crimes and those of his closest associates.
> Many important resolutions—even those on removing Stalin from
> the mausoleum and renaming cities, streets, squares, etc., bearing the
> name of Stalin—were adopted at the congress itself and not in
> advance.[9]

The stenographic report of the congress supports this view. In many
speeches one finds that directness which usually disappears when Party
leaders prepare the texts in advance. In any case, I am convinced that,
for example, the speech of the old Bolshevik D. Lazurkina was not
previously checked by Party censors. Otherwise, the delegates to the
congress and the readers of the stenographic report would not have
been able to enjoy her beautiful, spirited digression (she was speaking
of removing Stalin from the mausoleum):

> I always carry Ilich in my heart. And always, comrades, at the most
> difficult times, I have survived only because I had Ilich in my heart.
> I asked him what to do. (Applause.) Yesterday I asked Ilich what
> to do, as if he were before me, alive. He stood there and said: "I
> don't like being next to Stalin, who did so much damage to the
> Party." (Stormy, prolonged applause.)[10]

was Peter Grigorenko.[11] The chairman interrupted and moved that he be deprived of the floor, but the audience rejected the motion and voted that Grigorenko continue his speech. He finished his speech, which was by no means anti-Soviet or seditious or even sharply critical. But Grigorenko had raised a question that the Party leadership wanted to avoid, and for a Soviet general and Party member this speech was of course a very "undisciplined" act. It was after that speech that the persecution of General Grigorenko began.

As for speeches at meetings that have not been planned or organized by the authorities, the latter (insofar as possible) not only do not allow such speeches—they do not allow such meetings.

Although the right of assembly is guaranteed by the Constitution, in practice an assembly or meeting can be held only if it is organized by associations or authorities recognized by the state. And there are no norms in the law specifying how citizens can organize an assembly or meeting or demonstration, or what procedure there is for getting permission from the authorities to hold such an assembly or meeting.*

Of course people can gather at someone's private apartment, and they do so, sometimes even to discuss social problems. However, even this form of assembly may be considered in juridical practice—or by neighbors—an unusual thing.

* On the other hand, there is a provision that makes it possible to prosecute persons who interpret too literally the constitutional right to hold meetings, assemblies, and demonstrations. Article 190-3 of the RSFSR Criminal Code provides punishment of up to three years' deprivation of freedom for the organization of, or active participation in, group actions crudely violating the public order, or accompanied by clear disobedience to the lawful orders of representatives of the state, or involving disruption of the work of transport, state, and social institutions or enterprises. It was on the basis of this article that Pavel Litvinov, Larisa Bogoraz, Victor Dremluga, and others were convicted for their demonstration in Red Square protesting the 1968 Soviet intervention in Czechoslovakia.

According to Soviet doctrine it is quite natural that adult citizens should gather for educational purposes only under the supervision of their mentors. Holding an assembly or a meeting without following the established custom of gathering only under "proper" supervision is regarded by the authorities as an attempt to escape ideological leadership and the control of the authorities. The laws of the state are silent on this point. But since Party-state dualism is recognized in the laws on the administration of the state, it is appropriate to cite the Party Rules:

At congresses, conferences, and meetings called by Soviet trade-union, cooperative, and other mass organizations of the workers, and also in the electoral organs of those organizations, where there are no less than three Party members, Party groups are organized. The tasks of these groups include the all-around strengthening of Party influence and the implementation of its policy among non-Party people . . .[12]

Lenin was quite frank in his program for guaranteeing democratic liberties:

A general proclamation of very broad principles is important for the bourgeoisie: "All citizens have the right of assembly, but of assembly under the open sky—we won't give you any buildings." But we say: fewer phrases and more substance. We must seize palaces—not only the Tauride but many others. As for the right of assembly, we say nothing—and this must be applied to all other points of the democratic program.[13]

Although after Lenin's death his promise to keep silent on the right of assembly was formally violated and this right was guaranteed by the Soviet Constitution, on balance it can be said that Lenin's advice was successfully applied "to all other points of the democratic program."

Despite the guarantees in the Constitution, Soviet officials (following Lenin) do not conceal the fact that in the Soviet Union the manner of assuring freedom of speech, of the press, and of assembly is completely different from what it is in bourgeois systems of "formal democracy." Law textbooks point out that the exercise of these freedoms "has primarily not an individual but a collective character."[14] Needless to say, this is no deterrent to the affirmation that these freedoms are adequately exercised:

The free speech of Soviet citizens is heard in schools and colleges, assuring freedom in teaching; in theaters and clubs, on the radio and on television, guaranteeing freedom of creativity; at assemblies, conferences, and meetings, making it possible to exchange thoughts, knowledge, and experience.

The above words are not from a newspaper editorial: they are from the same textbook.[15]

In limiting freedom of the press the authorities act rather openly. Although the Constitution guarantees freedom of the press and civil legislation[16] stipulates the right of the author to the publication, reproduction, and dissemination of his works by all lawful means, the commentaries on the Civil Code openly distort the sense of these laws, interpreting the right to mean only the prohibition of publication without the author's consent, whereas the laws in question do not contain that particular guarantee.

The author's right to dissemination of his work disappears in the commentary: "A work cannot be published without the author's consent. But the question whether it should be published is decided by socialist organizations which have the function of selecting and disseminating useful works."[17] Soviet ideologues explain frankly how freedom of the press is understood and guaranteed in the Soviet Union. In a speech at the Twenty-third Congress of the CPSU, in 1967, I. I. Bodyul, a Party leader of Moldavia, said:

As is generally known, in our country everyone who considers himself an artist has the right to create freely and is free to write at his discretion without any restrictions. But to the same extent, the Party and our government agencies exercise the right of free choice as to what to print.[18]*

There is an elaborate system of organs that decide what to print.[19]† First there are the editorial boards of the publishing houses and journals to which the author submits his works. The amount of red tape involved in their decisions to publish a work, or not to publish it, is considerable. These editorial boards have the function of selection—in particular, of selection on the basis of artistic worth, topicality, or scientific value. The last word, however, lies with the censorship agencies, which exercise ultimate ideological and political control over all printing.

The organs of Soviet censorship were created shortly after the Revolution. The first decrees stated that limitations on freedom of the press were being introduced only temporarily, pending the complete victory of the Soviet regime.[21] Did people understand then that this meant until such time as the regime was so strong that it could limit freedom of the press without reference to temporary necessity and without justification? In any case, as the regime became stronger, so did the system of Soviet censorship. At first the censorship office was usually called Glavlit, for the Main Administration for Literature and Publishing RSFSR. People still call it Glavlit, although now its official name, apparently, is the Administration for Protecting State Secrets in Print. As the regime grew stronger, information on the system of censorship gradually ceased to be published. So far as I know, Glavlit's instructions are not published at all now, but one can get an idea of its functions from

* The USSR's recent accession to the 1952 Universal Copyright Convention has caused many people to fear, with good reason, that henceforth the Party and government agencies will also determine what is printed abroad.[20] (See Appendix 10.)
† It should be remembered that in the USSR there are no private printing establishments, and that permission is required to organize printing and engraving establishments and to use duplicating equipment. In institutions, duplicating equipment is kept under special control.

the published documents of the thirties. And there is reason to believe that since that time Glavlit's functions have not been reduced but rather expanded. I know that today the list of items whose publication is prohibited fills a very thick tome. According to the 1931 regulations, Glavlit was responsible in particular for prior and subsequent control of publications with reference to their political-ideological and military-economic aspects, and also over radio broadcasts, lectures, and exhibits; for the "confiscation of publications which should not be circulated"; for "authorizing the founding of publishing houses and periodicals; for closing publishing houses and publications; for prohibition and authorization of imports and exports of literature, pictures, etc., in accordance with statutes in force"; and for "preparing a list of works whose publication and dissemination are prohibited."[22] In time Glavlit was made responsible for checking not only the content of published materials but also their appearance. For example, a 1935 order issued by Glavlit instructs its staff members to "carry on a decisive struggle against all manner of formalist tendencies in the design of publications—especially their covers."[23] Similar prior censorship exists with respect to artistic exhibitions and radio and television concerts.*

Although the concept of a state secret in the Soviet Union is very broad, checking on the protection of state secrets in printed matter and in the dissemination of literature is only a small part of Glavlit's job. A Glavlit staff member has the unusually complex task of checking content from the ideological viewpoint, meaning he must read

---

* A general principle of the Soviet attitude toward the dissemination of information is to censor, in theory, all forms of the public dissemination of information. In many cases this censorship is exercised by organizations that are not as reliable as Glavlit. For example, schoolchildren's speeches on holidays are subjected to prior censorship, although it appears that only local educators do this. In certain cases it is not clear who is responsible for the censorship. For instance, I do not know what agency censors the sculptures and inscriptions on gravestones, but so far as I know, such censorship does exist.

not only the text—what is explicitly written—but also what is implied between the lines. More than once I have heard that editors refused to publish authors' works with the argument that certain passages in them stirred up "uncontrollable associations."

It should not be thought that Glavlit's activity is directed only toward prohibiting the publication of works that openly contradict Soviet ideological doctrine. As a rule, such works never reach Glavlit. Book and journal editors are vigilant enough to immediately refuse publication of such a manuscript, and often to report it to the authorities. Glavlit's functions are much more subtle than merely prohibiting publication of manuscripts or deleting passages from them. Soviet literature is required to promote vigorously the Communist education of the workers. Therefore Glavlit must combat such phenomena in literature as indifference to politics or attempts to distract the reader from the heroic significance of the more prosaic aspects of the building of communism.*

The foregoing applies not only to literature but also to publications in the social sciences, since for half a century these sciences have been subordinated to state ideological doctrine. Thus in the Soviet Union a book on history, even very ancient history, will not see the light of day if it lacks a Marxist analysis of the events described, or if the analysis contains mistakes as determined by Party policy on that

---

* A remarkable illustration of the problem of freedom of the press in the USSR is provided by the transcript of a courtroom debate in a civil suit brought by Lydia Chukovskaya against a publishing house because the latter had refused, despite a signed contract, to publish her novella *Sofya Petrovna* (later published in America by E. P. Dutton as *The Deserted House*). Explaining why the publishing house had changed its mind, a representative of the house said: "At the publishing house the manuscript was praised. But then came the plenum of the Central Committee and the meeting of Party leaders with the intelligentsia, and the house readers and editors looked at the work with eyes which had been opened by the meeting and the plenum."[24]

question at the given moment. By way of example people usually recall the transformation of the image of Shamil* in Soviet historical works. At one time he was a national hero, at another time a reactionary opposing the progressive Russian conquest and, apparently, even a British spy. What he is now I can't recall. In the forties, in the field of the history of science, editorial boards and Glavlit were careful not to allow the publication of books lacking "truthful" (corresponding to the view that prevailed then) information on Russian pioneers in various sciences. Glavlit staff members have a lot of trouble censoring works dealing with the history of national minority groups in the Soviet Union, since the history of these peoples must be written correctly, taking into account the progressive role of their conquest by Russia—or, even better, taking into account the progressive role of their voluntary union with Russia. They must also be sure the author has not praised some national figure who did not support the "unification" of that people with the USSR. In literary criticism, not only editorial boards and the publishers of journals but Glavlit, too, must see that an author's opinions coincide with what Soviet ideologues think about the work of this or that writer. They must also see that the name of a writer or poet whose works have been banned does not appear by chance in a Soviet publication. There are many such banned poets and writers—especially among those who wrote just before and just after the Revolution—and both teachers and literary critics try to make sure that young people learn nothing about them.

As for literary classics—and especially Russian classics—it must be said that the Soviet literary organs have been unusually liberal. Perhaps some day the Party will call attention to an inadmissible oversight in the work of Glavlit

---

* A Moslem political leader in Dagestan during the mid-nineteenth century.—Translator's note.

which has made it possible, for example, to publish
Saltykov-Shchedrin,* since it is obvious to everyone that
much of Shchedrin's work stirs up very "uncontrollable
associations." However, this boldness on the part of Glavlit
apparently testifies not only to its intentional liberalism but
to its conviction that the Soviet reader will interpret
Saltykov-Shchedrin correctly and understand that his satire
refers only to times long since past.

Glavlit's liberal attitude toward many books written
before the Revolution is clearly seen in its library policy.
Pursuant to decrees of the twenties, books that were
ideologically harmful were removed from libraries and
destroyed. Many were sent to factories that recycle paper,
and some were burned on the spot "if they deserved such
treatment."† Despite all these measures, however, the libraries still contained many books published before the Revolution which, because of their content, could not of course
be published in our time. When dealing with a state system
like that of the Soviet Union—and especially during the
twenties and thirties, a time of unbridled revolutionary legal
consciousness—we should remember not only what was
done by the supporters of the system but what could have
been done. And if we are to count their good deeds, we
must of course take into account the fact that many old
books were retained in the libraries and even made available for general use, although not all of them would inspire
the reader to heroism in the building of communism.

Of course this liberalism in library policy does not mean
that a reader can get whatever old book he wants in a
library, even if it is in the collection. As a rule the large
libraries have special-custody sections (*spetskhrany*) containing many books that may not be issued to readers with-

---

* Mikhail Evgrafovich Saltykov (1826-1889), a Russian satirist who
  wrote under the pen name of N. Shchedrin.—Translator's note.
† These are the actual words of a statute of the twenties, testifying to a
  certain degree of personification of the inimical books. (I cannot give
  a precise reference here, since my notes were left in Moscow.)

out special permission. The books kept there are those Glavlit does not approve of: memoirs of people who combated the Soviet regime; all émigré publications, however harmless; foreign publications, if they criticize the Soviet Union and its policies or interpret international events differently from the way they are interpreted by the Soviet newspapers; philosophical works that are reactionary in Soviet eyes; and much, much more. I even know of an instance when French fashion magazines were put in a special-custody section.

The existence of special-custody sections is not publicized, but a library patron may be told that the book he wants can be obtained only with special permission and only if he needs it for his work. The permission must be issued by the institution for which he is doing the work, and approved by the First Section of that institution. (The First Section consists of the local representatives of the KGB. I do not think this is the only link connecting the special-custody sections with Glavlit and the KGB, but there is no published information on the connections between Glavlit and the KGB.) Cards for books in the special-custody sections are as a rule (except in cases of oversight) not in card catalogues open to the public. The general catalogue of the Lenin Library in Moscow cannot be considered fully open to readers, since, for example, a reader in the science room who wants to consult the card catalogue must give the person on duty a card showing his last name and the subject matter of the bibliography he is interested in. If he begins to look into drawers of cards unrelated to the subject matter he has indicated, the librarian on duty will come up to him (not always, but depending upon the degree of efficiency), offer his services in an unmistakable way, and lead him to the card file corresponding to the subject matter he has indicated. This general catalogue contains cards which, instead of a number, have SKh (special custody) written on them.

What I have said about the special-custody sections does

not mean that all books not in these sections will be issued on request. I have often heard disputes between readers and librarians about why the latter would not issue a Bible. In one dispute the librarian said, "We do not propagandize religion." Needless to say, this would not have occurred in the social sciences room. Yet even in the room for physical and technical sciences, obtaining certain books not kept in the special section involves great difficulty or proves to be impossible. According to my observations, the works of Freud, for example, often turn out to have been sent to the bindery. For such authors as Nietzsche or Przybyszewski* the refusals are more open, without reference to bindery work.

There is also a special solicitude for the morals of library patrons. Pornography is interpreted very broadly in the Soviet Union, and the Soviet's scrupulous attitude toward its obligations under the Convention Prohibiting the Dissemination of Pornographic Publications may serve as an encouraging example of its capacity to fulfill international agreements. Naturally, it is Glavlit (again) that is responsible for this.

We see that the activity of Glavlit staff members covers a wide variety of subject matter. Although there is apparently some specialization among them, on balance it would seem that Glavlit personnel have to be erudite in many areas. Judging from the fact that their personal numbers, which are generally—though not invariably today— printed in the books they are responsible for,[25] consist of a five-digit figure and one letter, it may be concluded that there are many such erudite people in the Soviet Union. Some of them even have to know foreign languages for work in customs and (according to Zhores Medvedev) in the post office.[26]

The customs duties of Glavlit workers are apparently very

---

* Stanislav Przybyszewski (1868-1927) was a Polish novelist.—Translator's note.

demanding. Organizers of ideological sabotage against the Soviet Union have dreamed up all kinds of tricks to get their printed matter into the country. For example, the book *Ideological Sabotage: a Weapon of Imperialism* contains a photograph of a man in whose money belt copies of the New Testament were discovered (the title was discernible in the photograph).[27]* Thanks to the vigilance of Soviet customs agents and Glavlit workers, the New Testament was held up at the border and not used as an opiate to stupefy Soviet citizens with preachings of goodness and meekness. The law permits importation of books, but not all books are the same; religious literature, including the Bible, is not allowed into the Soviet Union. (In response to a question from Boris Zuckermann, one of the active defenders of human rights, the chief inspector of the Ministry of Foreign Trade confirmed that importing religious literature into the USSR is prohibited.[28]) Books whose importation Glavlit does not allow are removed from packages and generally, so far as I know, are not returned to the sender. Since Western propagandists and ideological saboteurs resort to multifarious tricks, the customs agents and Glavlit workers must be very vigilant. One example of such vigilance, according to Medvedev,[29] is the ritual of burning the paper wrappings of equipment purchased abroad.

Keeping track of exports of printed matter from the Soviet Union likewise demands vigilance. This is necessary so as not to allow the export of books whose distribution is prohibited—those that are ideologically obsolete, for example, by former leaders who have been labeled enemies of the people—and also to see that no one sends out "secret" literature (including local newspapers, whose export is prohibited). It is further necessary because old editions are considered items of cultural value, and anyone exporting

---

* The caption for the photograph reads: "From this photograph we can see how a foreigner tried to bring anti-Soviet propaganda into the Soviet Union under his clothes."

them must pay a customs duty. In practice, the vigilance of customs agents is demonstrated by their having certain travelers take off all their clothes, and even performing internal physical examinations. Apparently the same considerations are a factor in the prohibition of newspapers and other printed matter being used to wrap articles being sent out of the country.

The role of Glavlit in connection with the mails has been discussed in detail by Medvedev. I myself have not studied this question thoroughly, but from personal experience I am familiar with the disappearance of letters. As it happened, I was unable to ascertain who was to blame for the disappearance of letters sent to me from abroad. I estimate that during the period of my public activity in Moscow in defense of human rights I received no more than 10 per cent of the total number of letters sent me from abroad. In particular, among the letters that disappeared were some from the New York headquarters of the International League for the Rights of Man and Professor John Carey, who was then its president, and from the International Institute for Human Rights and its president, Professor René Cassin. I sent an inquiry to the Ministry of Communications about this systematic disappearance of my correspondence and received an answer from the chief inspector at the ministry. He stated that the letters whose registration numbers I listed had not been recorded at the Moscow Post Office—a piece of information I can readily believe, even if my letters were held up by the censor. The Moscow Post Office gets foreign letters from the International Post Office there, and according to Medvedev's information, letters are censored at the International Post Office. Out of almost two hundred letters sent from New York in 1971–72 by Leonid Rigerman, who was then my representative there, I received about twenty. Rigerman has told me that the letters I did not receive contained the Russian texts of UN documents on human rights. Since such a percentage of lost letters creates the impression of a systematic loss, it would be interesting to ascertain whether it is the Soviet or American postal service which takes such a disapproving attitude toward UN documents on human rights. It seems, however, that neither postal service intends to admit any fault in the loss of those letters.

People in the West and in the Soviet Union are so accustomed to the fact that letters to and from the USSR frequently vanish that no one is surprised. On the contrary, people are more likely to be surprised that some individuals are trying to investigate this matter. International legal guarantees of the inviolability of the mails represent an important achievement of our civilization that could help the development of freedom of information even in the Soviet Union, but when someone in the West writes to the Soviet Union he is likely to think (in terms of the thirties and forties) of how not to harm his Soviet acquaintance with his letter, rather than of how to achieve uninterrupted mail delivery. Meantime, the use of registered mail and a systematic follow-up on what happens to the correspondence would—if this follow-up were carried out by many correspondents—promote the realization in practice of the guarantees of inviolability.

Yury Levin, a native of Leningrad, did some very important research on the problem of assuring postal guarantees. For example, he sent registered letters to a Voice of America staff member. These letters regularly failed to reach their addressee. Complaints to the Leningrad Post Office did not clear up the reasons for the disappearance of the letters. The finale of Levin's experiments is tragic. He sent the United States Embassy in Moscow a registered letter making a statement on the criminality of the movement of Soviet troops into Czechoslovakia. He assumed that the KGB would take measures of some sort and thus expose its actions in violation of the secrecy of correspondence. Levin was soon placed in a psychiatric hospital, then released, and then, after some time, arrested. Not long before his arrest, at a KGB district division headquarters in Leningrad, Levin was presented with a document certifying that a letter from Yu. L. Levin addressed to the U.S. Embassy had been discovered and confiscated in the course of a customs examination. This letter was sent to the *partaktiv* (the most active members of the Party organization) at the institute where Levin worked, and the *partaktiv* asked the procurator to institute criminal proceedings against Levin for anti-Soviet, libelous opinions conveyed to enemies.[30]

Here are two more examples. On February 8, 1972, the newspaper *Penzenskaya pravda* reported the conviction of A. Lokolov, who under the pseudonym of A. Karpov had sent letters to one of the announcers at Radio Liberty, in Munich, the headquarters of the American-financed station that broadcasts to the USSR. The newspaper reported that "these libels were exposed by ordinary Soviet citizens." It is doubtful that this was done by "ordinary Soviet citizens" from Radio Liberty, but the newspaper gave no details of how these letters were discovered by the investigators.[31]

The indictment of Yakov Khantsis, in Kirov in 1972, stated that the witnesses Nikitchenko, Pervakova, and Demina, "workers at the Amutinsky Telegraph Office, explained that on January 14 and February 11, 1972, Khantsis brought to the telegraph office two telegrams containing fabrications discrediting the Soviet state and social system. The telegrams were addressed to [a person in] the city of Kishinev."[32]

As for telephone communication, methods for lawful violation of the secrecy of telephone conversations are not specified in Soviet legislation. But a recent amendment to Article 83 of the USSR Communications Regulations provides: "The use of telephonic communication (long distance, urban, or rural) for purposes prejudicial to state interests and the public order is prohibited."[33]

It may be too bold to suggest that methods of enforcing

this legal requirement involve the tapping of telephone con-versations.* However, even if it turns out that they do involve tapping, there is no basis for assuming that Glavlit workers take part in this.

Glavlit's activities do, however, extend to radio and tele-vision. For the state radio and television stations Glavlit is of course the highest instance; basic ideological control is the responsibility of the station staffs. Although there are no powerful private radio stations in the Soviet Union, there are amateurs who use low-power transmitters for personal purposes, usually as a hobby. There is a licensing system for such transmitters, and their use without permission from the authorities is punishable by a fine under adminis-trative procedure.[34] In recent years there have been prose-cutions for transmitting "without appropriate authoriza-tion." The amateurs were sentenced to punishment under the article of the criminal code on hooliganism—that is, for crude violation of the public order combined with an evi-dent lack of respect for society.[35] Depending on the con-tent of the transmissions, it is also possible to prosecute under other articles, such as the one forbidding anti-Soviet agitation.

I do not know whether it is Glavlit or other agencies that monitor information broadcast by foreign radio stations; but it would appear that the information broadcast by them in the languages of the peoples of the USSR is monitored very strictly. Although I have no documentary evidence, like many other people in the Soviet Union and the West I cannot escape the strong impression that certain Western transmissions to the USSR are subjected to jamming sanc-

---

* The "monitoring" of telephone conversations is mentioned in an act of 1922 (Decree of the Central Executive Committee and Council of People's Commissars of the Crimean Autonomous Soviet Socialist Re-public on Expanding the Use of the Tatar Language): "In view of local conditions in the Crimea and by virtue of the impossibility of establishing monitoring, for the time being the only telephone con-versations permitted in the Tatar language are official conversations."

tioned by government authorities. Soviet sources usually
that certain foreign stations are spreading anti-Soviet propa-
keep silent about this systematic jamming when they claim
ganda in Russian and other languages of the USSR.* But I
will not be surprised if official Soviet sources were to confirm that fact some day.

KGB investigators in their talks with dissidents—and
also certain Soviet journalists—very much like to complain
that hostile radio stations in the West are poisoning "our
Soviet air waves" with anti-Soviet or religious propaganda.
Testimony that a defendant has listened to foreign radio
broadcasts in the Russian language has proved so worthy
of attention in investigations that it may be included in the
indictment. In and of itself, listening to foreign radio transmissions is not a crime, but it does indicate a certain degree
of disloyalty. If, however, someone records a transmission
from a Western radio station on a tape recorder, this may
be characterized as the preparation of a libelous document.[37]

After I came to the United States I listened to several
broadcasts of Radio Liberty (not without difficulty, since
the jamming reaches even this far). I really couldn't understand, judging from those broadcasts, why a radio station
operated by such a friendly country as the United States
should be considered hostile by the KGB. But possibly this
is because it broadcasts, in Russian, information not cleared
by Glavlit. Who knows? Perhaps some day, thanks to
détente and the development of increasingly good relations
between the United States and the USSR, Glavlit's guidelines will affect American radio stations as well. In any
case, the draft convention that the Soviet Union proposed to
the UN in 1972 for the prospective relaying of television

---

* According to Volpin, among those being held in the Leningrad prison-
type psychiatric hospital was a man named Lysak,[36] who had been
arrested because he asked a Party lecturer about the jamming of
foreign radio transmissions in the USSR.

broadcasts via artificial satellites was written in conformity with the principle of state control of information disseminated over its territory.[38]

Although the draft text does not fully correspond to the conventional Western attitude toward freedom of information, I would not be surprised if the UN ultimately accepted this proposal. The fact that the UN has adopted a convention abolishing statutory limitations for certain crimes prompts me to expect the international law created by the UN to conform closely to that recommended in Soviet legal doctrine.

The Soviet state devotes a great deal of attention to controlling the information that reaches its citizens. Particularly careful attention is devoted to the control of information reaching young people, and especially to programs for the education of youth. A great many laws and decrees are concerned with the correct ideological education of children. As for university students, a recent decree of the Central Committee and the Council of Ministers on measures for the further improvement of higher education in the country obliges institutions of higher learning "to insure high quality in the teaching of the social sciences . . . to develop in student youth a class approach to the phenomena and events of social life and skill in the argumentative criticism of anti-Marxist views."[39] There is a similar decree governing education on other levels. In the recently adopted Fundamental Principles of Legislation of the USSR and the Union Republics on National Education, the state's expectations from education at various levels are expressed in a single text, which makes it possible to observe the increasing demands for ideological correctness in education as a child grows and progresses from preschool education to secondary school and higher.[40] Preschool institutions, in close collaboration with families, "educate children in a spirit of respect for their elders, a love for the homeland and their own region." General secondary education has the task of developing a Marxist-Leninist world view in the younger generation, of inculcating in students a feeling of internationalism, Soviet patriotism, and a readiness to defend the socialist homeland. One of the chief tasks of higher education is to develop high moral qualities in students—a feeling of duty and readiness to defend the homeland. Soviet educational policy makers apparently understand that these tasks would be carried out more successfully if children were subject to centralized education under the exclusive control of the state without the interference of parents, who may still retain some vestiges of the pre-Communist era. The Fundamental Principles of Legislation on Marriage and the Family stipulate that parents should rear their children in conformity with the moral code of the builders of communism, and provide that violation of that obligation is punishable by deprivation of parental rights or taking away the child.[41] Soviet ideologues understand that it is precisely through the family that "alien" influences can reach the consciousness of the younger generation.

Despite the obvious advantages of taking children away from their parents for a centralized and ideologically correct education, the Soviet Union does not apply that effective measure.* In a certain sense Soviet legal doctrine implies the right of the state to adopt such measures. Apparently this is what enables the legal commentary to note that the right of parents to rear their children is *granted* to parents by the state, because that right "makes it possible to satisfy one of the strongest and noblest human feelings—the feeling of parental love."[42]

Very strict ideological and political requirements are demanded of people involved in the process of formal education.[43] In particular, to obtain a teaching post at an

---

* But whereas the former marriage and family code stipulated that agencies of guardianship and wardship were required to permit parents who had been deprived of their parental rights to visit their children, the present code merely states that such agencies may permit visitation.

institution of higher learning one must present not only documentation of scholarly attainments but also ideological and political references. Instances of teachers being dismissed from educational institutions for actions contravening the regime's ideological requirements are well known.

5
Freedom of Movement

I~N~ S~OVIET~ L~AW~ there is no direct guarantee of freedom of movement, but travel within the USSR is usually quite feasible for most Soviet citizens. True, this freedom of movement is limited in areas where there are special installations and in the so-called border zone along the frontiers.[1] It is also limited by the possibility of criminal prosecution for vagrancy.[2] Legal commentary explains that "vagrancy consists of repeated moves or trips (wanderings) from one populated area to another, together with the avoidance of socially useful labor."[3] Criminal prosecution is instituted only in the event of systematic vagrancy: "one or two instances of moving from one place to another do not constitute criminally punishable vagrancy." The maximum punishment is deprivation of freedom for a period of two years or, in the case of recidivism, four years. The legislation does not associate punishable vagrancy with other kinds of violations, but in practice it is punished only when combined with the avoidance of socially useful labor, so that freedom of movement is fully recognized only for those engaged in socially useful labor.

The right to choose one's place of residence, although guaranteed by law, is subject to very serious restrictions not based on statutes. The Soviet Union has a so-called passport system whose norms are established by an unpublished decree of the Council of Ministers. This decree requires citizens living in nonrural areas to have passports, and these passports, in addition to other data, must contain information on the citizen's *propiska*—a permit issued by local authorities for residence in a particular city or town. Violation of the passport system or of the *propiska* incurs criminal liability after administrative warnings.[4] The passport system creates a very great limitation on freedom, especially for the Soviet Union's large rural population. They do not have passports and cannot move to urban areas without permission, since they must obtain both a passport and a *propiska*. Experience indicates that local police agencies have instructions to obstruct rural people's attempts to get passports and permits (*propiski*) to reside in urban areas.

Moreover, members of collective farms (and the majority of the Soviet rural population are collective farmers) have no guarantees of the right to leave their collective. Although the model charter for an agricultural artel provides that a member of a collective farm can submit a request to leave it, neither the charter nor the law assures the right to do so. A collective farm is considered a voluntary association, but as early as 1930, during criticism of the policy on persuading people to join collective farms, it was explained that "voluntariness" did not mean "transforming collective farms into way stations."[5] Although a lot has changed in Russia over the past half-century, the extralegal demands of the authorities and of juridical practice that tie people to the land they till suggest an analogy with the serfdom that existed in Russia more than a hundred years ago.*

Ex-convicts are also systematically hampered in their choice of where to live if they were convicted of one of the many crimes enumerated in the very long list under Article 40 of the Regulations on Passports (unpublished). Among other especially dangerous antistate crimes, this list includes anti-Soviet propaganda and agitation. By way of example we may again mention Vladimir Bukovsky, who was sentenced to two years in prison plus five years in a labor camp plus five years of exile. The expiration of this twelve-year sentence will not mean that Bukovsky can return home. For eight more years he will not be able to obtain a residence permit for Moscow. Thus Bukovsky was actually sentenced, not to twelve, but to twenty years of limitation of freedom.[7]

Substantial limitations on the right to choose one's domicile have been imposed on former "specially resettled persons": persons belonging to such national groups as the Crimean Tatars, the Meskhi Turks,† and the Volga Germans, who in the Stalin era were forcibly resettled away from their own territory. Today, as a rule, members of such groups cannot obtain permission to live in those regions from which they were deported.

What I have said about restrictions on residence permits for certain categories of citizens does not mean that a citizen outside these categories can choose his domicile and register wherever he wishes. If the place in question is Moscow or Leningrad or some other large, "regulated city,"‡ he will sometimes encounter insurmountable difficulties in trying to get a residence permit, even if he has

---

* Without special permission, a member of a collective farm cannot be hired for temporary work elsewhere even during the season when he is not busy on the collective farm.[6]

† A Turkic ethnic group indigenous to the Georgian SSR.—Translator's note.

‡ That is, one under special regulations to control population.—Translator's note.

relatives there. An exception is usually made when a citizen is moving to join a spouse, but this is not always true. In the summer of 1973 the authorities refused Aleksandr Solzhenitsyn a permit to live in Moscow, even though his wife was living there.[8]

Permits for "nonregulated" cities are easier to get, but apparently this is still not a trivial matter, since the local authorities always want to know the reasons for moving. Of course there are many reasons that justify a move in the eyes of the authorities—particularly reasons associated with family or job. But if a citizen who wants to relocate goes to the police department and says he is moving simply because he wants to, such an argument will produce an unfavorable impression on the officials in the passport section. This does not rule out the possibility of further discussion; but various government agencies receive so many complaints about the refusal of local authorities to grant a residence permit, that to satisfy all these claims and overrule the decisions is very difficult.

There is one problem that, in my opinion, has to do with freedom of movement within the country but that, in the opinion of Soviet officials (the police and the KGB), apparently has to do instead with the right to leave the USSR. This is the question of freedom to visit foreign embassies. Muscovites know that one must not visit foreign embassies. As far as I can find out, however, no restrictions on such visits have been published. I have been very much interested in what arguments might be advanced by jurists to justify the forcible restraint of citizens who try to visit foreign embassies, even people with official invitations. I know that often a person who has managed to get past the policemen and into a foreign embassy has subsequently been followed and invited to the KGB for an educational talk. I also know that they try to arrest people, and do arrest them, for an attempt to enter a foreign embassy. But only once did I hear arguments trying to justify the prohibition, and I remember how anomalous they were. When my friend

Leonid Rigerman, who then lived in Moscow, decided to renew his right to American citizenship, he found it necessary, after a telephone conversation with an American consular official, to go to the U.S. Embassy in Moscow. He did not come back, and late that evening some of his friends found out that he had been arrested and was being held at a precinct station of the Moscow police. His mother and several friends, myself among them, went to the precinct station. There I heard an unforgettable dialogue between the police captain on duty and Rigerman's friend Boris Zuckermann.

Zuckermann: "We heard that your colleagues arrested our friend Rigerman. What for? Did he do something wrong?"

The captain: "Yes, he disturbed the public order. He was walking along the street and he tried to violate the frontier of the USSR."

Zuckermann: "He tried to violate the frontier on the street?"

The captain: "No, he tried to violate the frontier on the sidewalk."

The subsequent talk made it clear that the police captain was seriously convinced that a foreign embassy is encircled by a line—not one that is marked out anywhere on earth but a definite line nonetheless—which the police must defend as the national frontier. Such a notion of the extraterritoriality of a foreign embassy made it completely obvious, in the eyes of the police, that they must detain any Soviet citizen who tried to cross that line. It seems, however, that such "violators of the frontier" are only detained (and sometimes sent to psychiatric hospitals); they are not subjected to the same persecution as violators of the actual frontier of the USSR. Nevertheless, the obstacles placed in their way by the authorities cause a great deal of trouble for people who need to visit a foreign embassy for some juridical procedure—to renew their citizenship, perhaps, or to try to locate relatives abroad.

Despite all these limitations, freedom of movement within the country and the freedom to choose one's domicile within the territory of the USSR seem well protected in comparison with freedom to leave the USSR.

In Soviet legislation there is no direct guarantee of the right to leave the country. True, that right is recognized as a civil right by the Soviet Union's ratification of the UN Convention on Eliminating All Forms of Racial Discrimination. The convention does not, however, contain a guarantee. Indirectly, the right to leave the country to resettle abroad is recognized in Soviet legislation by the guarantee of the right to choose one's place of residence,[9] which does not specify the geographic limits for the exercise of that right. The right to leave the country to travel is indirectly recognized in Soviet legislation by the guarantee of the right to choose one's occupation, since travel to other countries is undoubtedly a kind of occupation. It is doubtful whether the Soviet authorities recognize such interpretations of these guarantees of rights as a basis for defending the right to leave the country. One attempt—in Dora Kolyaditskaya's case—to defend in court the right to leave the country by pleading the freedom to choose one's domicile proved unsuccessful.[10]

Despite the lack of guarantees of the right to leave the country, the possibility of leaving is recognized by Soviet laws and regulations. The statute on entering and leaving the USSR[11] stipulates that Soviet citizens permitted to leave the country will be issued a general citizen's foreign passport, and that exit from the USSR is authorized in conformity with it. Violation of the established procedure makes one liable to punishment by deprivation of freedom for a period of up to three years, and for up to ten years if one leaves illegally in a plane.[12]

This, however, applies to cases in which the court does not find, in the acts of the person violating or trying to violate the procedure for leaving the country, elements of a more serious crime. In cases of so-called fleeing abroad (or refusing to return to the USSR from abroad), the crime is treason. The article on treason specifies execution as a possible punishment if a Soviet citizen flees abroad with intent "to do damage to the national independence, the territorial integrity, or the military power of the USSR."[13] Although it is not clear how the emigration of a private person can damage the national independence, the territorial integrity, or the military power of the USSR, in practice there have been many court decisions limiting the right to choose one's domicile that refer to the article on treason.

The statute on leaving and entering the country provides that documents for leaving the USSR, living abroad, and returning to the USSR are issued according to established procedure "on the basis of written applications from the interested ministries, departments, and organizations of the USSR, and also on the basis of applications from citizens going abroad on private business."[14] This might lead to the assumption that the procedure for citizens to obtain passports by application is simple, and the impression is reinforced by the fact that, unlike applications filed by ministries, departments, or organizations, this statute does not indicate that an individual's application must be written. (This presumably corresponds to the Soviet legal tradition of not allowing discrimination on the basis of literacy.*) Experience shows, however, that the procedure for obtaining a foreign passport is complicated. Moreover, the initial procedure of applying for a passport or a visa is very complicated. No regulation governing the procedure the authorities use in considering citizens' applications for permission to leave the country is known. The first and the final stages are obviously handled by the USSR Ministry of Internal Affairs and its local offices, since the staff of that ministry accepts applications and authorizes or communicates refusals. One can only assume that people outside the Ministry

---

* Who knows? Perhaps this tradition accounts for the wretched habit of many Soviet officials of giving, insofar as possible, oral answers to citizens' complaints.

of Internal Affairs are involved in the intermediate stages. At least even senior officials there sometimes say, in reply to the demands of Jews for exit visas to Israel, "You must understand that this is not up to us."

There are no known procedural codes governing applications for permission to travel abroad. But many details of this procedure are known from experience, and instructions on how to apply are posted in the waiting room of the Visa and Foreign Registration Section (OVIR) of the Ministry of Internal Affairs.

Although a great deal of paper work and long delay is generally required for approval of travel to any foreign country, it is relatively simple to obtain permission to travel to socialist countries. For travel to capitalist countries, as a rule, the citizen must first of all present an invitation from close relatives living there. The criteria for closeness are usually evaluated by OVIR staff members. The citizen may be informed that first cousins are not sufficiently close relatives, or that a sister he has not seen for a long time is not a sufficiently close relative to justify such a long trip. He is also required to fill out long questionnaires containing, in addition to trivial questions, such specific questions as whether he belongs to the Party; and to present a reference from his place of employment signed by the director of the institution, the secretary of the local organization of the Communist Party, and the secretary of the trade union. This reference must show the attitude of the signers toward the citizen's intention to go abroad. Virtually no one is surprised that the signature of the secretary of the local Communist Party organization is obligatory even for references issued to persons who are not Party members.

If the specified officials do not endorse the citizen's wish to go abroad, they will give him a negative reference. Or they may even try to avoid giving him a reference at all. Usually, however, such references are obtained. Yet because the law contains no guarantee of the right to a reference, and there is no effective procedure for overcoming the difficulties of getting one, this requirement causes trouble and anxiety for many people.

In addition to all these requirements, a person who wants to go abroad for permanent residence must present an affidavit of his spouse's agreement to his departure (if the spouse is remaining in the USSR) and a document showing his parents' attitude toward his leaving. Since the law contains no reference to cases when a competent adult citizen must request the agreement of his parents or spouse to the exercise of his rights, notaries refuse to attest the signatures of parents or spouse on such affidavits, and this often causes further difficulties for the would-be traveler.

I think citizens of the USSR would be patient in putting up with such a complex procedure for applying to go abroad if the applications were usually approved. But most often they are denied. As far as I know from many hundreds of cases, the OVIR staff never issues written refusals. People are usually notified by telephone, and the reasons for refusal are given only if the applicant is exceptionally persistent. Even then, it often seems that the real reasons for refusal are not being given; the OVIR personnel sound as if they simply do not know them.

Despite the fact that applying to go abroad involves such great trouble—including keeping the applicant away from his regular occupation (there are frequently long queues at the OVIR)—no one can act through a lawyer or other agent. On the basis of unpublished regulations, lawyers are not allowed to represent a client in foreign passport matters. One cannot retain a lawyer to handle the formalities required in making application, or to talk to the OVIR staff, despite the fact that the statute on the bar does not restrict the possibilities for retaining counsel in administrative processes.[15] Nor can one send documents to the OVIR through the mail: it will not accept them.

One may of course protest the OVIR's refusal to grant permission to leave the country. Complaints may be made to the Ministry of Internal Affairs, the Presidium of the

Supreme Soviet or Council of Ministers, and other instances. Usually, all complaints are returned to the OVIR, and the OVIR then reports that the complaint has been considered and there are no grounds for satisfying it. Again, replies to complaints are as a rule made orally. Out of hundreds of people who applied to emigrate to Israel, I know of only one, Vladimir Mogilever, who received a written reply to a complaint.[16]

Although no statistics are published, there is reason to believe that applications to go abroad are very frequently refused. In addition, many citizens who in principle would like to travel abroad or emigrate do not even attempt to apply, assuming that they will be refused.

The restriction of Soviet citizens' rights to leave the country has attracted the attention of "world public opinion" in connection with the problem of the emigration of Jews to Israel. The obstacles the Soviet authorities have placed in the way of this emigration may testify, not necessarily to a policy of anti-Semitism but (on equally valid grounds) to a policy of philo-Semitism—to the state's partiality toward keeping its own Jews. But any mass restrictions of rights affecting Jews attracts the attention of "world public opinion," since historically any form of restriction on the rights of Jews is a critical question for our civilization. Although public opinion has concentrated on the problem of Jewish emigration, it should be remembered that this is a problem of the emigration of people in general. It is a question of forcibly keeping people under the jurisdiction of a state whose territory they want to leave.

It is very gratifying that the persistence of the Jews who want to emigrate and the support of foreign public opinion have prompted the Soviet authorities to take a comparatively realistic position, and to permit Jewish emigration on a scale one could scarcely have hoped for at the outset. Except for temporary indulgence during the N.E.P. period, the right to leave the country has always been violated in the Soviet Union, to the point where people bold enough to express their wish to leave the country were often subjected to criminal punishment or psychiatric repressions. Over the decades this attitude of the state has driven some individuals to desperation and even to attempts to violate the law; for example, Dmitri Mikheyev tried to leave the Soviet Union using the documents of a Swiss citizen, de Pérrégaux. This was the background of the 1970 trial in Leningrad involving Edward Kuznetsov and others who, made desperate by illegal restrictions on their freedom to leave the country, planned (according to their sentence) to steal an airplane in order to leave the country in which they were being detained against their will. For this they were sentenced to long periods of deprivation of freedom. Many other citizens have been convicted of attempts to cross the frontier without permission.

The mass of Soviet people do not suffer acutely from restrictions on the right to leave the country. This is not only because there are only a few who want to leave the country but because those few do not usually strive to have their difficulties or secret wishes brought to the attention of public opinion. After all, the wish to leave the country is, in and of itself, traditionally regarded by the Soviet public as a sign of a certain degree of disloyalty. It is fortunate that some Jews disregarded tradition and brought their case to the attention of "world public opinion." The Jewish emigrants were the first large group in the history of the USSR to break through the fifty-year-old barrier. Thanks to the efforts of the Jewish emigrants it has become possible, to some extent, to study the problems associated with the procedure for obtaining permission to leave the country.

The Jewish repatriates have accomplished a lot. The Soviet Union has not only ceased to deny the existence of the problem of Jewish emigration but has made it possible for many thousands of Jews to leave the country. However, the problem cannot be regarded as solved. Today Jewish scientists and technical specialists still encounter serious difficulties.

The exaction of huge fees for education from those Jews who are emigrating to Israel has been temporarily halted, but an oral promise to suspend a law is no basis for regarding that law as abrogated. The emigration of specialists whom the state considers to be particularly valuable, or to whom (as alleged by the authorities) secret information was entrusted, is still very difficult. There are no criteria for judging the accuracy or the legitimacy of an assertion that a person was privy to secret work. This, combined with the fact that before being made privy to secret work the person was not warned of future restrictions on his right to emigrate, indicates a certain degree of arbitrariness in using clearance for secret work as grounds for refusing permission to emigrate, and that recourse to such grounds is unlawful.*

---

* In 1971 a judicial experiment was carried out in Moscow. About ten Jewish scientists whom the authorities had prevented from emigrating to Israel on the grounds that they had been made privy to secret documents filed complaints, identical in content, with various district courts of the city of Moscow. The gist of the complaints was that since the receipt of clearance for secret work affects the right to emigrate from the USSR, the receipt of that clearance is in the juridical sense a contract between the citizen receiving the clearance and the organization issuing it (according to Soviet civil law, "actions of citizens and organizations aimed at establishing, changing, or abrogating civil rights and obligations" are contracts), since the right to leave one's country was recognized by the Soviet Union by the act of ratifying the Convention on the Elimination of All Forms of Racial Discrimination. Because the plaintiff was not warned that receipt of a clearance for secret work would limit his right to leave the country, this was a contract executed under the influence of a deception. The plaintiff therefore has the right to demand that the contract be declared null and void, and he appeals to the court to do so.

The reactions of various district courts of the city of Moscow to these identical complaints were themselves identical in that all the courts refused to consider them on the grounds that the dispute did not fall within the competence of judicial organs. However, different reasons were given as to why it did not. One judge stated that receipt of clearance for secret documents is one of the conditions of a labor contract, and the conditions of a labor contract are not justiciable matters. Another ruled that the dispute in question fell within the competence of administrative organs. One of the judges went so far as

The USSR's ideological uniqueness is usually seen as the main reason for restrictions on its citizens' right to travel. The kaleidoscope of information unverified by Glavlit can have a baleful effect on a Soviet citizen traveling abroad if he is not politically literate and is not capable of adequate resistance to the intrigues of bourgeois propaganda. I think, however, that is not the sole reason for restricting the right to leave the country, since it is not much easier to travel to socialist countries. Also, of course, this is not the reason a citizen is refused permission to leave the country for permanent residence abroad.

People often try to explain the restrictions on the freedom to leave the USSR by saying that without them a mass exodus of "malcontents" from the Soviet Union would begin. I do not think this is the explanation. There are plenty of malcontents in countries easy to leave, but the majority of them stay in their own country. It is hardly likely that in the USSR one could recruit enough malcontents ready to leave the country to begin a mass exodus capable of doing demographic damage to the USSR. And a

---

to say that questions associated with clearances for secret work could be considered only by special courts. However, his frankness was not reflected in the written decision refusing to consider the complaint.

Subsequently all the plaintiffs protested the district court decisions to Moscow City Court, taking issue with the district courts' grounds for refusing to consider the complaints. On all the protests the decisions of the Moscow City Court were virtually identical. It ruled that the district courts had been correct in refusing to consider the complaints, and without going into a detailed examination it found correct all the various reasons cited by the district courts as grounds for refusing to consider them.

Using documents from these cases, I wrote a protest to the president of the Moscow City Court, calling his attention to the fact that the court, in finding correct all the reasons invoked by the lower courts for refusing to consider the complaints, had approved several decisions that contradicted one another. Unfortunately, this marked the end of the judicial experiment, since I received no answer. (I hope that in telling of this experiment I have not made errors of substance; I do not have detailed documents on these emigration cases; they were apparently lost in an attempt to send them to the West for publication.)

few emigrants would not even prejudice the Soviet Union's claims to being the happiest of countries. On the contrary, the prestige of the Soviet Union would be enhanced if it became a state that, although proud of its own way of life, displayed its liberality by assuring freedom of emigration.

I think restrictions on the right to leave the Soviet Union are due to traits of social psychology that are deeper and more ancient than the ideological uniqueness of the USSR. I think these restrictions are rooted in the custom of obstructing the self-government of society, of obstructing the individual's departure from the hierarchy, class, or guild ordained for him. This heritage from former social systems has proved fully harmonious with the present-day system. Moreover, the architects of the present-day system have apparently had an interest in preserving these vestigial social patterns. There are many examples of this. The system of residence permits, including the follow-up to make sure that an able-bodied citizen is "inclined to work"; the obstacles put in the way of people who change jobs frequently; the obstacles to leaving a collective farm; the fact that the authorities do not recognize a citizen's right to renounce his citizenship—all these are related phenomena. The bylaws of social organizations in the Soviet Union, which as a rule recognize that joining the organization is a voluntary act, do not mention the right to leave the organizations voluntarily, or the procedure for doing so. For example, we know from experience that a request to resign from a trade union results, quite simply, in expulsion from that organization—for the wish to resign or for some other reason. Apparently the powers that be find it very convenient to foster such restrictions on the individual's right to self-determination, possibly because they believe that such restrictions make it easier to rule.

Assuring actual freedom to travel abroad for all Soviet citizens, not merely for those especially tested and found to be loyal, is even more problematical than assuring freedom of emigration. This is all the more true since the Soviet authorities apparently suffer great pain each time a Soviet citizen fails to return from his travels. Permission to travel abroad is obtained only by those loyal citizens who, the authorities hope, will not only come back, but will come back relatively uncontaminated by foreign ideology.

Of course (or apparently) there are plenty of such loyal people in the Soviet Union. Nonetheless, in terms of percentages foreign travel is rare, and by no means all of those whom the authorities would consider loyal go off to travel abroad. It is not only those who dislike traveling who refrain from such trips, but those who lack the money. (The 400-ruble visa fee for a trip to a capitalist country amounts to some four months' earnings for a young Soviet intellectual.) In addition, there are quite a few people who refrain from traveling abroad because they remember earlier times when the fact that a citizen had traveled abroad was *per se* grounds for henceforth suspecting him of disloyalty and for repressing him.

For the ordinary Soviet citizen a trip abroad is a major event in his life (and in the life of his family). But it seems to me that on the average such trips are very boring. Either it is an official assignment, in which case the traveler is subordinated to the strictest discipline, or it is a group tourist trip in which the traveler visits the points of interest and the stores along with his group under the supervision of a mentor in civilian clothes who is attached to it. More varied impressions, apparently, are gained by people who visit foreign relatives, but such trips are even more rare.

Any attempt to deviate from the strict usages that Soviet tourism prescribes may be fraught with the danger of losing permission for that trip, or for trips in the future. One scientist who had received permission to visit Poland decided to vary his mode of travel. Having already received his visa, he asked an OVIR official if he could go to Poland not in the usual way—in an airplane or train—but on his own, on a bicycle. The next day that sharp-witted man was called in for an examination at a psychiatric dispensary. He never went to Poland—not even on the train.*

As we have seen in recent years, the USSR's position on the right to leave one's country has gradually changed. The Soviet authorities have been compelled to agree to emigration from several groups in the population: foreign citizens who lived in the USSR for a long time; people who received political asylum in the USSR; Jews who wanted to be repatriated to Israel; and many Germans resettling in the Federal Republic of Germany. Certain changes have also taken place in the authorities' attitude toward the emigration of individuals. In particular, they have recently begun to allow emigration even of dissenters who have spoken out in defense of human rights in the USSR, or who have exercised their freedom of creativity to an unacceptable extent. Those who have left the USSR with permission include Zuckermann and Volpin, well known for their defense of human rights, the writer Andrei Sinyavsky, the poet Joseph Brodsky, and others. It is known that in some instances the authorities even insisted upon granting permission to leave, so that in Western opinion this freedom to leave verged on exile. Some writers have used such terms in commenting on cases in which persons were granted the right of leaving the country temporarily, after which they were deprived of Soviet citizenship (as happened to Zhores Medvedev and to me).[17]

---

* It would appear that officials of other states also take a suspicious attitude toward people who are fond of unusual means of traveling. When I was getting ready to go to England from the United States the British consul in New York demanded that I show him a return ticket for the trip back from England. (This demand I consider offensive and unacceptable, but it is routine for stateless persons.) From purely theoretical considerations, I observed that this demand limited my right to travel in a rowboat. The consul (perhaps only in my imagination) looked at me as if I were a madman. I was not called in for expert examination, but at the French Consulate in London, when in a similar situation I refused to present a return ticket from France, I made sure not to talk about traveling in a rowboat.

These experiments in getting rid of dissidents and critics by permitting them to go abroad have apparently been successful from the standpoint of the authorities. True, they may be afraid that critics who go abroad will begin to criticize even more vigorously, but the experiments made so far could rule out such anxiety in the future. Experience has shown that dissidents who held moderate views while in the Soviet Union continue, when they are in the West, to be no more than moderate critics. Even if at first they are drunk on the freedom of expression they enjoy here and begin to say uncharacteristic things, their criticism is still much milder than the Soviet Union has been accustomed to hearing from the West for the past fifty years. As for those who in the Soviet Union held sharply critical views vis-à-vis the authorities, once in the West these people do not find much of a serious audience for their criticism and are all the more harmless to the Soviet Union. This statement may sound strange, but I have noticed that the average Western intellectual is almost more afraid of being suspected of anti-Soviet views than the average Soviet intellectual, who sometimes criticizes out of sheer snobbery. I am speaking of my impressions of the Western intelligentsia in general, not of either the professional anti-Soviets or those who are especially sympathetic with everything that comes out of the Soviet Union and are capable, for example, of being enraptured at how "intelligently" the Soviet troops occupied Czechoslovakia, by contrast with the behavior of the American troops in Vietnam. For that matter, I am no expert on the views of the Western intelligentsia; I am merely speaking of personal impressions, which strengthen my conviction that from the viewpoint of the Soviet authorities the resettling of a Soviet dissident abroad is not at all dangerous.

If the Soviet authorities allow dissidents to resettle abroad instead of putting them in prison or a psychiatric hospital; and if, as I assume, they know that the voice of a critic inside the Soviet Union affects public opinion much more strongly than the voice of the same critic after he has gone to the West, why don't they amaze the world with their humanity and send abroad all dissidents who are incarcerated and who agree to leave the country? I have repeatedly called upon the Soviet leaders to do this, and I have not lost hope that some day my advice will be accepted (even though I have offered considerable advice which they have not taken). My hopes are based on the obvious consideration that the civilized world would be much less surprised by the bad manners of Soviet juridical practice if, instead of incarceration for many years in a psychiatric hospital, in a camp or in a prison, the Soviet Union would use exile as a punishment for criticism.

I am not talking about exile, however, but about an even more humane measure: freedom to leave the country. The Soviet leaders cannot fail to realize how much their prestige would grow—and how much more justified their claim of being civilized people would be—if they let political prisoners who so desired go abroad, and if they continued this policy until they had enough courage and confidence in the stability of their regime to stop persecutions for criticism. I think the Soviet authorities—especially now, when they have such an interest in improving the international situation—would have done this if they had not feared that those allowed to go abroad would begin to give interviews (not controlled by Glavlit) to Western journalists, and would talk too frankly and in too much detail about an aspect of Soviet life that is hushed up in the Soviet Union: the Soviet penal system. But these fears seem to me unfounded for at least one reason besides Western indifference. Such interviews could hardly do substantial damage to the prestige of the Soviet Union against a background of its amazing humanity in letting the political prisoners go. This is all the more true since a great deal is already known about the Soviet penal system, thanks to those who spoke of it while in the Soviet Union.

The question of the advisability of enabling Soviet political prisoners to go abroad is one that I am considering here only from the viewpoint of the importance of sparing them additional suffering, and from the viewpoint of the acceptability of such a step to the Soviet authorities, since it would strengthen the faith of "world public opinion" in Soviet humanity. To my way of thinking, reasoning about the right of political prisoners to be allowed to leave a country with whose laws and policy they disagree flows from the more general principle of the right of all prisoners to leave a country. This principle goes back to a fundamental philosophical principle of social relations proclaimed in the Universal Declaration of Human Rights: "Every person has the right to leave any country, including his own."

Although it is clear to me that reasoning about the right of convicts to leave a country creates an impression of unreality, I have nonetheless discussed that right in papers read at conferences in Uppsala and Washington, and I think it would be interesting to continue that discussion. I proceed from the assumption that the chief limitation on the right of leaving may be the consideration that no state wants to accept such a person. The attendant question of the right of a person to use parts of the world not under the jurisdiction of any state—for example, the right to use the open sea—deserves special discussion, despite the fact that such questions are not yet considered urgent.

In fact, however, the right to use the open sea is a rather pressing problem in certain cases.* Without the adoption of special international agreements on the right of a person to use the open sea, one is hardly likely to convince

---

* International laws take for granted the idea that the open seas are under the collective jurisdiction of the nations. The lack of proper attention to the right of an individual to use the open sea is apparently due to this concept, which is almost tantamount to a belief that each person must be regarded as under the jurisdiction of some state. And that is a principle whose antihumanistic nature is, in my opinion, evident without commentary.

the Soviet authorities that a Soviet citizen who has "fled" from the USSR despite illegal prohibitions, and is on the open sea, must be regarded as inviolable, and that the Soviet authorities do not have the right to seize him. But the authorities of other states may prove—and sometimes do prove—to be more receptive to the obvious argument as to the right of a person to use the open sea. In the summer of 1973 a Soviet citizen, V. Schneider, left the USSR in a rubber boat and headed into the Baltic. As later became known, Finnish fishermen picked him up on the open sea. At first the Finnish authorities were apparently ready to turn him over to the Soviet Union, considering it an obligation under their consular agreement with the Soviet Union. Seemingly, however, they took into account that Schneider was on the open sea and not on Finnish territory when he was picked up. In any case, the Finnish government released him to West Germany.

I have noticed that reasoning about the right of convicts and persons under investigation to leave the country creates an especially strange impression on those who consider a right to be only an instrument to assure "order" in human society. But when one is dealing with concrete cases discussion of that right does not seem so strange. Thus Israel is ready to permit entry to all persons convicted in the Soviet Union in connection with their desire to go to Israel. Vladimir Bukovsky, who was convicted in the Soviet Union in 1972, was invited by Leiden University to continue his studies there. And Yury Shikhanovich, accused of anti-Soviet agitation and under investigation at the time, was invited to England to lecture on mathematics at the University of Leeds.

A related problem, that of the right to return to one's own country, has not been discussed very much in relation to the Soviet Union but is nonetheless interesting. Although this right has been accorded international recognition, the difficulty of assuring it is considerable, partly because of the vagueness of the concept of "one's own country."* It may be considered that the right of a citizen of the USSR to return is guaranteed by recognition of the freedom to chose one's place of residence. In practice the right to return is not violated with respect to those whom the authorities regard as citizens of the USSR. Other people who regard the USSR as their own country may experience great difficulties in the exercise of that right. There have been requests for permission to return to the Soviet Union from people who emigrated to Israel and then wanted to return. Although there are not enough such people for their resettlement to be difficult, it is hard for them to obtain permission to reenter the USSR.[18]

There are also instances of people who have "fled" abroad, violating the established Soviet procedure for going abroad; or who have refused to return to the Soviet Union once they were abroad; or who, God forbid, have asked for political asylum in another country. Although the right of such people to return to the Soviet Union is usually recognized by the authorities, exercising that right involves one extremely important consideration—the fact that a person may not know in what capacity he is returning: that of a

---

* Associated with the right to return to one's own country is the problem of emigration from the USSR of ethnic groups which, returning to the land of their forefathers, had immigrated into the USSR. We know that this problem is acute for certain Armenians who came to the Soviet Union from the United States, Turkey, and other countries. It is also known that the Nekrasovite Cossacks, who came to the USSR from Turkey, had difficulties in becoming acclimated to their new home, and that some of them—especially the young people—want to leave the USSR.

† According to recent communications,[19] there is a policy in Soviet juridical practice of prohibiting certain persons from entering the USSR "forever." The case cited had to do with a person of Latvian origin who had a right to consider Latvia his own country. The deprivation "forever" of his right to enter was effected on the basis of an unpublished act and by unknown procedures. Nor is it known whether the authorities are supposed to communicate such decisions to the interested parties.

citizen threatened by nothing, or of someone under investigation, or of someone already convicted.

In cases of voluntary return, fugitives or those previously unwilling to return are as a rule subjected to serious punishment, with the occasional exception of people not suspected of political motives for emigrating. The usual period of punishment for such repatriates is ten years' deprivation of freedom. Ten years or more was the usual period of punishment for most of those liberated from German imprisonment by Soviet troops at the end of the Second World War, and then convicted of having surrendered.

In certain cases former fugitives are not subjected to criminal punishment. The physicist Yury Sayasov, who for nonpolitical reasons remained abroad for some time and then returned to the Soviet Union, was not subjected to criminal punishment. However, the social condemnation of his behavior was so strong that for several years he was deprived of the possibility of doing creative work. (He has since gone to Israel.)

For those who are returning to the Soviet Union not of their own free will but because they have been turned over to the Soviet Union as criminals, the situation is of course much clearer.*

Apparently criminal proceedings are always instituted against fugitives and those who refuse to return. If the person under investigation is outside the USSR, this fact is not usually communicated to him or to his relatives. On only one occasion did I learn from documents that such a case had been instituted, then dropped (the case of Alexei Lyovin, now a resident of the United States). Soviet legislation allows conviction *in absentia*[20] but does not require

---

* As far as I can judge from available information, this category included Strolman, who sought asylum in Yugoslavia and was turned over to the Soviet Union, and also the seaman Simas Kudirka, who asked for asylum in the United States but was turned over to the Soviet ship's officers at their demand. (See Appendix 11.)

the court to inform a defendant outside the Soviet Union of the fact that his case is being tried. The confiscation of property provided by criminal law in convictions of treason, even if it is carried out, does not constitute definite evidence that a court decision has been handed down, since a law of 1928[21] provides for the administrative confiscation of the property of persons who have "fled" abroad for political reasons. (On the other hand, few people may remember this old law, and it may not be applied now.)

I have no data on juridical practice in this sphere, but it is theoretically interesting to consider whether the execution of death sentences passed *in absentia* is possible elsewhere than on the territory of the Soviet Union, and to what extent this is likely. The important thing is that since the law provides for the death penalty by way of punishment for treason, and since questions of executing death sentences are not regulated by a published Soviet law, in principle there is no reason for assuming that this possibility of executing death sentences passed *in absentia* is ruled out.

6
The Price of Freedom

Why, what evil hath he done? But they
cried out the more, saying, Let him be crucified!
—*Matthew* 27 : 23

I HAVE DESCRIBED the care the Soviet state takes to make
sure that citizens absorb and disseminate only correct information—correct, that is, from the viewpoint of the state
—and that they travel only within the limits the state considers it necessary to fix for its citizens. In the Soviet Union
everything has been arranged so that in doubtful cases
citizens are able—with the help of propaganda, newspapers,
or simply talking with their ideological mentors—to separate "correct" information from "incorrect," and to ascertain, even in the most complex cases, what should be talked
about and what hushed up. At present a person is not
usually persecuted for saying something incorrect by mistake—provided, of course, that he does not insist on keeping
the same opinion after his mistake has been explained to
him.

Preventive measures, such as "little talks" at Party and
Young Communist League offices, are used rather widely.

Frequently people who have been bold in their speech or actions (signing a petition in defense of a political prisoner, for instance) draw "the appropriate conclusions" after the little talk and fall silent. The persuasiveness of such little talks is based on the very fact of the talk rather than on the dialectics, logic, or eloquence of the mentor. An example is the talk a Party official had with the Leningrad scientist Revolt Pimenov. Here is the main thing said by the highly placed Party mentor (V. Medvedev, secretary of the Leningrad City Committee of the CPSU for Ideological Matters): "Of course we do not have power enough to force all people to think alike. But we still have enough power to prevent people from doing things that will harm us. In the matter of ideology there will never be any concessions whatsoever."[1] For Pimenov this little talk did not prove to be persuasive, and he was soon arrested.

If a person persists in his mistakes and spreads incorrect information after his mentor's explanations, the state sometimes comes to his aid. In a speech at the Twenty-second Party Congress, Shelepin, chief of the KGB at the time, stated that his organization introduced on a large scale the practice of having little talks with citizens who, in the KGB's opinion, were coming close to criminal behavior.

It is still the practice to summon a person for a little talk at the KGB office; he may be summoned with no explanation, or as a witness in someone else's case. If the person is properly docile, and keeps quiet after his warning, most often he is not threatened with serious prosecution. Of course such educational work is not always practiced; there may be repression without warning, especially in the provinces, where there is apparently less "liberalism."

The present political persecutions have, of course, a different character from those under Stalin. Their scope is also different. Though all the figures are secret, one may assume that today the number of political prisoners (including people incarcerated as a result of religious acts) runs into the tens of thousands,* whereas under Stalin it ran into the millions.

The two periods, however, have many traits in common. Common to both is the regime's certainty that the doctrine it preaches is uniquely correct, and that any unorthodox opinions are consequently false and inadmissible. Common to both is fear of the free dissemination of information. Common to both is dread of public disclosure when political persecutions are involved. And they have much in common in the matter of disregarding procedural requirements in political trials, although of course in the Stalin era this disregard was much more marked and the majority of political repressions were effected without a court, or under simplified procedure.

In Soviet legislation there are two basic laws setting the price of freedom in expressing one's convictions. The first is the article on anti-Soviet agitation and propaganda,[4] which provides for punishment of up to seven years' deprivation of freedom, plus exile for up to five years, for agitation or propaganda carried on "with the aim of undermining or weakening the Soviet regime or committing individual especially dangerous antistate crimes, for the dissemination with that same aim of slanderous fabrications prejudicial to the Soviet state and social system, and likewise for the dissemination or preparation or custody of literature of like content." The same acts, committed by a person previously

* In accordance with tradition I use the term "political prisoners" for persons convicted for spreading information, for religious activity, and for "flight" from the USSR.[2] Strictly speaking, however, the term should also be applied to those convicted of other acts prohibited in the USSR by virtue of that country's ideological and economic anomalies. Such acts include, for example, the observance of folk customs and trading operations that violate no one's rights.

According to the official view, there are no political prisoners in the USSR whatsoever. Procurator Biryukova, in her charge in the Moscow trial of Nadezhda Emelkina, in 1971, stated that there were no political prisoners in the Soviet Union, and that the term was not applicable to Soviet reality.[3]

convicted for especially dangerous antistate crimes, or committed during time of war, are punishable by deprivation of freedom for up to ten years plus exile for up to five years. The harshness of this may be surprising, but it should be remembered that Lenin, whose humanity is so glorified by Soviet propaganda, proposed in his day that the punishment for such acts should go as far as death.[5]

The other basic law is applied when the authorities believe the defendant has not acted with the intent of weakening or undermining the Soviet regime. "The systematic dissemination in oral form of fabrications known to be false and prejudicial to the Soviet state and social system, and likewise the preparation and dissemination in written, printed, or other form of works of such content" is punishable by up to three years' deprivation of freedom.[6]*

Even if a person has wittingly spread false information prejudicial to the ideal state system, and done so with the aim of overthrowing that system, the punishments provided by Soviet law are not only unusually harsh, they simply should not be allowed in a civilized society. But these punishments for free speech are applied in cases of ordinary honest criticism. In all the cases known to me which involved political charges, neither the falsehood of the information disseminated nor the intention of the defendant to overthrow or weaken the Soviet regime was proven in court, and usually there was not even an attempt to provide such proof. Apparently this is a settled legal presumption: to consider the conditions as to the subjective aspect of such acts fulfilled if the person says or writes something disapproved of by the authorities.

In those rare cases when the lawyers or the defendants

---

* A special price is set on freedom to propagate religious convictions. Such acts as the overt preaching of religion or teaching religion to children are punished as a violation of the law on the separation of the church from the state and the school from the church, or as infringement of the rights and person of citizens under the pretense of performing religious rites (punishable by up to five years' deprivation of freedom).[7]

succeeded in steering the pleadings toward consideration of the subjective aspect of the act, the arguments of the prosecutors and the opinion of the courts were anomalous to say the least. I have already described how the procurator tried to establish a "deliberate falsehood" in the Amalrik case. So far as I can judge from studying dozens of cases, mostly political trials involving such charges, there was no proof of either a deliberate falsehood or any falsehood at all. As a rule the court never seriously considered whether the defendant's utterances were false. For both the prosecution and the court it suffices that the defendant's utterances contradict the official point of view, even if they do not concern the state system but are merely critical of some state institution. For example, the statement that a court passed sentence unjustly in some political trial is considered false and prejudicial to the Soviet system—as in the 1968–69 trial of Irina Belogorodskaya—despite the fact that the bulletins of the supreme courts publish many reports of judicial errors. The same thing applies to criticism of the KGB, and, for some time now, to criticism of the expert opinions of psychiatrists. Basically, it was for just such criticism that Bukovsky was convicted.

Soviet courts are at a far remove from formalism in deciding what should be considered fabrications; they approach the solution of that problem very creatively. Thus the phrase "For your freedom and ours" was found by a Moscow court—and subsequently by the Supreme Court RSFSR—to be a fabrication known to be false and prejudicial to the Soviet state and social system. Vadim Delone held up a placard bearing this phrase at a Red Square demonstration on August 25, 1968, against the movement of troops into Czechoslovakia. His lawyer, Sofia Kallistratova, said in her speech during the appellate proceedings, "On October 11 the court handed down a decision according to which the slogan 'For your freedom and ours' was found to be criminal, and Delone, who had displayed that slogan, got two years and six months' deprivation of free-

dom. Yet on October 12 the newspaper *Komsomolskaya
pravda* published a banner head reading 'For your freedom
and ours.' "[8]

An ability to find the hidden meanings of words is also
demanded of Soviet courts and prosecutors. For example,
in the indictment in the Khantsis case the defendant was
incriminated on the basis of the following incident: "When
the lady of the house, A. I. Zaikina, asked him whether he
had bought the newspapers for her, he answered equivo-
cally, 'There is no *Pravda, Rossiya* is sold out, only *Trud*
was left.' "* It was not stated whether Khantsis was being
incriminated for the ambiguity of what he had said, or for
the sentence itself, interpreted in one specific sense.[9]

It appears that to the Soviet courts "systematic dissemination" means a very broad range of acts. In principle,
oral communication of a "criminal" utterance to one person may be sufficient for conviction for anti-Soviet propaganda. The preparation of a text with such opinions is
per se sufficient for conviction, even if the author has
shown the text to no one, and even if the text exists only
in a rough draft.[10]

The publication of literary works or critical articles and
statements defending political prisoners or protesting
against the authorities' violations of their own statutes or
international law—these are the usual reasons for the harsh
punishments dealt out to recalcitrants. Even when a person
has not expressed his dissidence publicly but has entrusted
his innermost critical thoughts to the beloved Party and
government—or, more accurately, to their leaders—he is
in for punishment all the same. I don't know why it is, but
the prosecution of people for their letters to high state and
Party officials seems to me particularly cruel. The fact that
the Soviet leadership fears public disclosure is not surpris-

---

* *Pravda, Sovetskaya Rossiya* ("*Rossiya*" in the colloquial), and *Trud*
  are Soviet newspapers. Khantsis was being accused of saying, "There
  is no truth (or justice), Russia has been sold out, and only work is
  left."—Translator's note.

ing, but it is very unpleasant to realize that high state and Party officials are informers who forward citizens' letters to punitive organs so that their trusting authors can be punished. (It is not important that they do this through their assistants; their awareness of what goes on may be presumed.) There have been several known cases of this kind. E. Trakhtenberg and the scientists Sher and Glezer were convicted for having sent letters to high government and Party officials. The newspaper *Moskovskaya pravda* reported the Glezer case in an article titled "Poison in an Envelope." It was a useful article. People should know about the vigilance of those whom they might have trusted.

HOW TRIALS ARE HELD

Perhaps the reader is amazed by something other than the harshness of these punishments for such ordinary human behavior—for expressing an opinion (punishments all the more harsh in that, as a rule, these opinions are by no means incitements to crimes or to the overthrow of the state system). Perhaps the reader also wonders why the general public puts up with such trials at all.

I think the authorities come close to realizing that if the public systematically learned about these trials, ultimately it would be more difficult to conduct them. Apparently it is precisely because of such considerations that the authorities, with rare exceptions, cover up the very fact that such trials are being held. Usually the public never hears of them.* In the rare instances when a political trial is reported

---

* In addition to court prosecutions there are, of course, many administrative persecutions and many having to do with employment. I must at least mention known cases of expulsion from professional associations, which is almost tantamount to dismissal from work. Aleksandr Solzhenitsyn, Alexander Galich, Vladimir Maximov, and Boris Pasternak were expelled from the Writers' Union for ideological dissent. Boris Zolotukhin was disbarred. According to recent reports, Benjamin

in the press, the accounts are full of substantive distortions. Apparently the aim of the journalists is to provoke the reader's wrath by their description of the acts of the defendants—more wrath than would have been provoked by the communication of actual information. Sometimes, however, the press says almost nothing about the acts of the defendants but a great deal about what frightful villains the defendants are. For example, the articles in the Siberian papers about the trial of members of a Buddhist group in Ulan Ude (Buddhist scholar Bidya Dandaron and others) were primarily devoted to describing what a terrible person Dandaron was: how much he drank and how poorly he worked. That the publication of such information did not prevent the administrative workers at the institute where Dandaron was employed from evaluating his work positively before the court was in itself a rare phenomenon. Usually, regardless of how a person has actually worked, the administration gives him a bad report merely upon learning that the procurator's office or the KGB is interested in him.

In its account of the trial of the Moscow demonstrators against the movement of troops into Czechoslovakia in 1968, *Moskovskaya pravda* for October 12 said of Litvinov, Larisa Bogoraz, and the others: "Common to all of them were not only antisocial views but antisocial acts and an uncontrollable passion for alcoholic beverages, debauchery, and parasitism." An example of substantive juridical distortion in newspaper reporting is an item about the trial of Bukovsky and others for their January 22, 1967, demon-

---

Levich, a corresponding member of the Academy of Sciences and an active defender of the right of Jews to emigrate, is threatened with expulsion from the academy.[11]

I must also mention something widely practiced in recent years: administrative arrests (detention of up to fifteen days) for participation in Jewish protests. A stronger measure is also used against protesting Jews; sometimes a person who seeks permission to emigrate to Israel is sent off to serve in the army, as happened in the well-known cases of Jonah Kolchinsky and Evgeny Levich.

stration in defense of Yury Galanskov and others. *Vechernaya Moskva* for September 4, 1967, reported that all the defendants had pleaded guilty. Yet in the text of both the lower court and appellate decisions, it is noted that Bukovsky did not plead guilty.

As a rule it is impossible to get into the courtroom during a political trial without permission from the authorities. The few who have decided to protest against political trials in the USSR have tried to get in, but usually the courtroom is filled, long before the trial opens, with people who are strangers to the defendant and his friends. No one else is allowed in the courtroom, except for the rare occasions when close relatives of the defendant are permitted to attend, or when some friend of the defendant has managed to get in. When I was in the courtroom during the trial of Natalya Gorbanevskaya—who was found not responsible for her actions—I was amazed to see that the room was full of young people all of whom seemed to be acquainted with one another. At most political trials the public is not so homogeneous, but the courtroom is nevertheless full of people there by special permission.*

It is rather difficult to challenge this violation of the law that trials should be public. First, there is the reply that the number of seats in the courtroom is limited. Second, court officials may simply not respond to complaints of denial of public disclosure. On the rare occasions when one manages to obtain replies, they prove to be contradictory.

---

* The *Chronicle of Current Events* (No. 6) published an account of a man who along with other "representatives of the public" attended the trial of those who demonstrated on Red Square in 1968:

> At eight o'clock on October 9 all those who had been picked to make up the public at the trial reported to the Proletarsky District Committee of the Party, where they were informed they were going to a trial of "*antisovetchiki.*" Then they were taken to the courthouse in a bus that drove into the courtyard, and were led into the building through a rear door. They whiled away the time before the trial in an empty room, where they were given sets of dominoes and other games. Then they were let into the courtroom.

This is possible because neither procedural legislation nor any other laws establish criteria for the observance of public disclosure or the procedure for allowing access to a trial by those who want to attend—even relatives.*

It is not known who is responsible for assuring public disclosure. When the lawyers Kallistratova, Kaminskaya, Pozdeyev, and Monakhov, in the trial of Litvinov, Bogoraz, and others, supported the defendants' request that certain persons be allowed in the courtroom, the president of the Judicial Collegium of the Moscow City Court replied that this question came within the competence of the "commandant" of the court.[13] When I wanted to get into the courtroom during the trial of Natalya Gorbanevskaya, I went to see the deputy president of that same Moscow City Court and I was told that my request could not be granted by the deputy president because the question came within the competence of the president of the judicial collegium.

Most often, lawyers not only have no real chance of getting a public trial for their clients but do not even make such a demand. In an open letter to Kheifits, who was defending Pimenov in a trial in Kaluga, I pointed out that the defense of public disclosure was a lawyer's responsibility, since the guarantee of a public trial means not only the public's right to be present but the defendant's right to public examination of his case. Judging from what is known of the developments in the Pimenov case, it seems unlikely that his lawyer demanded public disclosure.[14]

---

* Soviet law does not oblige investigative and judicial agencies to inform relatives of the accused—the person under preliminary investigation—or the defendant of the progress of the case, including information about arrest and time of trial. When by agreement with relatives or friends of the defendant a lawyer is taking part in the case, it is possible to find out the date set for the trial, although sometimes this is only the day before it begins. Sometimes, however, relatives are not told even when the trial has started. This happened, for example, when Nazarov was being tried in the town of Dushanbe, in Tadzhik S.S.R. Nazarov's relatives did not know when the trial would begin, and it was not until the third day that they were able to get into the courtroom.[12]

Friends of defendants and members of the movement for the defense of human rights have repeatedly called the authorities' attention to the necessity of making trials public, as well as to the fact that judgment rendered as a result of a court examination that is not public must be considered unjust.* As a rule, these appeals to the authorities are not answered. Attempts to "reserve" a seat in the courtroom by appealing to the court authorities long before the beginning of a trial have been equally unsuccessful.*

Intellectuals who are more or less free in their thinking apparently understand that there is good reason for the anxiety of those who have spoken out for public trials. As to how this matter is regarded by the public, which is little concerned with meditating about legal problems, it is hard to say.‡ There is, however, much of interest in the statement of the teacher A. V. Novozhilova, who spoke at a trade union meeting at a Moscow secondary school during a discussion of the behavior of the teacher Valeria Gerlina,

---

* I am speaking here of ordinary courts. In the USSR there are also military tribunals established by law, and public disclosure of their activities constitutes a special problem. In addition, there are so-called special courts for trying cases associated with penal institutions. Nothing is said about these courts in the published laws. It is difficult to talk about guaranteeing public disclosure of proceedings in courts whose very existence is not publicly disclosed.

Another important problem is that of guaranteeing public disclosure of trials of previously convicted persons at their places of confinement. Usually such trials are held on the territory of the place of confinement, which cannot be entered even by relatives of the defendant.

† Attempts by foreign correspondents to prevail upon the Soviet authorities to allow them to attend trials have also proved unsuccessful. Some foreign correspondents requested the Ministry of Internal Affairs to allow them to attend the trial of Peter Yakir and Victor Krasin, in 1973. A few days later, in lieu of an answer, their letter was returned to them.

‡ One can judge how the rulers of the USSR feel about public trials from their Bulgarian colleague, First Secretary Todor Zhivkov, who once replied to a question from a correspondent: "Will the trial be public? We're not going to put on a show. It would undermine the authority of the government." (The trial referred to was a political one.)

who had signed a letter of protest against the trial of Galanskov and others. Novozhilova said:

The trial was not entirely public. But is this really important when it is a question of such downright enemies? They must not be allowed to make their anti-Soviet statements in court in the presence of Soviet people. We must not compel our people to be subjected to the influence of such slander. There may be other reasons, too, why everyone on the street should not be allowed in the courtroom. After all, we are not supposed to know all the reasons. We must trust the authorities, not suspect them.[15]

The last sentence of this beautiful statement on the natural limits of the principle of public disclosure in Soviet society is very typical.

Related to the principle of public disclosure is the question of the right of access to the materials of a case. It is clear in any event that this is the right of the lawyer and the defendant. But if the case is associated with a political charge, it is sometimes difficult for the lawyer and the defendant to gain access to the file. Despite the fact that the hearing of the case is considered open, and despite the legal principle of oral disclosure according to which all materials relevant to the examination of the case must be made public in court, the file on political charges is considered secret. Materials on such cases are kept in the so-called *spetschast* * of the court; and lawyers as a rule do not have the right to take their own notes on a political case out of the building. At the conclusion of the preliminary investigation, the accused has the right to familiarize himself with all the materials on the case. However, he may not transmit excerpts from the file to his relatives or friends. A convicted person receives a copy of the judgment in his case but usu-

---

* "*Spetschast*" or "first section" is the appellation given to "representatives" of the KGB at institutions. These sections also have custody of secret documents.

ally he may not transmit it "at all." Copies of judgments are not furnished to relatives. All this despite the fact that the law does not limit the right of any person in any case to file a protest by way of supervision.*

People who have been convicted have the right, even before their period of punishment expires, to petition for rehabilitation. It is natural that such a petition should contain a rebuttal of the arguments in the indictment. But this would require a new study of the case, and experience has shown that this is impossible. Bogdanov, a judge of the Moscow City Court, in response to an inquiry from Leonid Rendel, a former political prisoner, stated that the Moscow City Court could not make it possible for Rendel to familiarize himself with the materials on his criminal case, "since the file was being kept in the archives of the KGB CM [Council of Ministers], USSR."[16]

In another case, in response to Fridrich Ruppel's inquiry about the fate of his mother, the Procurator's Office of the USSR officially confirmed that copies of judgments were not furnished to the relatives of persons who had been unjustly convicted and punished.[17]

The Soviet Constitution guarantees the right of an accused person to defense. Violations of this right—in legislation and in practice—are not so flagrant now as they were in the Stalin era, when not only in "special conferences" but even in court trials on certain charges, the case was heard without the participation of the parties. Even today, however, the violations are very substantial. First of all it should be remembered that the right to defense is also a right to self-defense. The law takes this right into account among several provisions on the rights of the accused† and of the defendant. However, the law also violates this

---

* I.e., under the procedure whereby the procurator's office "supervises" the correctness with which cases have been handled.—Translator's note.
† A person under preliminary investigation, as distinguished from a defendant actually on trial.—Translator's note.

right, putting an accused person and defendant who prefer to defend themselves in an unequal position relative to accused persons and defendants who repent in court or during the preliminary investigation, and actively help to uncover a crime.

Such repentance and help are considered a mitigating circumstance.*[18] This is a very important problem, particularly as regards self-defense in political trials. (In the document in Appendix 5, I discuss this problem.) Here I shall say only that the conditions of preliminary investigation are harsh. In the first place it is harsh to detain a person for nine months or more† in complete isolation from his friends and relatives, not even—with rare exceptions—allowing correspondence. Because of such conditions he may not only become depressed but even have a "breakdown." This is not hard to understand if we add that during that long period he must deal with an investigator who tries to extract depositions and repentance from him using a broad spectrum of methods, including threats, promises to mitigate punishment, and lies—in particular, lies about the depositions of other persons or the behavior of other persons.

The right to defense counsel, especially in political trials, is subjected to limitations that very much complicate the defense of an accused person or a defendant. With rare exceptions, defense counsel is allowed to take part in the case only upon completion of the preliminary investigation.[21] An accused person cannot have recourse to defense

---

* I should not be surprised if a similar concept exists in the legislation of other countries. I have always realized that in this world it is not only Soviet laws that may surprise one.

† By law the maximum period for detention under guard during the preliminary investigation of a case is nine months. Sometimes this law is simply violated (as apparently happened in the recent persecutions of Ukrainian intellectuals).[19] Sometimes the period of detention under guard has been illegally extended by the Presidium of the Supreme Soviet, as apparently happened in the cases of Yakir and Krasin.[20]

counsel in the process of interrogations during investigation or in the process of expert examination; nor can he have counsel while defending his rights in connection with being held in preliminary detention.

It is natural to assume that the right to defense includes the right to use the services of defense counsel chosen by the accused person himself. Although as a rule defense counsel is chosen by the friends or relatives of the accused, the latter may demand replacement of counsel or refuse counsel proposed to him. However, the choice of defense counsel for a case involving political charges is limited by the practice, which has no basis in the law, of issuing "clearances." Not all members of the bar, but only those who have a so-called clearance, are allowed to handle political cases and certain categories of especially serious criminal cases. When Nina Bukovskaya, by agreement with her son Vladimir Bukovsky, tried to get permission for the lawyer Dina Kaminskaya to handle his case, she submitted her request to the Presidium of the Moscow Collegium of Advocates. The president of the presidium replied with a note on her letter: "I cannot assign the lawyer Kaminskaya, since she does not have a clearance for secret files. K. Apraksin, November 24, 1971."

It is amazing that there should be such a notorious distrust of lawyers, despite the statute on the bar that says that people whose moral and professional qualities do not correspond to the calling of a Soviet advocate are not admitted to the bar. It is also amazing that accused people, who do not usually have clearance for secret files, are allowed to familiarize themselves with the materials on their cases. Whatever the reasons that prompt the authorities to allow only specially trusted lawyers to handle political trials, this procedure, which is not based on the law and which offends the professional honor of lawyers, sometimes leads to very substantial violations of the accused person's right to defense. Cases like Bukovsky's, in which defendants are not allowed to have the lawyers they choose, are far from rare.

Since the use of clearances gives the lawyers who have them career advantages over other lawyers, fear of losing clearance is natural. In addition, if a defense lawyer displays more boldness in a political trial than the authorities approve of, he may not only lose his clearance but be disbarred—as happened to Zolotukhin, who boldly defended Alexander Ginzburg. Today the situation is such that lawyers like Kallistratova, Kaminskaya, Pozdeyev, and others who have uncompromisingly defended political defendants are no longer allowed to participate in political trials. Lawyers who have not yet lost their clearances may be warned by their colleagues' loss, and as a result the quality of their defense in political trials may deteriorate. Perhaps to some extent this would be a good thing: if all honest lawyers lost their clearances for political trials it would leave only lawyers ready to join the prosecutor in indignation at the acts of the defendant. Defendants would decline the services of such lawyers, which would leave them entirely without legal aid. Sometimes, however, a lawyer's caution in choosing his defense position is very anomalous. In Sverdlovsk, Valery Kukui's lawyer proved to the court that his client had not committed any criminal acts, and then asked the court to mitigate the punishment! A lawyer has to be very bold to ask for the acquittal of his client in a political trial.

There have been cases in which the defendant disagreed so strongly with his lawyer's position that he refused the aid of counsel. Nina Strokataya, accused of anti-Soviet propaganda in the Ukraine, fired her counsel because his defense position contravened the fact that she had not pleaded guilty.

Even the participation of an experienced advocate does not help the political defendant take advantage of all the procedural guarantees for protection against his indictment. A study of information on political trials in the USSR leaves the impression that to some extent the court makes common cause with the procurator from the very beginning, and this affects the matter of whose arguments the court will listen to more readily. In any event, the principle of equality of the parties in the presentation of evidence, guaranteed by Soviet law,[22] is systematically violated. The procurator's requests for calling witnesses or subpoenaing documents are usually granted by the court. The defense's requests for calling witnesses or subpoenaing documents— or having documents made a part of the record—are very seldom granted. In Bukovsky's third trial, in 1972, one of the items in the indictment was information in a deposition by Hugo Sebreghts, a Belgian citizen, that Bukovsky, in my apartment and in the presence of Volpin and myself, had given Sebreghts a copy of the *Chronicle of Current Events*. Sebreghts was not present at the trial, since he had by then been expelled from the Soviet Union. Bukovsky denied that he had given him a copy of the *Chronicle* and demanded that Chalidze and Volpin be subpoenaed as witnesses. The court refused.

When there is contradictory testimony from witnesses, the law requires the court to give the reasons for its preference and explain why it considers certain testimony not deserving of credence. This procedural principle is commonly disregarded. For example, at Marchenko's trial, in 1969, a witness named Dimitrienko stated that although during the preliminary investigation he had deposed that Marchenko had said, "The Communists have sucked all the blood out of me," he had never seen Marchenko before; and now in the courtroom, having seen Marchenko and heard his voice, the witness was firmly convinced that Marchenko had not spoken those words. Dimitrienko even stated that he knew the man who had spoken them. The court simply disregarded Dimitrienko's statement, preferring to believe the testimony of other witnesses. The judgment contains the statement that Marchenko uttered the sentence.

At the appellate hearing on the Marchenko case, the defense lawyer, speaking before the judicial collegium, subjected to doubt the testimony of the witnesses who had stated that it was Marchenko who spoke the words mentioned above. It is difficult for me to describe the indignation of the president of the judicial collegium, who in very sharp terms told the advocate Monakhov that the words were in the record and it was by no means necessary to repeat them. Of course it is possible that the president of the judicial collegium did not really intend to violate the principle of oral disclosure.* It is possible that her wrath was due to the fact that the appellate hearing was, amazingly enough, open on this occasion, and that among those sitting in the courtroom were Marchenko's friends—before whom, of course, in the opinion of the president, one should not repeat false information so insulting to the Communists.

Procedural law requires that after the reading of the indictment the defendant be asked whether he understands the indictment. Here is an example of how creatively judges deal with procedural principles in practice. At his trial in 1969 Ilya Burmistrovich gave a negative answer to the question whether he understood the indictment. The judge (Lavrova) refused to explain it, arguing that the law, in stipulating that the substance of the indictment must be explained, envisaged semiliterate persons and not those with a doctorate in science.

Judicial attempts to supplement procedural law are rather common. I recall that the journalist Feofanov, discussing in *Izvestia* the right of people in the courtroom to take notes during the pleadings, stated that a judge had prohibited the public in his courtroom from taking notes. When, in a private talk, Feofanov tried to get the judge to explain the legality of such a prohibition, the judge explained that the law sometimes had loopholes and that they, the judges, must supplement the law. Needless to say, if one recognizes

* Yet the principle of oral disclosure of court examination is systematically violated in political trials. Usually, documents that the prosecution considers anti-Soviet or libelous are simply mentioned by title and not read aloud in court, even though the public sitting in the courtroom has been selected by the authorities.

the correctness of supplementing the law—as by affirming that the requirement that the substance of the indictment be explained to the defendant applies only to semiliterate persons—it is only one step from such supplementation to a more general amendment of the law—which is quite often realized in practice. I have in mind the general principle of Soviet legal doctrine which holds that democracy and legal guarantees exist for one's own side, while dictatorship exists for one's enemies.

Since transcripts of pleadings are as a rule not published, it is very difficult for someone who has never been in court to imagine to what extent procedural usages worked out by the Soviet judicial system during a half-century prove stronger than the procedural principles (themselves none too perfect) formulated by Soviet legislation. There are certain peculiarities of Soviet pleading which apply to trials not involving "dissidents." A brochure published by Gospolitizdat (State Publishing House for Political Literature) in Moscow in 1960, under the title *The Trial of the Criminal Case of the American Flier and Spy Francis Powers*, contains a transcript of the pleadings in the Powers case. In studying this brochure one immediately notices three interesting circumstances. First, during the trial a great deal was said that was not, strictly speaking, relevant to the criminal case against Powers. Part of the procurator's indictment was devoted to stories from the sphere of international relations and evaluations of the acts of the United States of America. It was stated that the head of the Soviet Government, Nikita Khrushchev, in his speech before a session of the Supreme Soviet, had unmasked the falsehood of the American version of Powers' flight. And the government prosecutor, General Procurator of the USSR Rudenko, said that the American aggressors were latter-day imitators of Hitler. Rudenko also discussed the American policy of "brinkmanship," and the fact that countries bordering upon the Soviet Union had made their territory available to the "American militarists." Second, one got the impression that, in accordance with the thesis of Soviet legal doctrine on the educational role of Soviet law and courts, the trial of Powers was being held as an educational measure vis-à-vis international partners.

Third, I note that there was no rebuttal, although the prosecutor's statements were frequently unsupported by even a semblance of proof. For all practical purposes, insofar as one can judge from the transcript, the role of defense counsel in that trial boiled down to repeating all the prosecutor's statements: "First of all I consider it necessary to state that the defense has no quarrel, either with the facts of the charges brought against Powers or with the state prosecutor's evaluation of the crimes." Yet despite the fact that the defendant entered a general plea of guilty, in certain cases his answers could well have provided defense counsel with material for rebuttal. For example, the prosecution charged that the aircraft Powers was in had no identifying marks, but one does not get the impression that this was fully proved. It is quite possible that it had no such marks. Despite the data from the experts who studied the paint-and-lacquer coating on the wreckage of the aircraft, Powers had reason to doubt that such marks were missing. Defense counsel took no part in trying to clear up this question.

Another question in which the defendant had every reason to expect defense counsel to be interested was that of the pistol taken from Powers after he parachuted to earth. According to the conclusion of the experts, "the pistol was intended for noiseless firing at people in the event of an attack, by way of defense." With respect to that expert conclusion, Powers said: "As far as the pistol is concerned, it was given to me for hunting, and it was for that reason that I took it. Unfortunately, no one except myself knows that I could not kill a man, and that I wouldn't do it even to save my own life." There is reason to believe that any pistol intended for "firing at people" might also be used to shoot at animals. Defense counsel had every reason to express doubts about the experts' bold conclusion that the pistol was intended for "firing at people," but he apparently found no reason to answer the judge's remark that hunting is difficult from an altitude of 68,000 feet. He might at least have noted that Powers was likewise unable to fire at people from such an altitude.

During his questioning of Powers the defense counsel brought out the fact that his client came from a working-class family, and that the husbands of Powers' five sisters also came from working-class families. He ascertained the state of Powers' health, inquired about a birthmark on his right cheek,* and asked several questions about his background and education, his joining the intelligence service, and the working conditions in the service. In his summation for the defense, the lawyer called the court's attention to the unprecedentedly difficult situation in which he now found himself, since the law prohibits defense counsel from refusing to continue with the defense he has undertaken regardless of how much indignation the defendant's crimes has stirred up among broad strata of the Soviet public. Defense counsel then acknowledged that all the prosecution's arguments had been proved, and noted several circumstances mitigating the guilt of Powers, including the fact that he came from a working-class family and did not like to read political literature. In conclusion, defense counsel asked that Powers' punishment be mitigated.

The next-to-last sentence in the transcript is interesting: "Those present in the courtroom, many representatives of the workers of the city of Moscow, greet the sentence with approving applause." It is doubtful that the representatives of the workers applauded the fact that the court had mitigated the punishment and sentenced Powers to only ten years' deprivation of freedom. After all, the procurator's speech, which called for a sentence of fifteen years' deprivation of freedom, was also applauded by the representatives

---

* This subject was not developed in the summation for the defense.

of the workers. Perhaps they applauded because the death penalty had not been applied?

It may be assumed that, by comparison with ordinary trials, the Powers trial, which was covered by the press, was a holiday for Soviet legal proceedings in the sense that procedural norms were observed. It should not be thought, however, that this holiday mood was the reason for such unanimity of opinion between the prosecution and the defense.

In many trials defense lawyers do not contest the prosecution's arguments but merely ask the court to take mitigating circumstances into account. They take advantage of their opportunities to question the defendant and the witnesses only to bring out these mitigating circumstances, not to analyze the grounds of the indictment.

Needless to say, it is not this way at all trials. There are advocates who carefully look into the defects in the prosecution's case and debate vigorously with the prosecutor. There are even advocates who debate with the prosecutor in political trials.

THE PRISONERS

> In six years of prison and camp I ate bread
> with butter on it once—when it was brought
> by a visitor. I ate two cucumbers—one
> in 1964 and one in 1966. Not once did I eat
> a ripe tomato or an apple.
>   —*Anatoly Marchenko*[23]

The main thing I have heard from those who have been imprisoned is complaints about hunger, in both prisons and camps. According to information from Marchenko, whom I have reason to believe, the daily diet for a person incarcerated in a colony in the category called strict-regimen (where political prisoners are usually sent) is 700 grams of bread, 80 grams of dried codfish, 50 grams of meat, 450 grams of vegetables (potatoes and cabbage), 30 grams of groats or noodles, 20 grams of fats, 15 grams of sugar. This is all, meaning 2,400 calories a day. According to the same information, confirmed by the recollections of many prisoners, unfit products are very often used for food in the camps and prisons. With such a diet, people suffer from severe malnutrition. Yet the prisoners must do heavy work in accordance with "extreme output norms."[24] The slightest decrease in the diet causes acute hunger, which we know has a ruinous effect on the human organism, but the law provides that dietary norms for convicts depend upon their attitude toward work. It stipulates that less food should be given to those in disciplinary barracks or cells and in solitary confinement.* This kind of punishment is meted out to prisoners who refuse to work or who break any of the other rules. As one can see, hunger is an educational tool in the Soviet prison system.

This does not contravene Soviet penal doctrine. Two principles of that doctrine are known from the works of Soviet jurists. First, the Soviet Constitution, which holds that he who does not work does not eat, is also applicable to prisoners. Second, that the everyday, material conditions under which prisoners are kept should not be better than living conditions on the outside.[25]

The conditions in which prisoners live are well designed to assure observance of the constitutional principle that he who does not work does not eat. On the outside it is more difficult to prevent nonworking people from getting help from friends or relatives. In places of confinement the guard system and the restrictions on visits rule out the possibility of such help. Prisoners in a corrective-labor colony are entitled to receive food packages sent or brought to them

---

* It is known that the diet provided in punishment cells is similar to that known from the published decree on detention conditions for persons arrested for petty hooliganism. Hot food is given to the prisoners every other day. "On days when they do not get hot food, they are given only their ration of bread, salt, and hot water."

only after they have served half their sentence, and usually they are allowed only three packages, of limited weight, per year. People in prisons are not entitled to receive any food packages sent or brought to them.[26] For breaking any of the rules, including refusing to work, any prisoner may be deprived of the right to receive food sent or brought to him.[27] Out of the money he has earned a prisoner has the right to spend from two to seven rubles (depending upon the type of institution he is in) on articles of prime necessity and food at the camp or prison shop. Deprivation (for a period of one month) of the prisoner's right to buy food is stipulated by way of penalty for breaking a rule.[28] Under such conditions it is not surprising that prisoners' relatives try to get at least a little food to them during their very rare visits, but legislation has cut off even this possibility. In 1972 a decree was published stipulating a substantial fine for illegally giving food to prisoners.[29] Since then there has been an increase in personal searches of those who come to visit prisoners. Visitors may be stripped naked and their clothing thoroughly examined.[30]

There was a time when convicts were taken to Siberia in slow stages. Among them were murderers, rapists, and fighters for freedom. People from the surrounding villages came to the high road along which the prisoners were being convoyed and gave food to them. They had a right to help those who were hungry and suffering. Today prisoners are transported in closed trucks and railroad cars. People do not see them, and usually they cannot read about them in the newspapers. "Mercy toward the fallen"* is not permitted to distract them from the great task of building an ideal future. The fact that perhaps more than a million prisoners are suffering from hunger is one that people either are unaware of or keep silent about.[31]

Only in recent years have certain intellectuals publicly spoken out in defense of the right of prisoners (primarily

---

* This phrase is from a famous poem by Pushkin.—Translator's note.

political prisoners) to normal living conditions. We have
the text of a letter Marchenko wrote to several officials,
including the president of the USSR Red Cross Society.[32]
The answer he received from the executive committee of
that society is very significant: "People who have lifted
their hands against the achievements of the October Revolution are regarded by our legislation and our Soviet legal
consciousness as having committed the gravest crime against
their own nation and as deserving of harsh punishment
rather than soft treatment and indulgence." The head of
such a humane organization may of course feel that to feed
a hungry person is soft treatment or indulgence, but it is
interesting that the answer mentions "people who have lifted
their hands against the achievements of the October Revolution," when in fact its author very probably knew that the
majority of political prisoners are people who have been
convicted for anti-Soviet propaganda or agitation, or for
religious activity. That is, they were convicted not for "lift-
ing their hands" but for saying something.

Those who keep prisoners in a state of hunger "know what
they do." In the journal *Toward a New Life* (which is published for camp administrations and is not for sale) I read
that certain prisoners, trying to keep up their strength, prefer refusing to work and being put in punishment cells
rather than being fed a little better but having to do exhaust-
ing work. The author of the article explains that this is a
delusion, that the diet in a punishment cell does not, as he
expressed it, assure a human energy balance.

In terms of the overall situation of Soviet prisoners, it is
of the greatest importance to call attention to their hunger,
and to the fact that the law sanctions the use of hunger for
educative purposes.

In many countries there is much that should be criticized
in their methods of criminal punishment. But the problems
are especially acute in countries where the dissemination of
information is controlled by the state. In such countries
the authorities can do virtually anything they wish with peo-

ple isolated from society by sentence of a court. There is reason to believe, too, that the harshness of an embittered and weary administration at the place of confinement compounds the harsh policy toward prisoners dictated by central authority.* In the reminiscences of prisoners there are many examples of their constant humiliation by minor officials and local authorities.

In the Soviet newspapers anyone discussing the problem of reeducating criminals invariably mentions instances of former prisoners gratefully recalling their prison and camp mentors. There is no basis for completely discrediting such propagandistic articles. Even among camp administrators and overseers there are various kinds of people. They all have a hard life, but not all of them react to it with increased animosity against those they have to guard and "educate."

Among those who guard and "educate" political prisoners, however, one is much less likely to find people with a humane attitude toward prisoners. From the very beginning, the Soviet authorities have labeled regular criminals as an erring but socially "kindred" element. Political prisoners, though, are enemies from the viewpoint of those who run the Soviet penitentiary system; and this determines the authorities' attitude toward them.

Many intolerable restrictions on prisoners' rights are the same for political prisoners and regular criminals. Some, however, apparently cause greater suffering for political prisoners. These include restrictions on freedom to exchange information (restrictions on correspondence and receiving books; measures for checking up on what prisoners talk about) and on religious observance. The absence of any public control, along with the restrictions on information, create

---

* To this is added the harshness of fellow prisoners. Apparently this applies especially to political prisoners, who are frequently scoffed at by ordinary criminals. Instances of anti-Semitic persecution have come to light more than once, as, for example, in the cases of Kukui, Palatnik, and Burmistrovich.[33]

conditions under which the authorities, with no one checking up on them, can arbitrarily subject prisoners to punishments provided by the corrective-labor code (under administrative procedure for "violations of the regimen"). Under these rules they can also institute new prosecutions against prisoners for "crimes committed at the place of confinement." For political prisoners this means that the authorities can indefinitely prolong their term of punishment regardless of the period fixed by the original sentence.

To prolong a term in this way, proceedings are instituted against a political prisoner, the charge being that in talks with other prisoners he engaged in anti-Soviet agitation, or that he spread information prejudicial to the Soviet system. In a camp, among the hundreds of prisoners dependent upon the administration, there are usually people who will confirm such a charge. This practice was widespread in Stalin's camps, although in those days the authorities did not take the trouble to stage a new trial to prolong the term of a political prisoner. In recent years such well-known political prisoners as Anatoly Marchenko, Vladimir Dremlyuga, Lev Ubozhko, and Andrei Amalrik have been tried and resentenced in "camp cases." At present almost every political prisoner is under the threat of a new conviction—at any rate if the term of his imprisonment is nearing an end.

Judging from the numerous reminiscences of former prisoners and the letters and public statements of present ones, political prisoners must carry on a constant struggle for each one of the few rights guaranteed them by law. The right to correspondence, the right to have visitors, the right to receive books and packages, the right to use the camp shop—all these are things the administration tries in every way to restrict, with or without reference to the law.

Again judging from the reports of political prisoners, as a rule they are virtually deprived of skilled or humane medical care. Prisoners' complaints of bad health are often regarded by the administration as malingering, and even if a person is brought to the extreme of serious illness and gets into the hospital, he does not get skilled medical care. Yury Galanskov[34] died because for a long time he did not get skilled care, despite the fact that he and his relatives and friends had warned the authorities of his critical condition. This is the best-known, but not the only, instance of the death of a political prisoner which could have been prevented. It would not be an exaggeration to say that the conditions under which political prisoners are kept are such that there is good reason to fear for the life of each of them —even of those who were in good health when they were imprisoned.

EXORCISING THE DEVIL

> It has already happened more than once
> that people, going out of their minds,
> have suddenly begun to slander the Soviet
> social and governmental system, or have
> unrestrainedly given themselves over to
> anti-Soviet agitation and propaganda. This
> has necessitated the employment of the
> appropriate forensic medical measures—
> and sometimes simply prophylactic measures.
> (The time is not far off when only madness
> will explain this kind of behavior.)
> —*Boris Zuckermann*[35]

The price of freedom is sometimes different from a relatively honorable avowal of guilt or being declared an enemy of the people. Sometimes a person is simply considered a nonperson, denied the right to defend himself and the right to answer for his own actions. Of course in a certain sense he continues to be regarded as a person: it is acknowledged that he possesses the bodily structure of a human, and "humanity" is even displayed toward him, though in a rather anomalous way.

In short, it is considered that the one responsible for that person's unlawful free behavior—for his unlawful utterances—is not he himself but, as it were, a devil that has got inside him and has to be exorcised so that the person can attain that docile state that is becoming to him. It is taken into account that the devil being exorcised resents the interference and prompts the person to resist the humane procedure of exorcism.

As a result the person is virtually denied his rights under the law.

From prison one can write a protest to the procurator. Whether it serves any purpose is another question. The fact remains that the prison authorities are obliged to forward the protest to the procurator. But a protest from a patient in a psychiatric hospital is regarded as merely "written material of incoherent content," and nobody is obliged to forward it to the procurator. In prison a person can read books (such books as can be found, of course) and sometimes write letters. In a hospital the doctor can simply forbid the patient to read and write.* In prison a hunger strike is called a hunger strike, and although it is considered a violation of the regimen, it is recognized as a method of protest. In a hospital a hunger strike is regarded simply as a "refusal to take food, which indicates a pathological condition."

Methodologically, though, there is something in common between these ways of meting out punishment for freedom. In both prisons and hospitals it is expected that a person will alter his convictions and recognize the rightness of his punishment. In prison the mentor asks the inmate: "Do you understand that your sentence was just?" In the hospi-

---

* It is known that Peter Grigorenko was deprived of writing materials as a "therapeutic measure."[36]

tal the patient is asked: "Do you understand that you are sick and that it was right to hospitalize you for treatment?" For the prisoner, answering such a question in the affirmative can mean getting privileges in prison. For the patient, it can mean discharge from the hospital. In both cases a negative answer means greater suffering. For the prisoner it means he has "not begun to reform." For the patient it means he has not recovered his health; the devil has not been exorcised.

Most often a person is sent to prison or a camp* in accordance with the sentence of a court—or, in the case of administrative arrest, by the decision of a judge. He has the right to defend himself in court. (The violation of this right is another question.) A person is sent to a psychiatric hospital either without a trial[37] or as the result of a court examination conducted in accordance with simplified procedure especially provided by law.[38] The future patient is usually not invited to the court session. Why should the court listen to the arguments of a devil that must be exorcised? Usually the court does not see the person it is sending to a hospital. True, defense counsel does appear in court; but it sometimes happens that even he has not seen the person he is defending.†

The problem of the use of psychiatry to combat dissent in the USSR has perturbed many people in the West. This has been especially true since Bukovsky made available to Western psychiatrists the experts' reports in accordance with which certain dissidents were declared to be not responsible for their actions and were confined in general or special hospitals.[39] Judging from statements by the Western psychiatrists, these expert reports were incorrect

---

* I have already mentioned the "undocumented" imprisonment of Moscow Jews before President Nixon's visits.

† The lawyer Dobuzhsky did not want to meet with his client Valeria Novodvorskaya, who was arrested in 1969 and adjudged not responsible for her actions.

from the medical point of view.[40] Analysis shows that they are also incorrect from the juridical point of view, since the experts sometimes exceeded the authority provided by law, or were not impartial.*

In discussion of this problem many people oversimplify a great deal. They assume, for example, that the problem consists simply in the fact that the KGB uses psychiatrists to hospitalize healthy people for their dissent. The tragedy, however, is more profound and more complex. It remains a particular puzzle why in such cases psychiatrists prove more docile than the courts, which (as is supposed) upon instructions from the KGB can also hand down the decision wanted by the KGB, regardless of the amount of inculpatory material.

It is my opinion that the organs of the KGB, once they have decided to isolate a dissident and once they have their superiors' permission to do so, always find a way of carrying out their intention. It is hardly likely that in certain special cases they are compelled to use psychiatric persecution. It is interesting that when a dissident has been confined in a psychiatric hospital, the public frequently says, "They [the authorities] decided not to try him because there would have been a big scandal." When the dissident is tried, the public says, "They decided not to put him in a psychiatric hospital because there would have been a big scandal." Perhaps I exaggerate the power of the KGB, but such reasoning strikes me as naïve.

Of course psychiatric repressions can be quite convenient, both because the person being persecuted does not have the right to defense and because responsibility for the persecution is formally (in part) shifted to the experts. The legal procedure for psychiatric repressions is very simple as compared to the procedure for prosecuting those

* My opinion on this problem has been presented to the Human Rights Committee.[41]

who are still considered normal. It is clear, for example, that it was more convenient to try Grigorenko *in absentia,* as a person not responsible for his actions, than to allow him to make a speech in court that would subsequently have appeared in samizdat. But usually it is difficult to understand why the KGB chooses psychiatric repressions in particular cases.

The chief tragedy lies in the fact that society has been conditioned to accept the thesis that a manifestation of dissent may, in and of itself, be a symptom of psychic illness. The reason for that is the belief in a uniquely correct official doctrine* and a distinct notion that a manifestation of disagreement with official doctrine is unthinkable and useless and hence not characteristic of a normal person. As for the authorities, they want to be confident of their infallibility, and it is less perturbing to them if they consider their critics crazy.

The problem would be artificially simplified if one were to speak only of persecutions for ideological dissent. We should also mention the violations of the rights of thousands of people labeled mentally ill for other kinds of behavior (not necessarily ideological). Their rights are sometimes violated entirely "without objection." Sometimes they are violated with the help of mercenary (or merely weary) relatives who either do not want to—or cannot—try to defend those rights.

In my opinion, the belief of people (and particularly of psychiatrists) that there exists something resembling a proper "norm" for man, is altogether unjustified and fraught with the danger of its being used for discrimination. This danger is especially great in a country where the authorities try to educate the inhabitants according to a

---

* This belief has actually been implanted in society, despite the fact that each citizen may (and probably does) have doubts about particular questions.

single standard. It seems that according to Soviet notions, the criteria for determining the normality of a person are much more stringent than in the West, and there are correspondingly broader criteria for determining whether a person should be confined in a psychiatric hospital. (I am not merely speaking of cases of ideological dissent.*) Associated with these social peculiarities are specific traits of Soviet forensic psychiatric practice that I think exist independently of the fact that it has become convenient to get rid of militant dissidents with the help of psychiatrists.

A study of the problem leads me to the conclusion that the situation is very susceptible of abuse, and that the abuses exist. Their victims call upon the world in the hope of help.

The plight of these victims is cause for great anxiety. It is not simply that they have been illegally isolated. It is not simply that they are suffering and are subjected to treatment incompatible with humane behavior. In addition to all this, these people are running the risk that their individuality will be subjected to irreversible changes because of compulsory treatment with drugs that destroy the intellect and the will.† It should not be thought that in using such treatment physicians in the USSR always deliberately abuse science, although of course the use of such treatment on political dissidents provokes special alarm and justified suspicion. But even with innocent motives a physician may do damage and cripple a person if he proceeds from the assumption that a person who is considered mentally ill

---

* Habituation to the situation of social fear that has taken root during the past half-century has led, for example, to setting up the following criterion: It is normal to experience fear in the face of a threat. The absence of fear—for instance, fear in the face of repression for dissent—is a symptom of a pathological condition.

† Details on the conditions under which patients are held in psychiatric hospitals of the special type may be found in the letters of Victor Fainberg,[42] and in the works of Professor Volpin[43] and Volpin's testimony before the United States Senate.[44]

must be subjected to treatment—that he does not have the right to be mentally ill.* This is an unusually complex area in the life of all mankind, and a satisfactory solution to this complex problem has not been found in any country. However, the risk that a so-called mentally ill person will be crippled by treatment is much greater in countries where intolerance toward "deviations from the norm" is preached. And in countries where the authorities want to educate all people according to a single standard, it is even a risk for ordinary people not usually considered ill.

---

* We know how enthusiastically some psychiatrists greeted the discovery of lobotomy, which brings a person out of a profoundly pathological state and assures contact capacity and tranquillity, but is accompanied by other irreversible changes. It is frightening to think that in the future science will provide totalitarian systems with more advanced methods of making people over.

7
The Rights of Minorities

SOCIAL MINORITIES

THE TIME is past when the regime had to actively battle against the majority of the population. The regime conquered the majority. The regime and the majority have adapted themselves to each other. Of course to a certain extent they are dissatisfied with each other, but the regime is cleverer than the majority, and has secured itself against dissatisfaction by convincing the majority that it is the only possible regime, that any other regime would be frightful, and (most important) that the USSR is surrounded by such predatory enemies that it is better to put up even with a regime that is not too good but is one's own, since there is the danger of falling under the power of enemies. It would appear that the majority of the population of the USSR actually thinks this is so, and in this lies the chief victory of the Communist regime in the USSR.

One important thing about such a victory over the majority, however, is that the regime must continue to conquer the majority. In particular, it must continue to educate the majority—and especially the new generations—in a spirit useful to it. And during the half-century of mutual adaptation between the regime and the majority, the regime has elaborated, so to speak, an image of the acceptable average Soviet person.

We know of course that the chief condition for the successful building of an ideal future is the formation of an ideal person. But in practice the Communist government understands that even in an ideal future people will be of somewhat different kinds. Therefore, along with laying down the parameters for the ideal Soviet person, the rulers have elaborated norms for acceptable (tolerable) deviations from the ideal for each category of people. It is considered that in a socialist society all the social prerequisites exist for voluntarily living up to such acceptable norms. A deviation from the ideal of the Soviet person that is greater than the acceptable deviation is, on the one hand, considered a result of vestiges of capitalism and feudalism in people's consciousness. On the other hand, it entails more or less harsh educative and punitive measures.

The official Soviet belief in the natural goodness of man and the beneficial influence of socialism on people is so great that all human faults are attributed to vestiges of capitalism or feudalism. This even applies to crime, which can hardly be said to have been greatly reduced under socialism. Otherwise, why conceal information about such an important propagandistic factor?* Unfortunately, such an explanation of the causes of human faults does not simplify the process of overcoming them. Sometimes even the contrary is true. It is known that one Soviet jurist said in a lecture, "The struggle against crime in the USSR is

---

* According to data from Peter Reddaway, a senior lecturer at the London School of Economics, it may be assumed that there are at least a million prisoners—including political prisoners—in the Soviet Union at any given time.

complicated by the fact that in our country there are no social roots of crime."

Although all conditions have been created so that a person can voluntarily, with the aid of his mentors, satisfy at least the acceptable average requirements, there are many people who deviate from the acceptable average with respect to certain parameters. As a rule these people do not come out against the regime and have fully adapted themselves to it in everything except some of their forms of behavior. But the regime persecutes them for these forms of behavior—these deviations from the prescribed norm. This applies to groups of such people whom we may call social minorities.

Of course the defense of the rights of the majority is an important task. But since the majority has adapted to a greater extent than the social minorities, I dare say the defense of the rights of minorities is more urgent. This is all the more true in that some of these minorities—historically or because of persecutions—have proved to have a higher level of legal consciousness and legal education than the majority, so that sometimes they act in defense of their own rights.

A very common method used to oppose groups of people with qualities different from the prescribed average is legal discrimination on the basis of the possession of those qualities. Here it is convenient for the regime to practice discrimination on the basis of a vaguely defined criterion. As we have already noted, the campaign of persecution against the kulaks was carried on by the authorities without clearly defining the conditions under which a peasant was considered a kulak. The usual pattern of discrimination against a social minority is for the regime to announce persecution for a quality condemned by the majority, but in practice the persecution will affect a broader group of people than those who possess that quality.

Over the years the Soviet authorities have worked out many methods for suppressing social minorities. In all likelihood history has not known another such war against minorities "on many fronts." It is important to study and analyze these methods, both to help the minorities and because the Soviet methods may be used by other states.

We may illustrate the methods used in suppressing minorities unwelcome to the authorities with the example of the struggle against certain groups of that "class" which heretofore has been considered the ruling class in the Soviet Union. I mean the workers. We know how widely the image of the ideal worker has been advertised. He is a worker endowed with several fine human qualities who takes pride in his title of worker, who overfulfills the plan, who helps his comrades, and who moderately criticizes shortcomings. It is best if, in addition, he is a Party member. It seems that at every plant or factory there is a certain number of workers who come close to such an ideal and serve as an example to the rest. Of course since it is no doubt harder to be such an ideal worker than to be an ordinary one, it is possible that the administrators help such chosen persons to be ideal workers. The tolerable deviation from the ideal is represented by the merely conscientious worker who fulfills the plan and does not avoid meetings. At the opposite pole from the ideal is the person who avoids socially useful labor, who drinks and disturbs the public order—the so-called parasite, prosecuted in accordance with the law and forcibly made to labor.[1]

But there is a great range between the tolerable average and the vice that must be prosecuted. There are also simply poor workers (poor from the viewpoint of the authorities). It is not always convenient to persecute this group openly, since their faults are not so great and, even more important, they are very numerous. To persecute them, the method of discrimination on the basis of a vaguely defined criterion is brought into play. This intermediate category of the blue-collar population is persecuted as if its members had a punishable vice. For example, it is usual to prosecute as parasites people who are merely not working, even if they do not disturb the public order as stipulated in the published act. Also persecuted are so-called "rolling stones" (people who change jobs frequently) and people who have been fired. Propaganda abuses the "rolling stones" just as vigorously, and in almost the same terms, as it abuses the parasites. At the same time they are dealt with, through administrative measures, in almost the same way as parasites. This is done not on the basis of a published legislative act but on the basis of directives from administrative or even Party organs. Thus a directive of the Moscow Soviet[2] lays down the procedure whereby such persons are hired on the basis of a job assignment from a special commission on employment rehabilitation. Unpublished recommendations on this subject state that basically such persons should be assigned to unskilled work involving heavy physical labor. (I have read a directive of the Tallin City Committee of the Party on this subject.) Obviously "rolling stones" may join the ranks of the parasites if they dislike the assignment from the employment rehabilitation commission. (According to unpublished police instructions, prosecution for parasitism is begun when a person has not worked for four months.)

Like any discriminatory measures, of course, the campaign against parasites is adapted to the persecution of anyone the authorities disapprove of who wants to work but has been discharged and cannot find work. (Examples include those who want to go to Israel,[3] or dissidents, or writers and artists out of favor with the regime.[4])

The treatment of "rolling stones" exemplifies the liberalism of the Soviet authorities in recent years. Stalin dealt with "rolling stones" more simply. A decree of 1940[5] simply forbade quitting a job without permission of the authorities, under threat of criminal punishment. Today the prosecution is administrative—for the time being. Still, if a discharged person refuses to work at the job assigned by the employment rehabilitation commission, he is forcibly sent to work as a parasite. And if he refuses that work as well, he will be criminally punished by deprivation of freedom for a period of up to one year and, in cases of recidivism, up to two years.[6] The liberalism here consists in the fact that a person is given much more time for reeducation before he is imprisoned. Perhaps the fact that the victim has time to think things over is the boon that distinguishes this liberalism from despotism.

Another unwelcome minority is collective farmers who do not want to be collective farmers, or who in the opinion of the authorities are poor ones. As in the case of the blue-collar worker, the ideal collective farmer is of course an advanced collective farmer endowed with many traits of the positive hero of socialist realism. The tolerable average is represented by the collective farmer who, to the best of his ability, does the prescribed volume of work—at least the so-called minimum of work days. (Formerly failure to fulfill this minimum entailed criminal responsibility. Today it entails, in any case, social pressure, being deprived of various privileges, and so on.) At the opposite pole from the ideal collective farmer is the person who wants to leave the collective farm. Neither the law nor the charter of the collective farm prohibits leaving the farm, but neither guarantees that right. And very tangible obstacles, especially in the matter of internal passports,[7] are placed in the way of leaving.

I do not know whether one can leave a collective farm and become an independent farmer.* Even if it is possible,

---

* Independent peasant farmers may still exist in the USSR. A discriminatory act of 1938 concerning a tax on horses on individuals' farms[8] even provided for cases of more than one horse. A 1961 textbook on financial law says of this tax that "during the first years after it was passed it yielded rather large revenues for the budget. Today the revenues from it are very negligible."[9] I trust that the abolition of the law in 1971[10] does not mean that private farms have been entirely eliminated but was only a manifestation of legislative concern for the vanishing class of real peasants.

in practice that too is very difficult, since the land belongs to the state. The only laws I know of that specify how a peasant can receive land apply to the small personal plots of collective farmers.

The intelligentsia as such, if it is not a suppressed minority, is in any case a minority under special control. The intelligentsia is the chief source and custodian of information, and, as we know, the Soviet rulers attribute special significance to the control of information. The intellectuals who are persecuted are those who think most boldly, people who, passively or actively, resist control over information and creativity. Persecutions of people who express a critical view of social problems have been especially strong and notorious. The intelligentsia also represents a special threat to the Communist regime in that, in principle, the liberalization of Communist ideology is a source of danger. The times have passed when a Party official wore a leather jacket and a holster. Now he wears the same clothes as the intelligentsia and wants to appear one of them. The danger is that they will infect him with liberalism, criticism, and what is called bourgeois humanism. The authorities, understanding this very well, put up with a decline in faith and a rise in the cynicism of ambition among higher Party officials. For the cynical struggle for a place on the career ladder—for all the big privileges—is what gives an official tangible reasons for docilely carrying out the instructions of his superiors, even if he has been inwardly infected with "the ideology of the intelligentsia." I have noticed that Party or Young Communist League activists, feeling ill at ease with intellectual friends, assert themselves by flaunting such cynicism. And I am not the only one to have noticed careerist cynicism among many Party officials. I hope what I say does not sound blasphemous, but by comparison with the fanaticism of Party members in the twenties and thirties, I see in this a slight social advance, possibly giving promise that Russia is moving closer to actual liberalism.

A great many examples of suppressed social minorities

could be cited. I shall give only two more before going on
to discuss national and religious minorities.

Persons whose sexual behavior is either very active or
deviant also constitute a persecuted minority in the USSR.*
Extramarital relations are condemned by society, and the
ordinary sexual diversions of youth may be illegally persecuted by Young Communist League activists. For example,
during the Youth Festival in 1957, Komsomol members
shaved the heads of girls who went out with foreigners.
This was widely known in Moscow, but unfortunately I am
not aware of a single protest.

Sexual deviation is strongly censured. For example, a
male homosexual act between consenting adults is criminally punishable by up to five years' deprivation of freedom.[11] There is a rather strong hope that the socialist
system will create all the conditions necessary so that a person can overcome his "shortcomings" in this sphere. It is
apparently plain to Soviet ideologues that both extramarital
relations and male homosexuality are vestiges of capitalism.
On the subject of male homosexuality, I read in a textbook
on Soviet criminal law that the "objective" of this crime
was to create "the social pattern of sexual relations in a
socialist society."[12]

There is also a unique kind of discrimination against a
special social minority in the USSR. Membership in this
group is not considered blameworthy, at any rate not by
the authorities, because this is the social minority constituted
by Party activists and officials. The fact that representatives
of this minority are involved in governing the country
should not delude one as to their freedom. These people
enjoy a great many privileges, but in many respects their
rights are very limited—sometimes, indeed, much more
limited than the rights of the average citizen. The chief

---

* Not only there, of course. The lawmakers of many countries have a
very nasty way of interfering in people's intimate lives. Soviet legislation is relatively liberal in this respect.

restrictions on their rights are not those proceeding from the juridical system of the state but those imposed by Party discipline. I have not yet had occasion to defend the rights of this social minority, but so that the reader should not be too surprised by my statement that this ruling minority is in a tight position, I shall quote from Medvedev's book by way of illustration:

Although there were many who were dissatisfied and who disagreed [in the Khrushchev era], they had to keep their opinions to themselves. As a result, mistakes were redoubled, and this put the country on the brink of a political and economic crisis. After the October Plenum of the Central Committee* it became possible to discuss and analyze rather freely many of the mistakes of the preceding decade. But this freedom of discussion and criticism was not extended to decisions taken after October 1964.[13]

It is difficult to say to what extent the representatives of this enslaved and yet powerful minority are subjected to legal discrimination. I shall, however, give one example which in any case testifies to "symbolic" discrimination against Party workers. According to an account in the magazine *The Worker-Peasant Correspondent*, at one plant a Party member named Migush, the editor of the wall newspaper, shot himself, leaving behind a note in which he accused the plant administration of persecuting the worker-correspondents. The case reached the courts and several people were punished for malfeasance. The magazine further commented: "Migush failed in his Party duty to struggle. The court emphasized this social crime on the part of Migush. The court did not admit the charge that the defendants had 'driven Migush to suicide,' since a Party member cannot abandon the struggle."[14]

* After this plenum, in 1964, Khrushchev's retirement was announced.

BELIEVERS

While implanting in the nation a belief in the unique correctness of official ideological doctrine, the Soviet authorities have from the very beginning vigorously suppressed other beliefs. The chief victims of this intolerance are the advocates of concepts based on a faith whose vitality has been tested through centuries of human history. Of course I mean religious systems. Many Western studies have been devoted to persecutions of priests and believers in the Soviet Union. Likewise, many Soviet studies have been devoted to showing how perfectly freedom of conscience is assured in the Soviet Union. These Soviet studies sometimes refer to the testimonials of foreign "experts" on the rights of believers—experts who have apparently studied the situation of religion in the Soviet Union and expressed their opinions. Thus it was reported that Lieutenant Colonel Saad, former military attaché of the Republic of Iraq in the USSR, declared, "I am convinced that Soviet citizens are free in the performance of religious rites."[15] There are many such examples.

Meantime, there are many problems in the area of assuring the rights of believers and the rights of religious associations in the USSR. To speak less academically, it may be said that in this sphere, quite simply, tyranny reigns. The authorities, paying no attention to existing statutes and the constitutional guarantee of freedom of conscience, issue instructions contravening or supplementing the laws. Officials sometimes violate both laws and instructions, often not bothering even to put their own decisions or directives in writing.

Many studies and statements published in the West and in samizdat have been devoted to detailed investigation of how the rights of believers are violated in the USSR. A discussion of the various aspects of this problem, based on analysis of law and practice, may be found in Igor Shafarevich's paper, "Legislation on Religion in the Soviet Union," which was presented to the Moscow Human Rights Committee in 1973.[16]

Soviet ideologues do not conceal their enmity toward religion, or the fact that they are determined to overcome the religiousness of the population once and for all. Discrimination against those whose faith is other than communistic is continuous. One might praise the Soviet leaders for not having prohibited religion completely, given their enmity toward it, but such praise would be misplaced. Apparently they were not in a position to go that far. Religion would have continued to exist anyway, despite their prohibition and the arrests of believers and priests—arrests of which there have been too many as it is. Religion would have existed underground, just as certain sects banned by the authorities now exist. The existence of an underground ideology is very dangerous to the regime if that ideology has many adherents. It is much less disturbing to permit the population to profess that ideology, so as to keep an eye on its preachers and followers and gradually increase the restrictions on their rights. This was the course the government followed when it realized that hopes for a rapid rise in the "consciousness" of the population were unrealistic—that people's religious convictions are frightfully tenacious.

Along with crude and forcible mass education in atheism,* the regime gradually increased restrictions on the possibilities for religious observance. Churches were closed, the founding of religious associations hampered, religious teaching prohibited even in the family, and the activity of church officials constantly and illegally monitored.

According to the Constitution of the USSR, the church is separated from the state. It would appear that by separation of church and state the authorities mean something very anomalous—perhaps that the church does not partici-

* This education is enforced primarily in schools and state institutions.

pate in governing the state.* For its part, the state actively interferes with church, often not on the basis of open instructions but via verbal orders from officials. There is reason to believe that these officials are not acting on their own but on the basis of secret state (and perhaps Party) orders. N. Eshliman's and Gleb Yakunin's "Open Letter" states that virtually all appointments and consecrations of priests have to be cleared with the government Council on the Affairs of the Russian Orthodox Church.[18]

Is the Church in the USSR fighting such oppression as the Polish Catholic Church, say, is doing? It would be better to ask whether the Soviet Church *can* fight. And the answer to that question is no doubt clear. It seems that people frequently expect more of the Soviet Church than it is able to give. I am not an expert on evaluating the activity of church hierarchies, but it seems to me that the chief (and very difficult) task of the Soviet Church is to exist. Fulfilling that task apparently requires the church hierarchs to render unto Caesar—and sometimes, one would think, not to Caesar alone. I should not be surprised to hear the reply that ten forced recantations from church hierarchs are not too great a price to pay to assure the possibility of implanting hope in one despairing soul. Not only would I not be surprised: I understand the naturalness of such an approach, even though my own ethic is different.

Of course when I say it is natural that church officials sometimes render unto Caesar excessively, in the name of preserving the Church—in the name of preserving the possibility of consoling sufferers—I do not have in mind the

---

* It has become customary in houses of worship to glorify the atheistic Soviet Government. In a Moscow synagogue I saw the text of a prayer for peace in which the Most High was called upon to bless the Soviet Government, "the stronghold of peace throughout the world." The government is praised in especially colorful terms in certain sermons by the hierarchs of the Moslem religion.[17] These facts are not so interesting if the church is doing the praising on its own, but I should not be surprised if the authorities have given out instructions or hints on this subject.

instances of church hierarchs' making common cause with Caesar in persecuting or deceiving believers.* Such cases are very depressing; and I can understand the indignation of the late Boris Talantov, a defender of the rights of believers, who in 1968 accused Metropolitan Nikodim of lying.[20] In a protest to the General Procurator of the USSR, Talantov set two facts against each other: first, that KGB agents had proposed that he disown his signature on an open letter from the faithful of Kirov to Patriarch Alexi; second, that Metropolitan Nikodim, while abroad, had declared the same letter to be anonymous and entirely unworthy of credence. In his protest Talantov, who was arrested in 1969, also declared himself ready to attest the truth of his statement by swearing on the cross and the New Testament.

I find unnatural the attempts of certain contemporary Orthodox theoreticians to modify the teachings of the Church so as to harmonize them with the commands of Caesar. For example, I get the impression that Metropolitan Nikodim and certain Orthodox theoreticians allied with him preach that the struggle for peace is a Christian obligation. Although I am not a specialist, I doubt that such a thesis has any canonical basis if it is a question of an obligation. In this connection I feel compelled to recall that in the decision in the case of Father Adelheim the description of one of the "criminal" documents contains the following sentence: "The author writes that the struggle for peace on an international scale should not be a Christian duty."[21] Although the Tashkent City Court did not hand down a definite ruling on whether the struggle for peace is a Chris-

---

* The authorities must have an interest in helping to place in the religious hierarchies people whose behavior might compromise the religion in the eyes of believers. Eshliman and Yakunin have called attention to this problem: "The Council on the Affairs of the Russian Orthodox Church promotes the infiltration among priests, and the subsequent promotion, of persons who are morally unstable, of little faith, sometimes entirely unprincipled, capable of serving an evil cause—the dissolution of the Holy Church—and, at the appropriate moment, of renouncing Christ."[19]

tian obligation, the very mention of this problem in a court decision that had much in common with the theological innovations of Metropolitan Nikodim's followers is, in my opinion, cause for vigilance.[22]

Associated with the suppression of an alien faith is the campaign against alien symbolism. The removal of ikons and the profanation of relics of saints,[23] the destruction of monuments of the past (which still goes on), vandalism even on the ikons kept in the storerooms of provincial museums and being destroyed anyway by neglect, the prohibition against pilgrimages to holy places,[24] and much else is motivated by the regime's striving to suppress alien symbolism.

Of course the campaign against alien symbolism is carried on in other ways besides destroying things that play the role of symbol. It is also carried on by means of implanting new symbols. In this sphere it is hard to be completely inventive, and the new symbolism sometimes grotesquely copies the old forms. In place of ikons, portraits of leaders. In place of relics, the holy Soviet mausoleum.* The Soviet ideologues claim that the new symbols are surrounded—as the old ones were—by an atmosphere of sanctity, and the epithet "sacred" is used. Nor has the concept of the sin of blasphemy been forgotten. Disrespect for, or the vandalizing of, the new symbols may be regarded as a manifestation of ideological enmity. Apparently it was this concept that inspired certain vigilant Soviet citizens to inform on their neighbors if it was noticed that they used scraps of Soviet newspapers, with portraits of leaders on them, as toilet paper. And apparently it was this same concept that inspired legislators to include in criminal legislation punishments for "vandalizing" the state seal or the flag (up to two years' deprivation of freedom).[26]

Speaking of symbolism, it is appropriate to mention the

---

* Nikolai Podgorny, speaking at the Twenty-second Congress of the CPSU, called Lenin's mausoleum in Red Square a holy thing for the Soviet people and for all workers of the world.[25]

attitude of the Soviet ideologues toward the dead. Some of the dead are sacred symbols, and some of them are inimical.

Every effort is made not to mention the names of the inimical dead, with one rare exception: when the name of a dead person is made a symbol of frightfulness. (For example, in the thirties the names of certain "oppositionists" who had been destroyed were symbols of this kind.) But as a rule the names of inimical dead people are surrounded by a taboo. Not only the books written by such people, but even books mentioning their names, are removed from libraries. In the Stalin era, when the number of inimical dead people was constantly increasing, it caused a lot of trouble not only for the workers of Glavlit and the libraries but also for private owners of books. People understood that if during a search they were found in possession of a book containing a mention of an inimical dead person—although only in passing and without praising him—this might suffice to make the owner of the book, in the eyes of the "organs," an "unliquidated" partisan of the dead person mentioned. Today one can find for sale old books in which either the name of the editor or a name in the text has been carefully deleted—which means that the original owner was vigilant.

Fear of the inimical dead has also been officially recorded in directives. Thus in 1923 a special circular[27] prohibited the mention in churches or in public prayers of persons who had been convicted of, or were on trial for, grave anti-state crimes.

Akin to the implanting of the new symbolism are the attempts to teach the population to replace customary, traditional rituals (usually associated with religion) with new rituals stuffed with new ideological content. The campaign for such new rituals has been quite vigorous in recent years. These rituals are offered to the population in lieu of religious marriage ceremonies, christenings, and funeral services. Sometimes the ideologues note that the public is not eager to get into the habit of honoring the proffered surrogates. We know, for instance, that the Azerbaijanian Party leader F. Aliyev remarked in one of his speeches that "in several towns and regions the new traditions and rituals are still being poorly propagandized."[28]

NATIONALITIES

I have not observed that the Soviet authorities, in principle, favor any particular nationality. Their approach to all is the same: to overcome a person's historical, spiritual, and even family attachments in the name of establishing one main attachment (or, more accurately, devotion): to the Communist regime and ideology. Everything in a person that is stronger, or potentially stronger, than devotion to the regime must be suppressed, including attachment to one's nationality (or, as the Soviet ideologues express it, nationalism).

Although Russians of course occupy a special place in the Soviet power system, the government is just as ready to suppress Russian nationalism as any other. In the opinion of the authorities, an enthusiasm for "Russianness" is just as dangerous, ideologically, as an enthusiasm for "Jewishness." Of course the regime allows—and sometimes even encourages—people to speak, say, of national pride. But apparently such pride is tolerable only within the limits of "national in form but socialist in content" (the formula the ideologues use in prescribing what a national culture should be).

The special place of Russians in the power system is due to the fact that for Russians the Soviet regime is largely their own regime. For other nationalities in the Union it is a Russian, alien regime. The central leadership understands this, and of course leans on Russians in governing national minority regions and in controlling the population of those regions. In particular, the central authorities encourage Russians to resettle in national minority regions. It is clear

that the "internationalist minority" leadership of these
regions cannot prevent this.*

Of course there is nationalism among minorities, and
chauvinism in the Russian public. The regime is apparently
willing to utilize ordinary Russian chauvinism in combating
nationalism, but I think this is a tactic rather than a doctrinal aim. It is difficult to judge, since the system seems to
involve the doctrinal aim of utilizing any tactics.

No particular nationality in the USSR seems to be persecuted as such. This is confirmed by Soviet history. National
persecutions have for the most part been carried out when
the regime feared the political disloyalty of that nationality.
(I would not swear, however, that Stalin himself, in addition to this fear, was not guided by certain other considerations when he resettled peoples or stirred up anti-Semitism.)

The nomadic peoples were subjected to persecution on
the basis of political considerations: their way of life con-
flicted with the requirements of organizing total control over
the population. Here and there the Kazakhs were forced to
take up agriculture and settle in one place (though without
any great success). Today, those still engaged in livestock
raising can roam from place to place with their herds, like
their forefathers. But their herds belong to a collective
farm, and they roam not by virtue of a national custom but
in connection with their job on the collective farm. Gypsies
have been very harshly persecuted for their custom of wan-

---

* A recent decree of the Council of Ministers, "On Privileges for Mi-
grants," apparently specifies very attractive privileges for people who
voluntarily resettle in the agricultural regions of the republics of the
Transcaucasus, Central Asia, the Ukraine, and Byelorussia; of the
autonomous republics of the Volga region; and those of Dagestan,
Bashkiria, Tuva, and others (including the extreme eastern regions of
the RSFSR).[29] Judging from this list, it may be assumed that the
authorities are openly encouraging the resettlement of inhabitants of
central Russia on the territories of national minorities. It is also known
that in recent years there has been active resettlement, by Russians,
of the industrial regions of the Baltic republics, and resettlement of
the Colchian Lowlands, in Georgia.

dering. A special decree of 1956 stipulates: "Gypsies must be prohibited from engaging in wandering, and invited to change over to a settled way of life involving work." Gypsies who scorned that "invitation" were subject to exile for a period of up to five years.[30] According to information in the *Chronicle of Current Events,* in 1970 Aeroflot ticket sellers were instructed not to sell tickets to groups of gypsies.[31] Did the official who issued those instructions understand that they were a violation of the Convention on the Elimination of All Forms of Racial Discrimination?

In the Stalin era certain peoples and ethnic groups were resettled away from their territories. The announced reason for this was the disloyalty or "treason" of those peoples.* The peoples of the northern Caucasus have now been returned to their territories,[32] but there has been no restoration of territorial rights for the Crimean Tatars, the Meskhi, and the Volga Germans. This is a very acute internal problem. In any case, it would seem that the Crimean Tatars and the Meskhi are determined to continue petitioning in defense of their rights to the territory taken away from them.

The problem of anti-Semitism is a special one. There have been many statements by Jews to the effect that official anti-Semitism exists in the USSR. I myself have gained the impression that in Russia anti-Semitism is primarily "social." As for the government, it restrains this anti-Semitism, as it does other "unregulated" behavior of the public. But at the same time it bears in mind that the restrained anti-Semitic feelings of the population can at any moment

* This resettlement was carried out with extraordinary harshness. Many people perished en route to their place of settlement. Many others died during the first months after resettlement because of the dreadful living conditions. According to official data, 9.1 percent of the Crimean Tatars died in the special settlements during the first nine months. According to data supplied by the Crimean Tatars, losses of their people due to resettlement amounted to 46.3 percent. In his speech at the Twentieth Congress of the CPSU, Khrushchev called the resettlement of peoples genocide.

be directed along the necessary "political" channel. Thus today, in connection with the desire of many Jews to go to Israel, the regime in the USSR, considering a desire to leave the country treasonous, apparently uses the anti-Semitic feelings of the public to prevent the example from becoming contagious—to discredit the idea of emigration.

As for official anti-Semitism apart from the problem of emigration to Israel, I am convinced that the government and Party officials are rather punctilious. They realize that one must not, say, issue instructions limiting the admission of Jews to institutions of higher learning or to executive positions. As far as I know, instructions of this kind do not refer to Jews but to persons belonging to national groups having ethnic ties with a bourgeois state.

The special position of the Russian national group in the USSR leads to internal conflicts of a purely national character, especially in connection with the fact that the Russification of the culture of national minorities is gradually being accomplished. In particular this is due to the fact that despite the recognition of a national language as the official language of many of the republics, the official language of the Union is Russian. The process of Russifying national cultures provokes passive resistance from national minorities. Sometimes the boldest and most active representatives of these minorities come out with public protests that are harshly suppressed by the authorities.*

The forcible Russification of the culture of national minorities means that small peoples with a unique culture and way of life, developed in the course of many centuries, have foisted upon them a new way of life and a new culture. This is called promoting progress and cultural improvement. Thus when the Soviet regime prohibited the payment of bride money in Central Asia, the northern Caucasus, and other regions with a Moslem population, it was

---

* There have been many persecutions for such protests, especially in the Ukraine. For details see the *Chronicle of Current Events* and the *Chronicle of Human Rights in the USSR.*

declared to be a measure aimed at the emancipation of women and the defense of their rights.[33] But it is clear that the payment of bride money is not *per se* a violation of the rights of a woman if there is no violation of her right to marry of her own free will. The latter is a value that is protected by other laws, and that for a woman is of practical importance only when that value is substantially higher than the values associated with the woman's respect for the social pattern of life in her ethnic group. Soviet ideologues, however, in trying to justify the prohibition of bride money, not only cited the principle that marriage should be a voluntary act but also argued that the custom of paying bride money required the ransoming of a person, which is demeaning to the dignity of that person. But it is reasonable to assume that the danger associated with the demeaning of dignity, as of honor, depends so much upon the age-old social pattern of the ethnic group that it is more natural to leave the solving of these problems up to the members of the group itself. Outside reformers dealing with such problems may base their solutions on values foreign to the members of that group.

From the purely legal point of view, the custom of paying bride money may be regarded as a custom of making partial reimbursement for the expense borne by the bride's family in giving her a proper upbringing and teaching her the crafts a woman must know according to the culture of the group. Apparently the Soviet ideologues were not very farsighted in affirming that the payment of bride money was demeaning to the dignity of the woman, in view of the more recent laws that establish the obligation of citizens with a higher education to reimburse the Soviet Union for the expenses incurred in their education if those citizens emigrate to capitalist countries.[34] As far as I know, this reimbursement is not regarded as demeaning to human dignity.

We may note in passing that the custom of bride money has not been forgotten in regions with a Moslem population. Apparently its payment is still rather common, even though some who honored that ancient custom have been subjected to criminal punishment.

Another example of interference by outside reformers in the social usages of ethnic groups is the prohibition of polygyny in regions with Moslem populations, where the polygynous family was sanctified by age-old customs. To justify criminal punishment for polygyny[35] the ideologues again cited women's rights.

It is interesting that neither the payment of bride money nor polygyny is a crime everywhere in the RSFSR. The RSFSR Criminal Code specifically stipulates that punishment for the payment of bride money and for polygyny applies only to the regions where these "socially dangerous acts" are vestiges of local customs.[36] As a rule, Soviet legislators are careful not to allow the publication of laws that discriminate on the basis of national origin. Perhaps the specification of territorial limits on the prohibitions of bride money and polygyny indicates that in this case the legislators were careless.

8
Prospects

IN 1966 about three hundred leaflets calling for freedom were pasted on walls and dropped into mailboxes in various districts of Moscow, by Irina Kaplun and Olga Iofe. (At the time the girls were not yet sixteen.) The majority of the citizens who received leaflets turned them over to the KGB.

What more can I say about the prospects?

True, the years that have passed since then have witnessed the development of the movement in defense of human rights and the activity of the Soviet Jews, who have broken through a fifty-year-old barrier and asserted their right to emigrate. But it is not likely that all this has seriously affected the mood of the majority or contributed to the average citizen's understanding of the law. But ultimately knowledge and understanding of the law is the factor that will determine whether the authorities can violate human rights with impunity or whether they must reckon with the possibility of mass resistance to tyranny.

Although there is sufficient reason for pessimism, perhaps the future may turn out better than one might expect. I say this not because it is always good to hope for the best, but because at every point in Soviet history, including the period of Khrushchev's "thaw," grounds for pessimism regarding the prospects for human rights have existed. Yet if we take a retrospective look at this development in the Soviet Union, we must recognize that today the situation is much better than during the years when violations of human rights were most comprehensive. As a yardstick for this comparison I am not using the purely statistical criterion of the number of repressed persons. This criterion is not appropriate because the goals of the repressions in the thirties and forties were basically fulfilled, and the so-called class make-up of society was altered. The regime was also quite successful in subduing the majority. In particular, the regime succeeded in changing the wants of the mass of the population, and they became so accustomed to restrictions on many civil rights that the term self-restriction might be appropriate.

But to subjugate the majority, the regime had to make a very substantial concession. In the twenties, in both theory and practice, communism proclaimed as the ideal for a citizen of Communist society the image of a proletarian completely indifferent to the blessings of property. In recent years, however, the regime has had to recognize that the striving to own property is in fact unconquerable, even if the possibilities for acquiring and accumulating property are very limited. And it has had to replace fanatical preachings against that "petty bourgeois vestige," the sense of ownership, with antithetical preachings about citizens' material interest in the successful building of an ideal future.

This does not mean, however, that the earlier goals have been forgotten and the earlier tactical principles rejected as morally discredited. The earlier goals still remain. Nor do these changes mean that the former fanaticism has been eroded by time and, if you will, by human nature. In terms of its basic principles—and, what is more frightful, its methods—the system has remained the same, but it has become more humane. And the prospect exists that this process will continue. We may hope that it is too late to return to the fanatical preaching that rejection of the sense of ownership is a basic Communist virtue. Therefore, the system will become increasingly less communistic, assuming a new form—likewise totalitarian, but different. How soon this new system will become one that is ideologically tolerable is difficult to predict. We may hope this will take place by peaceful means and hence more rapidly than if it were brought about by means of revolution. Possibly it will take place without the formal removal from power of the present ruling Party. Instead, the Party may be transformed and become more humane, thanks to the material interests of its leaders and members, and to their cynical careerism. Repugnant to decent people, cynicism is nonetheless more humane than fanaticism. Of course the transformation of the Soviet system into a liberal one will be accompanied by an increased general awareness and knowledge of the law. Perhaps, however, the sense of the law in the ruling Party will mature faster than among the citizenry, because the Party officials, to some extent and in their own way, imitate the intelligentsia.

What a beautiful prospect! And hope for its realization exists. But a return to reality suggests something else. It suggests that a further withering away of the law still lies ahead. It suggests that more than one generation will continue on the path of voluntary, docile self-restriction, denying themselves ordinary, fundamental human expression.

Of course the years of the movement in defense of human rights have left a definite trace. Not that the movement has achieved any democratic reforms, but it has convinced many people that things can be called by their right names, and that laws can be understood as they are written and not as they are interpreted by the authorities. (True, the movement has also demonstrated that for behaving freely a person can be sent to prison—something that was already realized very well.)

Many people are perturbed about whether the movement has merely left its trace, or whether it still exists. They also wonder: "Will new forces join the movement?" To all appearances, the repressions were so severe that little of the former activism remains.

The authorities can regard this as a success. Some of the people who took part in protests in defense of human rights are in prison or in psychiatric hospitals, some are abroad, and a great many, saddened by the impotence of such protests, have left the movement. Will new activists join it, replacing those who have been arrested, who have left the Soviet Union, or who have become disenchanted? I fear that new people will not come forth all that quickly. I mean "new people" in the sense of activists ready to come out just as openly in defense of human rights, despite the repression of previous years. It is clear that in the future people will continue to manifest dissent more or less actively and in one form or another; and in this sense new people will come along. But I am afraid these new dissenters will remember the disillusionment of many of their predecessors in dissent—disillusionment with open methods of debate with the authorities—and will prefer some sort of conspiratorial activity against the authorities. And it is clear that no prolonged conspiratorial activity is possible in the Soviet Union, with its total control of the population through the residence permit system and the job placement system. If the judgment of most Soviet citizens is valid, informers in every student group and every plant and institution also contribute to this control. The authorities will catch such conspirators easily; and it will be easier to try them in court, and easier to frighten people with stories about hostile secret organizations and call on members of the public to increase their vigilance—that is, to inform and spy upon one another. This will be an even greater tragedy for society.

It will be much easier for the authorities to suppress such a conspiratorial movement. It will be easier technically, because the trials can be held in secret without any "fuss" in the West. And it will be easier psychologically, since such conspirators better fit the stereotype of an enemy of the people that is stamped into the heads of those who run the Soviet penal system. It is quite noticeable that prison officials are sometimes embarrassed when dealing with today's activists, who are noted for the open nature of their activities. This is not only because any armed persecutor may sometimes pause in indecision when faced with a courageous and defenseless victim. It is also because today's overt dissenter does not fit the traditional notion of an enemy of the people, the notion inculcated in the persecutors, as in every other Soviet person, since youth. The KGB and the propaganda media have tried in every way to make these open participants in the movement resemble, in the consciousness of the people, the stereotyped secret enemies of the Soviet regime. To this end, the KGB in trials and the propagandists in articles try to distort the character of the movement in defense of human rights, declaring that its members act on "instructions from abroad." They try to discover instigators and bosses (thank heaven our movement had no bosses), and then to compromise the alleged ringleaders by forcing them to repent and acknowledge their guilt. Any future shift of the movement in defense of human rights to conspiratorial forms will increase the success of such tactics and increase the social atmosphere of distrust and denunciation. This is very sad. But perhaps the authorities believe that it is impossible, without such an atmosphere, to build a great and ideal future. Perhaps the regime, in trying to build such a future, will finally understand the inevitable consequences of suppressing honest, open, and lawful protests in defense of human rights. But if it turns out that nothing is heard in the future of protests in defense of human rights—if nothing is heard of people who are trying to defend human rights or trying to engage the authorities in a dialogue—this will not mean that the movement in defense of human rights has ceased to exist. It has always existed, and will continue to exist, at least in the camps where political prisoners, who earlier have protested only in private, learn to protest openly.

APPENDICES

1
The Legal Status of the Moscow Human Rights Committee

Letter to the Procurator of the City of Moscow

I was invited for a talk with Emelyanov, chief of the section of general supervision in the Procurator's Office, City of Moscow.

In the course of the talk it was stated to me that the existence of the Human Rights Committee, founded on November 4, 1970, by a declaration of Sakharov, Tverdokhlebov, and Chalidze, contravened the law, since the committee was not registered in accordance with the 1932 statute on voluntary unions and societies. The wish was expressed that the committee discontinue its activities. In response to this I stated that attention would be paid to the demands of the authorities whenever they were lawful and expressed in official (of course written) form. I was also warned of possibly being held answerable for the continued activity of the committee, under Article 200 of the RSFSR Criminal Code (on arbitrary actions).

Section Chief Emelyanov assured me that the members of the committee would receive a written demand from the

Moscow Procurator's Office that the committee cease its activity.

In this connection, with a view to presenting the Moscow Procurator's Office with more precisely formulated arguments as to the legality of our activity than would be possible orally—which I believe is important in inquiring into the legal basis of the demands of the Procurator's Office —I inform you of the following:

1. It is important to bear in mind the distinction between associations that are juridical persons, and other associations. Practically, the procedure for acquiring the rights of a juridical person is fully covered in the laws. And by virtue of the fact that many associations (societies, voluntary societies, unions, etc.) are juridical persons, a confusion of the concepts of an association and a juridical person may become common.

2. An appropriate example of an association of citizens which is not a juridical person is cited in Article 482 of the RSFSR Civil Code. This is a creative association of co-authors that does not require any registration but allows the adoption of a covenant among the authors. Neither the form of the covenant, nor the character of the requirements written into the covenant as to the procedure for adopting a common decision, nor the procedure for creative contacts in such an association, nor the requirements imposed upon new co-authors in such an association, are regulated by law, which means complete freedom in the choice of the form and conditions of joint activity in drawing up such a covenant. In the legal sense the committee, which was created for the theoretical study of the problem of human rights, is just such an authors' collective. The form in which we (Sakharov, Tverdokhlebov, Chalidze) adopted the co-authors' covenant is known to the Procurator's Office. I refer to the Principles and Bylaws of the committee.

Likewise, no one disputes the right of such a collective person to choose a name. Our choice was traditional and natural for an authors' association dealing with such a subject. But if the name, in someone's understanding, distorts the character of our legal status, I can only recommend paying heed not merely to the name of the authors' collective but to a study of the Principles and Bylaws, from which it is clear that the legal character of our activity is precisely as outlined above. Similar bylaws might have been adopted by the French mathematicians who published books under the pseudonym of "General Bourbaki."*

3. In founding a creative association without the rights of a juridical person, we do not claim to acquire such rights. But it is natural to assume that our subsequent scholarly activity in the sphere of rights would not be much hampered by our registration as a juridical person, although the concomitants of this transformation of a creative association into an organization would not be altogether attractive, since they could burden us with new concerns in addition to theoretical thinking. (Thus for an organization called the Human Rights Committee it would be natural to undertake certain actions in defense of rights in concrete cases, which would distract us from purely scholarly activity.) However, in principle the committee could acquire the status of a juridical person—all the more so since the authorities wish it. But in the existing laws there is no procedure for registering an association with so few members as a juridical person. The only norm cited to me in talks with the Committee of State Security (KGB) and the Moscow Procurator's Office was the 1932 statute on voluntary societies and unions.

This citation is surprising, since it is obvious that the statute on the registration of mass organizations—voluntary societies and unions—has no relation to such a small association. It suffices to say that this statute requires the presence of ten founders. It would be too paradoxical to consider that the right guaranteed by the Constitution (four years after the publication of that statute) of association in social organizations means a right to form associations with at least ten members. It is more natural to recognize a lacuna in the legislation regarding the registration of small associations than to suspect Soviet law of such paradoxicality.

* Yury Shikhanovich and Edward Kline have pointed out to me a mistake in this sentence: the French mathematicians called themselves merely "Bourbaki."

4. For that matter, even with respect to large associations the aforementioned statute is not always applicable, since it refers only to those voluntary societies or unions in which scientific research work is conducted on the basis of the Marxist-Leninist method. It is not entirely clear, however, what the legislators mean by such a *method*. But it is natural to assume that it is a question, if not of the full acceptance of the theories of Marxism-Leninism, at least of the application, in building other theories, of those methods which were utilized in building the theories of Marxism-Leninism. It is clear to everyone familiar with scientific work that even if it is possible in principle to limit oneself in creative work to only one definite method of investigation, this is a question of personal inclination, convenience, etc.; and it is not the business of the state to prescribe to the scientist or the association what scientific methods should be used. The law guarantees equality of rights regardless of religious belief. This should be sufficient basis for the Procurator's Office not to infringe upon the rights of individuals or collective persons without regard to their belief in the usefulness of one investigative method or another.

As for me, I have never considered that in physics, or law, or philosophical thinking I was using any definite method. Human culture is especially rich in methods of investigation, and variety in their use is pleasurable.

What I have said in this paragraph sufficiently confirms, of itself, the inapplicability of the 1932 statute to the registration of our committee, since, by its terms, if I did not profess Marxism-Leninism and its method, then I would be excluded from participation in the research of the committee. In other words, my right of association would be restricted by the state because of my religious belief, which contravenes the law.

The use of the term "religious belief" may provoke debate. I should explain that it is natural to apply the term "belief" to everything that a person accepts not as a result of direct observation or logical reasoning. For that matter, in this paragraph I could have spoken of convictions rather than beliefs. It is hardly likely that a Soviet procurator's office would, in the given case, agree to limiting citizens' rights to association on the basis of convictions.

5. It was very interesting to get a warning of criminal liability for participation in the activity of the Human Rights Committee on the basis of Article 200 of the RSFSR Criminal Code (on arbitrary actions). However strange the impression that this might produce on the public, for me the suggestion of instituting criminal proceedings is very tempting, since that would make it possible, in a public debate in court, to examine the status of law and of practice as concerns the right to association. Apparently such a possibility could arise only if criminal proceedings were instituted, for I doubt whether, if a civil suit were brought, the court would consider it possible to adjudicate this right. I make this statement on the basis of my own legal experience, knowing that courts prefer to declare cases which are unusual for them to be outside their jurisdiction; although in the given instance there is no doubt as to jurisdiction over cases involving defense of the right to association. This is because, in the Convention on the Elimination of All Forms of Racial Discrimination, this right is legislatively recognized as a civil right, which by virtue of Article 4 of the Fundamental Principles of Civil Legislation, and in the absence of statutes defining exceptions, means that it comes under the jurisdiction of a civil court.

True, there is a danger that under criminal proceedings the court would consider this case not worthy of attention, since "arbitrary action" means exercising one's actual or presumed rights only if there is *violation* of a procedure established by law, and not when the law fails to indicate the procedure for the exercise of the right, as is the case with respect to the formation of small associations. (This lacuna in the law is important in those cases where the association does not have such an academic character as our committee and where, therefore, the norms on an author's right regarding co-authorship are inapplicable.)

6. It goes without saying that the right to association is not especially encouraged by Soviet laws. And we know from history that practice, in this sphere of the official

obstruction of citizens' initiatives, has been even more severe. However, I consider it useful and timely to call the attention of the authorities to the fact that a great deal in the Soviet laws permits the possibility of creating various types of associations which, although not of the usual kind, are completely loyal. If such associations have not yet been founded in large numbers, it is not from a lack of initiative on the part of citizens or lack of interest in the right to association. It is rather because one cannot always find a knowledgeable person who would advise on legal means of founding independent associations. It is superfluous to stress the importance of such lawful independent activity on the part of citizens in promoting the growth of legal consciousness, in developing among the population the custom of constructively criticizing laws and the actions of the authorities, and in working out new social ideas. On the other hand, it is possible that the failure of citizens to found independent associations is due to the fact that that right has been forgotten. If so, any opposition to the existence of the committee on the part of the authorities will have the important result of reminding people of their right to association. Such is human nature.

7. Since there can be no question of liquidating the committee (the Procurator's Office is only raising the question of discontinuing activity so long as the committee is not registered), and since we do not claim the rights of a juridical person, considering ourselves as a collective of co-authors, it will be natural if we, recognizing the legality of the supervisory functions of the Procurator's Office, agree to constant monitoring of the legality of our creative activity; i.e., all our jointly signed documents will be sent to the Procurator's Office. Such a practice would be useful, especially as regards rooting out from among the public those rumors, false and damaging to the committee, which, as was wisely pointed out in my talks with the KGB and the Procurator's Office, might be used for purposes of political propaganda. The committee is ready to discuss the procedure for such monitoring by the procurator.

8. I of course consider this note an open one, meaning by "open" a communication copies of which I may give to anyone who wants them, with the right of distribution. This means that, depending upon the activity and interest of correspondents, the communication may also appear in the press. (This distinguishes a merely open communication from a communication or statement for the press, which in accordance with the nature of the genre I myself must transmit to correspondents.) Since with such open distribution there is no discrimination against Soviet journalists, the usual claims of the authorities as to the appearance of information, specifically in the foreign press, would be unfounded.

February 19, 1971

V. N. Chalidze

2
Appeal in Defense of Andrei Amalrik*

Thousands of newspapers and propagandists tirelessly repeat: "The Soviet Union is eternal and indestructible." Then suddenly a thoughtful man quietly asks: "Will the Soviet Union survive until 1984?"

The question is of course impolite. But if there is discussion of why the USSR may not survive, one should consider that impoliteness as a friendly service and ponder, with profit to oneself, the arguments advanced. The simplest thing is to get angry—that depends upon the culture of the listener. I dare say that fostering people's culture is the task of the intelligentsia. In particular, this means teaching people (and rulers) not to fear words. And if one must contend against words, let it be done with words and not with penal sentences.

But Amalrik has been arrested, and is awaiting trial and sentencing. He will not try to justify himself before the

* Moscow, October 25, 1970. Originally called "Appeal to the Intelligentsia."

court; he will not dispute the indictment; he will not ask for mercy. He is simply convinced of his right to pose and discuss any questions.

In terms of his cast of mind and character, Andrei Amalrik is not a politician and not a debater, not a fighter and not a tribune. In terms of his cast of mind he is a philosopher, and his journalistic writings are thoughtful and philosophical. But clarity of thought and inner freedom make for firmness of spirit; and he is ready to bear his cross like all the best people of Russia, who from century to century have suffered for their convictions.

I call upon you to intercede for him—some as they can, others as they dare to. Do it publicly, or at least do it in your own soul. Intercede regardless of whether you agree with his views.

Intercede for the word.

Chalidze

3

In Defense of Reiza Palatnik

To the Supreme Court of the Ukrainian SSR

By judgment of the Odessa Court, Reiza Palatnik was found guilty of disseminating literary and journalistic works objectionable to the Odessa authorities. Individual works of Anna Akhmatova, Lydia Chukovskaya, Alexander Galich, Osip Mandelstam, and others were found to be criminal. Once again the dismal fidelity to the tradition of judicial revisions of the literary legacy of Soviet writers.

Will the Ukrainian Supreme Court likewise be faithful to this tradition, or will it reject it? Will it confirm the unjust decision, or will it acquit Reiza Palatnik, Mandelstam, Akhmatova . . . ?

July 31, 1971

Chalidze

4
The Case of A. Gurevich

To the Procurator of the RSFSR

I have been informed of the difficulties of Citizen A. E. Gurevich, the wife of Yu. V. Vudka, who is serving a sentence in Institution ZhKh-385/19. Their visit was broken off because they were using their native language (Yiddish) for a family talk.

I call your attention to the fact that our laws recognize the right of everyone to use his own native language. If the administration wants to monitor a conversation, it is the institution's obligation to see that an interpreter is present.

I am especially chagrined by the fact that Gurevich did not receive a reply to the request addressed to you.

I enclose A. Gurevich's request dated March 14, 1971.

V. Chalidze*

---

* No date. Probably autumn 1971. After this letter Gurevich received a reply stating she would be allowed a visit in the presence of an interpreter.

To the Procurator of the RSFSR

From A. E. Gurevich, 25 Gulak-Artemovsky Street (Apt. 6), Chernovtsy

REQUEST

On 2/III/71 I was allowed to visit my husband, Yu. V. Vudka, who is serving a sentence in Institution ZhKh-385/19.

Unfortunately, the visit was broken off because the institution had no Yiddish interpreter and the guards present at the visit could not monitor that part of our conversation which had to be devoted to purely family matters and which therefore, according to our general family custom, could be carried on only in our language.

Considering that in accordance with the general rule, talks during visits with prisoners may be carried on in one's native language, and also considering that Institution ZhKh-385/19 was in a difficult position as regards interpreting, I request that, with your approval, I be allowed to pay for the services of an interpreter so as to take advantage of the visit due my husband in this six months' period but which did not take place on March 2, if this can be done without causing unforeseen difficulties for Institution ZhKh-385/19.

14/III/71

A. Gurevich

5

On the Repentance
of Accused Persons*

To R. A. Rudenko, General Procurator of the USSR

*Copies to N. V. Podgorny, Chairman of the Presidium
of the Supreme Soviet USSR; Y. V. Andropov, Chairman of the KGB, CM/USSR*

I. "In fixing punishment the following are recognized
as circumstances mitigating the liability . . . 8) sincere
repentance or confession." (Article 33, Fundamental Principles of Criminal Legislation of the USSR and Union
Republics.) This same article authorizes the union republics to make provision in legislation for other mitigating

---

* Published here in abridged form. Original title, "On the Repentance
of Accused Persons and Contributing to the Exposure of a Crime."

circumstances as well. Several republics, including the RSFSR, have taken advantage of this right and recognized as mitigating circumstances "sincere repentance or confession, and active contribution to the exposure of a crime." (Article 38, para. 9, RSFSR Criminal Code.)

Recognition of active contribution to the exposure of a crime as a mitigating circumstance is a novelty in Soviet law. In the old criminal legislation there is no mention of it, or of repentance. From the viewpoint of the principle of equality of persons before the law and the right to defense, the recognition of such mitigating circumstances is questionable.

First, the recognition of repentance and active contribution to the exposure of a crime as mitigating circumstances leads to a disadvantageous inequality before the court and the law for those accomplices in the act who see no need to repent and help the investigation but prefer to exercise their right to defend themselves against the charge being brought.

Second, the kind and degree of punishment is made to depend not only upon the nature of the act, the degree of guilt, the norm of the law, and the degree of socialist legal consciousness of the judges, but also upon the "pedagogical" skill of the preliminary investigator, since it is precisely the educative work of the investigator which often contributes to the repentance of accused persons. This is an inadmissible inequality, all the more so since the law does not give the accused person the right to challenge the investigator on the grounds of his incapacity to guide the accused along the path of repentance.

Third, with such a norm the law exerts psychological duress on the accused to give evidence, since in practice it is usually by means of giving evidence that the accused can contribute to the exposure of a crime.

Fourth, the law does not contain criteria for the sincerity of repentance. But in practice, unfortunately—contrary to the sense of repentance—the giving of evidence by the accused, and his informing against his accomplices, are considered an indication of repentance. (Cf. Commentary on the RSFSR Criminal Code, p. 100.)

Fifth, the law does not specify which crime it is whose exposure is a mitigating circumstance—the crime imputed to the accused, or some other crime. This may place in privileged positions those persons who previously, in the line of duty or out of enthusiasm, contributed to the exposure of crimes. And the same thing applies to persons who, being accused, give information to the investigators, contributing to the exposure of the crimes, say, of their cell mates. I dare say this is an obvious violation of the principle of equality before the law and the court.

II. The aforementioned shortcomings and lacunae in the law might be more tolerable if the efforts of accused persons by way of active contribution to the exposure of a crime were utilized by the authorities only as operative data. But experience shows that accused persons are used as witnesses in other cases, and that their testimony against other accused persons is utilized by the court as fully valid *evidence*. Yet by virtue of the fact that the giving of testimony by accused persons against other persons is regarded as a mitigating circumstance, their testimony should not be considered as fully valid evidence, since it is the testimony of *interested persons*. Specifically, they have an interest in giving not merely testimony but testimony actively contributing to the exposure of a crime. And psychologically, even without malicious intent, such an interest may be an obvious source of bias in the testimony—of unintentional distortion in the recollection of facts, etc. Such testimony would not be discredited by the fact of interest if the law did not contain the norm I am criticizing here—the norm on mitigating circumstances. (Para. 8, Article 33, Fundamental Principles of Criminal Legislation.) I think that what I have said can be easily understood by any judges, and taken into account in evaluating evidence. My arguments are not new. It has long been known that only the evidence of a disinterested person merits evaluation as fully valid evidence. The very fact that a witness is an interested party discredits his testimony regardless of the presence or absence of falsehood or perjury. It is amazing that Russian legislators understood this in the age of star chambers. Cf. Peter the Great's decree, "Concerning Non-Ascription of Merit if a Person Convicted of a Crime Informs on Others." (*Complete Collection of Laws of the Russian Empire,* Vol. 7, #4434.)

III. It is interesting that citizens do not usually receive any remuneration for testimony in court that contributes to the exposure of a crime. This is their civil duty. (It is only after committing a crime and becoming an accused person that a citizen receives remuneration in the form of reduced punishment.) The above is true only if a citizen's contribution to the exposure of a crime does not entitle him to mitigation of punishment in the future, in the event that he himself commits a crime. And as I pointed out *supra,* the legislation is not clear on this point. But if services in the exposure of crimes are useful in the future as mitigating circumstances, this should be made widely known to the public in the interests of social utility. It would help to combat crime, since it is likely that many devotees of crime would like to store up such quasi-indulgences.

IV. In Article 155 of the RSFSR Criminal Code, dealing with the procedure for subpoenaing a witness, the legislators provided only for cases in which the witness is at liberty, whereas in a similar article on the procedure for subpoenaing an accused person (Article 145) the provision is for the case in which the accused person is in custody. The commentator (cf. the Commentary on the Code of Criminal Procedure) arbitrarily filled in this lacuna in the law in Article 155 with a reference to Article 145. In and of itself, the fact of a lacuna does not of course mean that persons confined under guard cannot, in principle, be subpoenaed as witnesses. However, that fact does mean that persons confined under guard constitute a special category among witnesses, since the procedure for subpoenaing them is not regulated by law. But the lacuna is broader than has been noted. When persons are confined under guard, the adequacy of their perception may be impaired owing to the special conditions of their "ecological niche." (And this is not to mention the above-noted interestedness sanctified by law.) Adequacy of perception may be impaired not only because of changes in living conditions when confined under guard but because informational contact with the outside world is broken off. A person who has been arrested may be isolated for up to nine months. As experience has shown, he may be allowed no visitors at all. It is only from the preliminary investigator that the accused learns of changes in or the stability of the outside world—and, if you will, of the stability of those ethical and social values he previously honored. The law protects an accused person only against force and threats—not against lies, which the investigator can use for tactical purposes. An investigator does not have to be a skillful psychotherapist to elicit at will, from some accused person, the kind of testimony against other persons that the accused would never have given if he had been at liberty. It is doubtful whether such a method of eliciting testimony could have been prescribed by law. I am inclined to believe that the legislators intentionally (and temporarily) left a gap in the Code of Criminal Procedure regulating the procedure for subpoenaing witnesses. I believe they understood that in indicating the procedure for subpoenaing a witness confined under guard, the law must at the same time provide guarantees of the rights of such a witness that would eliminate the basic (from the legal point of view) fallaciousness of his testimony against other persons. This suggestion as to the intentional nature of the lacuna in the law should surprise no one. Let me cite an example from civil law. Article 447 of the RSFSR Civil Code provides that for damage done by the incorrect official acts of officials of organs of police inquiry, of investigation, of the procurator's office, and of the court, these organs are liable in those cases and within those limits *specially* prescribed by law. A reliable handbook (*Soviet Civil Law*, edited by Professor O. A. Krasavchikov, Moscow, 1969, p. 388) testifies to the fact that such a law has not yet been published, and that liability under Article 447 cannot ensue. As we can see, the legislators deliberately (for the time being) left a gap in the law, although it is clear to everyone that this gap makes it impossible to demand compensation for damages—perhaps in very important cases.

I dare say that juridical practice should also face the fact of a lacuna in the Code of Criminal Procedure relative to the subpoenaing as witnesses of persons confined under guard (and relative to the necessary guarantees of the rights of such witnesses); that is, not use the testimony of persons confined under guard, despite the fact that this is fraught with practical inconveniences. Presumably these inconveniences will be taken into account by the legislators, and they will be more diligent in filling in this gap in the Code of Criminal Procedure than in the case of the above-mentioned gap in civil legislation.

October 5, 1972

Chalidze

6

On the Confiscation of My Book, *Thoughts on Man*

To Andropov, Chairman of the KGB CM USSR

When your agents, in the course of their searches, confiscate my works on jurisprudence, I am surprised; but I am consoled by the hope that a reading of these works will help to raise the level of legal consciousness at your institution.

But I am especially surprised by confiscation of my philosophical work, *Thoughts on Man*. In the course of a search at the home of Shikhanovich, three copies of that book were seized. And in a search at my home last year, four copies of the second part of that book were confiscated.

Although *Thoughts on Man* is a work for popular consumption, it contains several new ideas I want to convey to the reading public, and I am grieved by the loss of each copy.

If the confiscated copies are not quickly returned, I shall once again get the impression that your institution is trying to defend official philosophy by means of confiscating non-Marxist (although completely legal) works.

I call upon you to use more academic methods of defending the official philosophy.

May 13, 1972

V. Chalidze

7

The Church Case
in Naro-Fominsk

To the Members of the Presidium of the Supreme Soviet USSR

I am sending you some documents on the case of the registration of a religious society in the town of Naro-Fominsk.*

In reading these documents you will see whether believers can gain recognition of their right to the unhindered performance of religious rites. And you will see how difficult it is to defend other rights if they appear to the authorities to be associated with attempts to found a church. But the fact that the authorities have practiced discrimination on the basis of religious belief is not self-evident, in a formal sense, from these documents. Let us see how this is done.

Unfortunately, the Naro-Fominsk case is not the only

* A number of the documents were published in the Russian-language edition of this book, *Prava cheloveka i sovetsky soyuz* (Khronika Press, New York, 1974). In this letter (somewhat abridged) I give the history of the whole case.

instance when believers have failed in their attempt to found a church or preserve an existing one.

I consider the defense of human rights to be important in such cases. In writing to you I am not overhopeful that the violations of rights that have been committed will be corrected, but I am calling upon you to do so.

I shall briefly recount the events that began with the insistent petitioning by the Naro-Fominsk believers for the registration of a religious society.

The first application was submitted on October 21, 1968. Twenty-four persons requested that they be registered as a religious society of the Orthodox faith in accordance with the decree of the All-Union Central Executive Committee and the RSFSR Council of People's Commissars, "On Religious Associations," dated April 8, 1929. They had to wait a long time for a reply. On December 8, 1968, about 700 believers signed an appeal supporting the request of the original petitioners. Not receiving a reply from the city authorities, the petitioners requested that their honored church hierarch, Metropolitan Pimen of Krutitsky and Kolomna, give them his blessing and assist them through prayer. It is not known whether he provided any help through prayer, but they received no answer or blessing. A protest to the city procurator's office against the silence of the city executive committee also went unanswered. It was only when the founders protested to the oblast procurator S. I. Gusev that the local authorities had not answered their application and protest, that they received an answer. It stated that their protest had been forwarded to A. Turshin, a commissioner of the Council on Religious Affairs. Turshin soon sent a reply that stated, without giving any reasons: ". . . it is not possible to grant your request." Meantime the town executive committee, which according to the law must answer requests for the registration of religious societies, remained silent as before. It was only after the believers published an appeal in a local newspaper on February 3—i.e., more than three months after the application had been submitted—that an answer came from the chairman of the town executive committee, Shultseva: "The registration of religious societies is not possible at the present time, because there is no building for that purpose in the city . . ."

Soon an answer also came from the procurator's office that confidentially stated the real reason for the refusal to register the society. The applicants, it seems, had not complied with the form for submitting an application, and the town executive committee had therefore refused the registration. The mistake was corrected, and an application in proper form was once again sent to the town executive committee. Chairwoman Shultseva replied that there were four churches in the Naro-Fominsk district; that they met the religious needs of believers; and that the executive committee "did not consider it necessary to create a new religious association in Naro-Fominsk."

What was this? Legal illiteracy? Or an international shifting of the focus of the problem so as to mislead the believers? Does the right of citizens to found a religious association really depend upon the number of churches in the region? Is it not obvious that even if no church existed in the region, the town executive committee would not deem it necessary to create a religious association simply because that is not within its province? A religious association is created by the citizens who are its founders. It is the business of the town executive committee to register that association —to record the fact that people have exercised their right to association. Is this understood by A. Shultseva and the thousands of other chairmen of executive committees?

But the town authorities considered their answer final. And in answer to their next request to the procurator's office, the petitioners received a subpoena with a threat of arrest if they did not appear. The "little talk" at the procurator's office was threatening and left no hopes. Apparently the gist of it was: "Stop all this scribbling. Don't distract people from their work." Moreover, the Procurator of the Naro-Fominsk district soon confirmed in writing that the refusal to register the religious society was correct.

Finally the believers were summoned for a personal explanation to the commissioner of the Council on Religious Affairs. For reasons of ill health and pressing business, they exercised their right to conduct their business through a representative. One of the group, V. A. Nefedova, retained a Moscow lawyer and paid a fee for legal services. A local notary public notarized Nefedova's grant of power of attorney to that lawyer. The notary, acting in conformity with the law, did not suspect that he was committing a politically harmful act, as became evident from what followed.

The legality of the representation did not assure the success of the lawyer's mission. The Council on Religious Affairs demanded the personal presence of the believers involved in the case, for purposes of explanation. It turned out that the retainer paid by V. A. Nefedova had been spent to no purpose, but this was not through any fault of the lawyer. Therefore, a suit for damages was brought against the Council on Religious Affairs. For this organization, acting contrary to law, had not recognized a citizen's right to conduct his affairs through a representative and was therefore liable for damages.

Nefedova entrusted the handling of this suit to Boris Zuckermann, likewise in accordance with the law, the arrangement having been formalized by a power of attorney. The record of the proceedings in this case contained an amazing argument by the representative of the Council on Religious Affairs. It seems that "the question of converting citizens to another faith must be taken up with the citizens personally and not with lawyers." The court agreed with this argument, and found against the plaintiff: "The defendant was correct in not dealing with the question of religion through a representative." It would appear that the Council on Religious Affairs also has a right to take a hand in the "conversion of citizens to another faith," and to settle questions of religion with them. In any case, the Council on Religious Affairs, the court, and the other authorities either do not understand—or else they forget—that the question here is one of exercising an elementary human right: the right to association in order to perform religious rites. None of the petitioners ever requested that a building be made available. And although other believers requested that their old church building be returned to them, they did not do so imperatively but expressed their readiness to build a new church at their own expense.

On the other hand, one thing became clear at the trial: that the semiliterate old ladies of the religious group had come up against a powerful organization. The Council on Religious Affairs declared: "We can give instructions to the Procurator's Office, but not the other way around." No less anomalous was the reasoning of the Moscow City Court, to which the case was appealed. The Collegium of the Moscow City Court found that a damage suit for ten rubles was simply a means of protesting decisions affecting religious affairs, and since such affairs do not come under the jurisdiction of the court, it ruled that the proceedings in the given case should be terminated.

The believers appealed to the Presidum of the RSFSR Supreme Soviet with a petition bearing 1,443 signatures. Persistence by the people on such a scale perturbed the town authorities. An article entitled "A Shady Business" appeared in a local newspaper, *Znamya Ilicha* (Ilich's Banner). It stated in sharp language that Nefedova, Chipegina, and Zhuchkova had submitted a fake petition with falsified signatures. In a complaint to the Naro-Fominsk Court with a demand for retraction, Nefedova, Chipegina, and Zhuchkova acknowledged that among roughly fifteen hundred signatures, semiliterate persons might make one or two errors, but stated that "uneducated people should not be put to shame before the whole nation for this."

It is significant that the case ensuing from this complaint was considered not by a local court but by the Moscow Regional Court. According to law, the burden of proof in this case was on the defendant. He had to prove at least two things: that the petition bore deliberately falsified signatures, and that Nefedova, Chipegina, and Zhuchkova had been parties to the falsification. But the representative of the newspaper employed a different kind of logic. The case was presented as if the plaintiffs and the other believers had had the intention of preventing the opening of a military museum in the building of the former church, closed forty years before. Incidentally, this theme had been heard before, in the statement made in court by the representative of the Council on Religious Affairs: "For a long time they did not submit any such requests; but when they learned of the opening of the museum, they registered protests." Obviously the believers had a right to demand that the old church be made available to them and the museum built in another place. This was their right, but they did not demand it. They were prepared to build a new church out of their own funds. Anatoly Krasnov-Levitin, representing the plaintiffs, pointed this out in court; and it then developed that the theme "museum or church" had been previously used by the city authorities for "educational" purposes. It turned out that another petition had been circulated in Naro-Fominsk for the opening of a museum. The witness Zolotova testified in court (p. 64, verso):

Two men came up to me and asked me to sign a statement. They talked to me, and asked if I was for opening a church or a museum. Naturally, I said I was for the church. They asked me if I would be willing to give 200 rubles for the church. I said I was willing—that I would work there as a charwoman and work off that amount. Those men were for opening a museum.

The witness Buchenkova testified (p. 63) as to the collection of signatures for the museum: "Even policemen were going around collecting those signatures."

Several witnesses testified in court that they did not know how their signatures turned up on the petition for opening the church. The grounds for these statements were discussed in my appeal of this case to the RSFSR Supreme Court. It suffices to say that the defendant used as evidence the testimony of the demobilized Red Army soldier Ivanchukov to the effect that he had not signed the petition. But his signature is not on the petition! A strong impression was created by several documents in the case proving that Citizen A. V. Volkov died in 1958, before the petition was circulated. But the signature of A. V. Volkov is not on the petition! It was impossible to prove this in court, since the petition with the signatures was not available, and the court rejected Krasnov-Levitin's request that it be produced.

There are several cases that are not so clear, but no one took the trouble to verify whether an error had been made or a fabrication perpetrated. And no one took the trouble to investigate the lawfulness of the educational measures taken by the local authorities. Yet there were grounds for doubting the lawfulness of those measures. The transcript contains the testimony of the witness Buchenkova: "The representatives of the town executive committee threatened me and others, too, when they asked us to sign the statement where people are asked to sign up for the museum." And if our judges were sharper-eared they would have paid attention to a shout from the courtroom: "They called us in and scared us!" In any case, signers of the petition were *called in*, although one hundred persons refused to sign.

Just what educational measures were employed to dissuade believers from supporting the request to open the church is not known for certain; but the shout of "They called us in and scared us!" reminds me of the documentation in samizdat of a similar case concerning the opening of a church in Gorky. There the believers wrote many petitions and finally appealed to the UN. They too were called in. Here is a note from one of the believers, written in an awkward, old-fashioned hand.

Explanatory note to the UN. In 1968 I signed a petition to the World Council of Churches and the UN Commission on Human Rights for the opening of a church in Gorky. In 1969, on April 16, I was called in to the district executive committee, and they threatened me as if by signing I was calling for war. I got frightened; they dictated and I wrote a statement saying I had not written an appeal abroad. Later I asked them many times to give the paper back to me, but they didn't give it back. I ask you to consider the paper I gave to the district executive committee null and void. I live at 70 Lenin Prospect, Apartment 57. Tikareva.

A similar note was written by E. I. Zhirnova.

People ask me why I *believe* what is told me by these uneducated people, who are interested parties. I believe them because I have never known them to lie. Also because, in this case, anyone who studies the appended documents can see the lying and trickery employed by the educated and powerful persons who are supposed honestly to defend the citizens' rights.

The court decided that the deliberate falsification of the signatures had been proved. And it seemed obvious to both the defendant and the court that the plaintiffs were responsible for it:

The organizing role of Nefedova, Chipegina, and Zhuchkova was confirmed by the fact that they gave powers of attorney to outside persons—Zuckermann and Zalessky—to solicit in their names for the opening of a church. This fact was not disputed by plaintiffs, and provided a basis for the statement in the article as to their active participation in the collection and submission of lists with falsified signatures. Nefedova and Zhuchkova did not deny that they had collected signatures, and Chipegina stated that she had collected only a few signatures, since she was busy on her job.

I note that Chipegina never made such a statement. On the contrary, at the appellate hearing she denied taking part in the collection of signatures. As for Nefedova and Zhuchkova, the burden of proof (as we have seen) was simply shifted to them, contrary to law. They offered no denial; and this was sufficient for the court to consider the fact proved. To what extent the grant of powers of attorney to the lawyer and Zuckermann could serve as evidence that the plaintiffs actively participated in the collection and submission of lists with falsified signatures, is apparently plain only to the defendant and the court. Yes, and to Gusev, the Procurator of the Moscow Oblast. Without any grounds, he affirmed that Nefedova, Chipegina, and Zhuchkova, "with the aid of Zalessky and Zuckermann, by various means collected signatures of town residents on a petition for the building of a church in Naro-Fominsk." One can only be grateful that the Procurator did not use the exacerbating theme "church or museum" but rather recognized that it was a question of building a church. But it was apparently plain to the town authorities that the lawyer and Zuckermann did not help to collect signatures. This notion was not expressed in the court. On the contrary, in the decision of the court Zuckermann and Zalessky were called outside persons.

In the foregoing I have quoted from a very interesting document signed by Oblast Procurator Gusev and authenticated by the official stamp of the Naro-Fominsk Procurator's Office. After the hearing of the case, this document was made a part of the record and designated page 17. When the file was examined after the appellate hearing, it turned out that this document had been pulled out of the file and put into an envelope. The document was headed: "Draft presentation." It was addressed to "Comrade A. V. Sudakov, Chief, Section of Administrative Organs, Moscow Oblast Committee of the Party."

The oblast procurator complained to the oblast committee of the Party about the district notary. The actions of the notary who authenticated the power of attorney given by "religious citizens"* to their representative were considered by the oblast procurator "illegal, politically harmful, and incompatible with her position." If the actions of the notary were *illegal,* the procurator should have taken steps to institute criminal, administrative, or disciplinary proceedings against the notary, as is prescribed by Article 15 of the statute on procurator's supervision.

Why did the oblast procurator not take such steps? Why did he decide to get in touch with the oblast committee of the Party ("I am communicating with you for purposes of taking steps")? Apparently this guardian of legality understood that the actions of the notary were absolutely legal; that they could be called illegal only by making an assumption that these actions were politically harmful. And according to our laws a procurator does not have the right to take legal steps against acts that are lawful merely because he considers them politically harmful.

---

* Incidentally, in writing this Gusev violated a decree of the Council of People's Commissars RSFSR that states: "Any mention of the fact that a citizen belongs, or does not belong, to a religious organization is to be eliminated from all official documents."

But who can discern anything politically harmful in exercising the right, guaranteed by law, to retain legal counsel? Perhaps it is to the point here to recall the words of the representative of the Council on Religious Affairs: "We can give instructions to the procurator's office, but not the other way around." This and many other questions will remain unclear until you order an investigation of this case.

You must decide whether these elderly, honest people, who have labored much and been exhausted by a hard life, will fall silent in their grief, having lost all hope, or whether they can find comfort in their old age with something dear and sacred to them even if incomprehensible and objectionable to you— prayer.

December 7, 1971

                                                    V. Chalidze

8

A Foreigner Came to My House*

Foreword

This is a brochure about how I was visited by a foreigner interested in my activities and what happened afterward. I feel that an account of this incident will be useful to foreigners visiting the USSR, and to Chekists.†

It will be useful to foreigners because it calls their attention to the need for behaving with a sense of responsibility.

It will be useful to Chekists because it is written in a spirit of good will. It is one more lesson in public disclosure —something they have run up against more and more often in recent years.

---

* Published here in abridged form.
† Formerly an agent of the Cheka (All-Russian Extraordinary Commission for Combating Counterrevolution and Sabotage); now any agent of the secret police.—Translator's note.

Report of Search

Moscow, March 29, 1971

Major Yuzepchuk, Senior Investigator of the KGB Investigation Section, with the participation of agents Sokolov, Khorikov, Bulanov, Boyarkin, and Ivanov, and in the presence of the witnesses Irina Anatolevna Okunevskaya, residing at 65 Prospekt Mira, Apt. 13, Moscow, and Boris Grigorevich Kaplunov, residing at 45 Bolshaya Akademicheskaya Street, Korpus 2, Apt. 68, Moscow, and also of Citizen Valery Nikolayevich Chalidze, on the basis of an order from the KGB Investigative Section dated March 29, 1971, in accordance with Articles 169-171 of the RSFSR Code of Criminal Procedure, conducted a search in the apartment occupied by Valery Nikolayevich Chalidze at 43 Sivtsev Vrazhek, Apt. 24.

It was explained to those present at the search that they had the right to witness all acts of the investigator and to make comments on any of his acts.

On the basis of Article 135 of the RSFSR Code of Criminal Procedure, it was also explained to the witnesses that it was their obligation to attest to the fact, content, and result of the search.

At the beginning of the search Citizen Chalidze was asked to surrender any weapons or anti-Soviet literature. Citizen Chalidze stated that he had no weapons or anti-Soviet literature.

As a result of the search, the following were found and confiscated:

1. A cardboard file case with the number "9" on the cover. Typewritten copies of the following documents were filed in the file case: a) *A Chronicle of Current Events,* Number 4/9/ for August 31, 1969, on 18 sheets; b) *A Chronicle of Current Events,* Number 5/10/ for October 31, 1969, on 28 sheets; c) *A Chronicle of Current Events,* Number 6/11/ for December 31, 1969, on 36 sheets; d) *A Chronicle of Current Events,* Number 12 for February 28, 1970, on 2 sheets; e) *A Chronicle of Current Events,* Num-

ber 13, on 31 sheets; f) *A Chronicle of Current Events,* Number 14 for June 30, 1970, on 27 sheets; g) *A Chronicle of Current Events,* Number 15 for August 31, 1970, on 25 sheets; h) *A Chronicle of Current Events,* Number 16 for October 31, 1970, on 27 sheets.

2. A cardboard file case in which typewritten copies of the following documents were filed: a) *Selected Texts from Samizdat* (STS), Number 1, on 43 sheets; b) STS, Number 2, on 42 sheets; c) STS, Number 3, on 52 sheets; d) STS, Number 4, on 52 sheets; e) STS, Number 5, on 55 sheets; f) STS, Number 6, on 53 sheets; g) STS, Number 7, on 57 sheets; h) STS, Number 8, on 44 sheets; i) a document in the English language on 6 sheets.

3. Four sheets of paper with a typewritten text (copy). The text begins with the words "which is a reference" and ends with the words "that to them as far as other facts."

4. A typewritten text on three sheets of paper with the heading: "From a Letter of R. Pimenov."

5. A document on two sheets with a printed text in the English language, beginning with the words "the steadfast" and ending with the word "imperialism."

6. A letter signed by Anatoly Yakobson—a typewritten copy on one sheet of paper.

7. A typewritten copy of a letter from Solzhenitsyn to the Nobel Foundation on one sheet of paper.

8. A letter from Turchin to the editor of *The Literary Gazette*, on three sheets.

9. A typewritten copy of a text headed "Bryusov on Lenin's Article about Party Literature," on six sheets.

10. A typewritten and handwritten text on six sheets containing a list of originals of articles and documents.

11. A list of documents, handwritten in a blue marker on three sheets of paper, beginning with the word "bindweeds" and ending with the word *Newsweek.*

12. A typewritten copy, on two sheets of paper, containing B. Zuckermann's comments on the book, *Ideological Sabotage.*

13. A typewritten copy, on two sheets, of a document headed "Declaration of the National Committee of French Writers."

14. A typewritten copy of a document headed "A Subjective Evaluation of the Inalienability of Certain Human Rights in the USSR," on five sheets.

15. A typewritten copy of a document headed "Foreign Correspondents in Moscow," on ten sheets.

16. A typewritten copy of a document headed "A Few Comments on the Soviet Democratic Movement," on eight sheets.

17. A typewritten copy of a document headed "Open Letter to the newspaper *Rude Pravo*," on four sheets.

18. A typewritten copy of a document headed "Concerning the Subjective Evaluation of the Inalienability of the Rights of the Individual," on six sheets.

19. A typewritten copy of a document headed "He and We," on three sheets.

20. A typewritten copy of a document headed "The Shedding of Leaves in Kaluga," on 21 sheets.

21. A cardboard file case bearing the handwritten inscription: "The situation of political prisoners; general questions of political repressions." The file case contained typewritten copies of the following documents: a) a letter on six sheets, beginning with the words: "Dear Aleshka"; b) a report on the case of Joseph Brodsky, on four sheets; c) a document on four sheets beginning with the words "What is exile?"; d) a letter to the deputies of the Supreme Soviet on 33 sheets; e) a document on four sheets headed "Open Letter"; f) a document on nine sheets addressed to the Presidium of the Academy of Medical Sciences.

22. A photostatic copy of the book by Nikolai Berdyayev, *The Philosophy of Inequality,* which has 245 pages.

23. A typewritten copy of *A Chronicle of Current Events,* Number 18 for March 3, 1971, on 32 sheets.

24. A document (typewritten copy) headed "To the Leaders of the Soviet State" and "Protest," on three sheets.

25. A document (typewritten copy) headed "Concerning the Civil Rights of Man," on 20 sheets.

26. A document (typewritten copy) addressed to the Ministry of Internal Affairs USSR on three sheets, in three copies.

27. A document (typewritten copy) headed "The Devel-

opment of the Law on Human Rights in Israel," on 26 sheets.

28. Seven sheets of paper with a handwritten text beginning with the words "October 23, evening" and ending with the words "I did not remember." Stapled to the first sheet is a piece of paper with a note beginning with the words "Not to be made public."

29. A document (typewritten copy) headed "Mode of Investigative Procedure in the Pimenov Case," on 164 sheets.

30. A typewritten copy of a statement of Chalidze on one sheet.

31. A brown file case on the lower part of which is pasted a piece of paper with the notation: "International law. Documents." The file case contains various documents on 133 sheets.

32. A white cardboard file case with a notation on the cover: "Bogdanovsky, Telesin, customhouse." The file case contains documents on 55 sheets.

33. A folder with a blue cover in which various documents on 58 sheets are filed.

34. A folder with a dark brown cover bearing the notation "Karhula" in which documents on 40 sheets are filed.

35. A typewritten copy of a document on 26 sheets with the heading "Brief Record of the Belgorodskaya case."

36. Various typewritten and handwritten documents on 39 sheets with the headings "Toward a Report on Aspects of the Problem of Human Rights in the USSR," "The Opinion of the Human Rights Committee," "A Decision of the Human Rights Committee," "An Opinion on Chalidze's paper," "Statement on the Principles and Bylaws of the Human Rights Committee," "Certain Comments on the Principles of the Human Rights Committee."

37. Three cassettes with tapes contained in three boxes.

38. A brochure, *The Universal Declaration of Human Rights*, on 54 sheets, paperback.

39. Sakharov's brochure, *Thoughts on Progress, Peaceful Coexistence, and Intellectual Freedom*—44 sheets of printed text.

40. Various documents (some of them in file cases)

totaling 2,593 sheets, packed in a linen bag, which was stamped and sealed with Seal #1 of Investigative Section #1.

41. A Remington portable typewriter with Latin letters, #281534.

42. A Moskva portable typewriter, #7627.

In the course of the search and when it was completed, no statements or claims were made by the witnesses or others present.

This report has been read by us. It is correctly set down.

Present—(Chalidze)

Witnesses   (signatures)—Okunevskaya,   Kaplunov, Yuzepchuk.

Search   conducted   by   (signatures)—Khorikov,   Bulanov, Sokolov, Boyarkin, Ivanov.

Chalidze refused to sign the report.

Major   Yuzepchuk   (signature),   Senior   Investigator, Investigative Section of the KGB, CM USSR.

This report was prepared in duplicate. The second copy was given to Chalidze.

Statement

The night of March 30, 1971

On March 29 agents of the KGB conducted a search of my home with a view to confiscating anti-Soviet materials.

In the course of the search the following were confiscated (basically without an inventory) as anti-Soviet: several thousand pages of documents dealing exclusively with the study of human rights and the defense of human rights in our country, including the texts of UN conventions on human rights and the text of the Universal Declaration on Human Rights; files of the Human Rights Committee; business correspondence with my friends dealing with the defense of rights and discussing our difficulties; articles on philosophy and law, including translations from René Cassin's international journal dealing with human rights; the files of a sociojuridical journal published by me, *Social Problems*. If the KGB considers such materials to be anti-

Soviet, it is difficult to conclude that this organization considers itself to be a Soviet one.

If the subject of human rights is a forbidden one, then I may expect any repression, since I am actively involved with this subject. Needless to say, I am ready for any repression.

V. Chalidze

Notes

Major Yuzepchuk left a handwritten "summons," bearing no seal, for me to appear on March 30 at ten o'clock as a witness. Given the nature of the summons, I could have avoided going. But I was interested, and decided to go.

In the morning I went to the Lefortovo Prison to see Yuzepchuk. The talk I had with him was pleasant. It lasted almost the entire working day, and was concluded with the following examination record: *

Question: What foreign citizens visited you during the month of March?

Answer: It is difficult for me to answer that question.

Question: Why?

Answer: I am not confident of the accuracy of my recollections.

Question: What documents have you transmitted to foreigners recently?

Answer: I don't remember. But if I transmitted anything to anyone it was, as always, only documents written and signed by me (or copies of the texts of such documents).

Question: Was there anything inimical to the Soviet state in those documents?

Answer: My texts and my actions in connection with the study of the problem of human rights contain nothing inimical to our country and state.

---

* I reproduce the questions and answers as I recall the text (pretty accurately, I believe), skipping the standard elements of examination records (warnings, etc.).

Question: Who was at your home on Sunday March 28?
Answer: I refuse to answer.

Question: What documents did you transmit to foreign citizens on March 28?

Answer: I remember very well that I transmitted nothing at all.

Question: Who was present during your talks with foreigners?

Answer: I refuse to answer.

In response to the investigator's question as to why I refused to answer, I said that the question had nothing to do with Case #7, and that he had no right to ask it. I had to explain that the question as to the reasons for refusing to answer the interrogation was material to possible proceedings against me for refusing to testify as a witness, proceedings which had still not been initiated.*

Statement on the Brecht Case

To Lieutenant General Volkov, Chief, Investigation Section of the KGB

I have learned that a week ago the Belgian citizen Brecht was arrested in the USSR. I am not certain that what follows refers to the particular Brecht who was arrested. Perhaps I was visited by someone with the same name.

I inform you, however, that about two weeks ago I was visited by a blond young man. (I seem to recall that he wore glasses, but I may be mistaken, since his appearance was such as to incline one to think that he wore glasses.) A friend of mine undertook the job of interpreter. (Naturally, I do not intend to supply the name of that friend, or names of the other interpreters who were present at our talks subsequently, although cognizant of my legal responsi-

---

* Investigators have the habit, after each refusal, of mentioning criminal liability for refusal to give depositions. It is reasonable to regard this as pressure and a threat, since the law obliges the investigator to warn of criminal liability only before the beginning of the interrogation.

bility I hereby attest that these persons did not commit illegal acts.) The stranger was called Brecht, and he
stated that he had come to me in the name of the Flemish
Committee for the Defense of Human Rights. I had previously heard of that creative group, and I expressed to
Brecht my pleasure at the possibility of creative contacts
with his committee.

I also stated that it was important to our Human Rights
Committee to have creative contacts with reliable national
and international associations studying the problem of
human rights, and I recalled with satisfaction my meeting
with Mr. Jerome Speiser, of the American Civil Liberties
Union. Having said this, I reminded the stranger of the content of Article 5 of the Principles of our committee, by virtue of which we are prepared to have contacts only with
organizations that do not have the aim of doing damage to
the Soviet Union. And I added on my own that we also do
not desire contacts with organizations pursuing any political aims. My visitor assured me that the activity of the
Flemish committee was remote from politics, and that that
committee was friendly toward the Soviet Union.

The conversation was not a long one. It was made difficult by the necessity of translation, and also by the typical
Western naïveté in understanding Soviet life—that same
naïveté that leads to distortions in reports in the Western
press, particularly as regards actions in defense of human
rights in the USSR. My guest, by the way, was interested in
the accuracy of reports about our committee. I repeated to
him the well-known information about the committee—the
standard text, like that published in *Newsweek*'s interview
with me.

We also talked about international organizations. I noted
that we had already sent information about the committee
to René Cassin's International Institute for Human Rights,
to the League for the Rights of Man in New York, and to
the Federation for Human Rights in Paris, but had not
received an answer. At this point I complained about the
mails and said that if our Western colleagues studying
human rights wanted contacts with us they should write

more. Then, even with the poor postal service, something would get through. I also talked about our difficulties in getting journals on human rights and UN documents.

Our conversation also touched upon an organization less to my liking—the NTS.* My guest had heard something about it, and I ironically said that the NTS would do us a great service by not publishing our texts in *Posev*† and other publications like *Posev*, since the spirit of such unreliable journals is clearly political, unlike our texts. As I understood it, my visitor could not be of help in this, since he was not connected with the aforementioned *Posev*.

Such was our conversation that evening. Shortly thereafter, on March 26, Brecht came to my home and gave me a sheet of paper with questions about the committee. He was interested in getting accurate information on the basis of which he could criticize the press for distortions. (The KGB organs know how many errors the press has made in accounts of the committee.) The questions were handwritten, in English, and there were about fifteen of them. The conversation that evening was very brief, and I managed to answer only a few questions. I agreed to receive Brecht on March 28 to continue the interview. He came on the 28th, and I answered the rest of the questions. I give the content of the questions and answers below. Here I want to state what happened to the sheet of paper with the questions written on it. After the conversation of the 28th, since I didn't need the sheet of paper, I tore it up and threw the pieces into a pan under the table where I usually throw papers I no longer need. The next day the search in connection with Case #7 was conducted at my home, and the contents of the pan were inspected in detail. Subsequently, hearing of the arrest of Brecht and assuming it was the same person I had talked to, I checked the contents of the pan and was rewarded by finding pieces of paper with English text on them. By arranging them in their original

* *Natsionalnyy Trudovoi Soyuz* (People's Labor Alliance), a Russian émigré organization.—Translator's note.
† Volpin has called my attention to the fact that in this text I unjustifiably associated *Posev* (Sowing) with the NTS. (*Posev* is an émigré journal published in Germany.—Translator's note.)

order I put together a document that may be important
in investigative proceedings if the investigators are interested in the talks between Brecht and me. My surprise that
these pieces of paper were not confiscated during the search
was rapidly dissipated when I recalled the nature of the
materials taken from me. These were international legal
documents, including the Universal Declaration of Human
Rights, documents on the legal practice of my friends, the
files of the journal I publish, *Social Problems*, and so on.
However strange the impression created by the seizure of
such documents, it was plain that the investigation in connection with Case #7 had more to do with the problem of
human rights than with my talks with Brecht, which
explains why these pieces of paper were not seized.

Using these pieces I was able to paste together only the
upper part of the sheet, on which the first nine questions
could be read in their entirety. I did not manage to recall
in detail the few other questions that were missing. I remember only that they were just as inoffensive as, and no less
naïve than, the first questions. And I recall one amusing
question: "What do you expect from the Twenty-fourth
Party Congress?"

Here is a translation of the text that I was able to restore.

1. Is the committee legal?
2. Do you have contacts with other committees?
3. How many people share your convictions?
4. You want to help the authorities. How?
5. Do you have a press service?
6. Who is the official representative of the committee?
7. What is your aim?
8. Is there a real possibility for contact between the committee
   and other national and international organizations?
9. What do the authorities think of the committee?

Anyone who has read my articles can easily imagine the
nature of my replies. In response to the first question I
simply handed over a note on the legal status of the committee which had been sent to the Procurator of the City
of Moscow. This was on March 26. Brecht took the note,
but expressed doubt that the customs would pass it, and said

he was afraid for me, since my name was given at the end of the text. So far as his fears were concerned, I simply laughed, saying that my name was known to the authorities, and that I act only openly. As regards the customs, I proceeded to argue that foreigners .have a distorted notion of Soviet democracy: that it is broader than is thought in the West. I now fear that I was too bold in extending my theoretical thesis on the breadth of Soviet democracy so far as to include the customs department. It seems unlikely, but was it my note that created a problem for my Western colleague? In any case, the note is patently lawful, and I hope it will not cause anyone to suffer.

In response to the question as to representation, I quoted the Bylaws, but said that in contacts with foreigners I would represent the committee. The other answers were stereotyped.

Such are the circumstances, insofar as I know them, of the visit paid to me by the Belgian, Brecht.

In the belief that my Western colleague did nothing inimical to the Soviet state, I should like to help in rapidly clearing up the troubles (short-lived, I hope) that have arisen for him, and should therefore like to be called as a witness at the investigation and in court.

While I believe that the unpleasantness that has arisen will be rapidly cleared up, I am nonetheless hastening to write to the president of the Flemish committee, whose address Brecht left with me, and to communicate to him what I have set forth here. To this end I am sending him this text. Needless to say, as is my practice, I am not keeping it secret from others.

April 4, 1971

V. Chalidze

P.S. I shall hand over the pasted-up document when we meet.

Notes

April 6
In the evening I received a telephone call from KGB agent Kartashev, who informed me that the general had

received my letter and had instructed him to set up a talk with me. I was not interested in who would handle the talk. I myself had suggested it, so why not have a talk? I was asked to come in the morning.

April 7

I was received by Major Sevastyanov, the one who had issued the warrant for the search of my home on March 29. He was affable and respectful. I had brought the pasted-up document promised to Volkov, and we spent an hour and a half drawing up the record on the transmittal of the document. Two of the typists in the office served as witnesses. I was well disposed and had no intention of caviling at details.

When the transmittal of the document had been formally recorded, the major reminded me that I had suggested to the general that I be summoned as a witness in the case of the Belgian, and proposed that we begin the interrogation. I was surprised that Major Sevastyanov was handling both the secret Case #7 and the case of the Belgian. Now it turned out that they were one and the same case. "If you remember the interrogation on Case #7," the major said, "it shouldn't be difficult for you to surmise that." I agreed, but noted that procedural law did not oblige me to surmise, whereas it did oblige the investigator to indicate on what case the witness was being questioned. Merely communicating the number of the case without stating who the accused is and what he is accused of is hardly correct observance of the requirements of the law.

At the beginning of the interrogation I offered to give a written deposition of what I knew about the case of the Belgian. It turned out that his correct name was Sebreghts, and I noted in the record that I might have made a mistake. In my handwritten deposition I put down almost everything that had been in my letter.

Then came the questions.

Question: With whom did the foreigner come to your home the first time?

Answer: I refuse to answer that question, since I do not want to mention the names of persons who were present during my talks with the foreigner, or who happened to come during that time.

Question: Who gave the foreigner your address?

Answer: I refuse to answer.

This was followed by some remarks to the effect that I was opposing the investigation, which produced an unfavorable impression of me. To this I replied that the search had made an unpleasant impression on me, and I did not want the same thing to happen to those whose names I mentioned in connection with the meetings with the foreigner.

Question: In addition to the note, did you intend to give Sebreghts any other documents?

Answer: I don't remember just what in particular. But in the course of the talk I showed Sebreghts my articles and some documents of the Human Rights Committee, and I would not have objected if he had wanted to take them.

Question: Did not your acquaintances, in your presence, transmit some documents to the foreigner?

Answer: That question is associated with those I refuse to answer.

In "off-the-record" conversation I asked whether there was any news of the Bukovsky case, since at the time my friends and I were disturbed by the lack of information about him. "There doesn't seem to be any," the investigator answered. Then he added; "You said you weren't going to mention any names, but you mentioned Bukovsky." I was satisfied that no news was good news, and in response I said I was worried about Bukovsky and had also asked Yuzepchuk about the matter.

After the examination record was signed, the major remarked in a melancholy way, "During the search at your place they found an apparatus . . ." To my surprise he explained that he meant a Minox camera and reproduction equipment. He asked me to bring them the camera the next day "for a little while." I made it plain that this was something unexpected. I confirmed that I did in fact have a Minox with a stand, but said I had had this property for a long time and it was not prohibited. I said I would not turn it over to the KGB, since I did not see that it had anything to do with the case. "You'll see what it has to do with the case," said the major in the portentous tone of the investigator.

For a long time he tried to talk me into turning over the camera voluntarily. I refused and said I would not do it, that he, if he wished, could conduct a second search of my home and confiscate whatever he liked. I saw he did not want to set up a search, but I did not consider it feasible to spare him that unpleasant procedure. We had to wait a bit, but soon, in the company of three agents, I was on the way home for a second search.

My mood was miserable, and the respectful attitude of the Chekists was my only consolation. I had already begun to believe that some nonsense against me would be found in the deposition of the frightened foreigner. On the way we stopped in at a police station to get some *druzhinniki* as witnesses, and they turned out to be two ordinary, quiet young fellows. At the apartment I was shown a warrant for the search—dated April 5.

The senior lieutenant directing the search took his time, anxious to do everything in proper order. I showed them the location of what they were interested in but refused to turn it over voluntarily. I suggested they seize it, which they did. They confiscated the camera, the rack, cassettes, undeveloped film, an exposed film with my picture, and a sheet of paper with the address Sebreghts had left with me.

Once again I did not sign the report. This visit by the Chekists took place in an atmosphere of greater calm and with more human contact.

Report of Search

Moscow, April 7, 1971

Senior Lieutenant Sokolov, an investigator of the Investigation Section of the KGB, CM USSR, and lieutenants Khorikov and Kozlov, agents of the KGB, CM USSR, on instructions from Major Sevastyanov, Senior Investigator of the Investigation Section, KGB, CM USSR, on the basis of his order dated April 5, 1971, in the presence of the witnesses Viktor Gerasimovich Kruchinin, residing at 21/23, Apt. 14, Second Lazorevsky Lane, Moscow, and Evginy Aleksandrovich Shevyakov, residing at 33 Arkh. Vlasov Street, Korpus 2, Apt. 58, Moscow, in accordance with Articles 167-177 of the RSFSR Code of Criminal Procedure, conducted a search at the apartment of Valery Nikolayevich Chalidze at 43 Sivtsev Vrazhek, Apt. 24, Moscow.

It was explained to the above-listed persons that they had a right to witness all acts of the investigator and to make comments on any of his acts. The witnesses were also informed of their obligation, in accordance with Article 135 of the RSFSR Code of Criminal Procedure, to attest to the fact, content, and results of the search.

(Signatures)

Before the search, V. N. Chalidze was shown the warrant for the search, dated April 5, 1971.

He was then asked to turn over any documents and articles which might have a bearing on the case; in particular, a Minox camera with film cartridges and equipment for it, etc.

Citizen Chalidze stated that he possessed no articles or documents that had a bearing on the case. At the same time he stated that he did in fact have a Minox camera with cartridges and a stand, with instructions.

According to Chalidze's statement the camera was in the right-hand drawer of the desk, along with the cartridges and film, while the stand was in a cupboard. At the same time [sic] he placed on the desk a sheet of white paper with notations on both sides.

The search was then conducted.

In the course of the search, the following were found:

1. A sheet of white paper with notations in a foreign language, made with a blue marker. The notation on one side began with "VAKOE . . ." and ended with ". . . 09/213324." That on the other side began with "VAKOE . . ." and ended with ". . .Belgium."

2. A Minox camera, #801593, without film, in a black cardboard case.

3. Six cartridges for the Minox camera, in black plastic cases, without film.

4. Four cartridges for the Minox camera, in black plastic cases, with film. The cartridges with film bore the numbers 5618, 7720, 7840, and 5614.

5. Three wrapping papers for the microfilm boxes with Minox written on them.

6. A roll of Minox film with 21 frames that had been removed and developed. Seven of the frames showed the image of a man.

The articles listed in paragraphs 2-6 were in a black tin box labeled "Black Magic," and were found in the upper right-hand drawer of the desk.

7. Two sets of instructions for the Minox camera, written in a foreign language.

8. Film wrapped in black paper and contained in a round, white tin box.

The articles listed in paragraphs 7 and 8 were found in the desk.

9. A reproduction stand with a cord. The stand was found in a cupboard.

At the conclusion of the search the articles listed in paragraphs 4 and 8 were wrapped in a parcel which was stapled and sealed with Seal #1 of the investigation section of the KGB, CM USSR.

Everything listed in paragraphs 1-9 was confiscated for the investigative section of the KGB, CM USSR.

The search was begun at 1635 and completed at 1800 hours. No additional comments or statements were made by the witnesses or V. N. Chalidze.

This report has been read by the investigator, and has been accurately drawn up.

After reading the report, V. N. Chalidze stated that he refused to sign it.

Witnesses: (signatures)—Kruchinin, Shevyakov.
Person searched: (signature)—Chalidze.
Agents: (signatures)—Khorikov, Kozlov.

Senior Lieutenant Sokolov, investigator of the investigation section of the KGB, CM USSR (signature).
Copy of report received: (signature)—Chalidze.

Notes

April 8

In response to a summons, I went for an interrogation, and my gloomy forebodings proved to be more than justified. Here is the examination record:

Question: During the search at your home on April 7 a Minox camera was confiscated. When did you acquire it, and for what purpose?

Answer: I refuse to answer.

Question: Among the cartridges seized at your home are some that are empty. What did you photograph?

Answer: I refuse to answer.

Question: The investigators have information to the effect that you were preparing microfilms of documents and sending them abroad.

Answer: I also refuse to answer that question. And I state that since the questions refer to me personally, and since the search of April 7 has no bearing on the Sebreghts case, I refuse to give a deposition.

"In a minute you'll see that all this has a bearing on the case," said the investigator. And after much hunting around he removed from a safe several typewritten pages, found the place he wanted, and began to write in the examination record:

"Question: At the interrogation, Sebreghts testified: 'Chalidze asked me to send certain documents abroad with the diplomatic mail. When that didn't work out, he decided to make microfilms to send abroad.' What can you say about that?"

I answered: "That is a lie." The investigator noted: "The foreigner's testimony was false." I was not disturbed by that crude distortion (my evaluation, "That is a lie," also applied to the question), since I did not intend to sign what followed in the examination record after my refusal to testify (and I signed only the refusal). But I went on with the conversation because it interested me.

"Off the record" the investigator wanted to know why I was aggressively and suspiciously inclined. I told him that after the search of the day before I suspected that a case was being fabricated against me, based on the testimony of the foreigner, who was easy to confuse since he did not know the Soviet laws. I said I did not want to be a witness in the case, since I was being accused of something. I demanded that I be presented with an indictment, so that I might be afforded the procedural possibilities for contesting the indictment.

After this exchange the major asked me to come the next day at ten o'clock. To this I replied, "You are right. It's time for a confrontation."

This time, rather than a summons, I had received an ordinary invitation.

April 9

I went to see Sevastyanov at ten o'clock. Soon Sebreghts came in. He was wearing a dark blue prison suit with a prison-style jacket. He looked depressed. He nodded sadly to me, bowed to the woman serving as interpreter, and sat down behind a little table.

Before the confrontation began, the major asked Sebreghts, very affectionately, if his requests had been satisfied. "Yes," Sebreghts said, "except that they haven't brought the pastry yet. But they promised to do that today." I should have protested this off-the-record talk about everyday matters on the grounds that the possibility of influencing testimony was concealed in this subject matter. But it was a sunny day, and I did not want to spoil the mood of those present.

Then the investigator asked Sebreghts if he knew me and what his attitude toward me was. The answer was that he knew me, that he had been to my home three times, and that his attitude was normal. Then I was asked the same question, and confirmed the acquaintanceship. "What is your attitude toward Sebreghts?" With this question the time had come to set about implementing my program for moral support to Sebreghts. I thought for a long time, and then dictated this answer: "My attitude toward Sebreghts is favorable. I do not believe he has committed a crime." An exchange of remarks began. The investigator felt that since I was not familiar with the materials on the case, I had no right to say whether I believed he had committed a crime or not. I felt that it was precisely when one lacked knowledge that one had recourse to belief. The investigator felt that the question as to a crime had no bearing on the question that had been asked about my attitude toward Sebreghts. I explained to him that in formulating my answer I had tried to think in terms of his categories. I asked whether he would not be surprised to hear that I had a favorable attitude toward a person while believing that he had engaged in anti-Soviet propaganda. This convinced him, and we finally arrived at a compromise: "Answer: I have a favorable attitude toward Sebreghts, since I do not believe he committed a crime." This answer was translated for Sebreghts, and it seemed to me that his face lit up.

Then the investigator quoted to Sebreghts the latter's testimony, at an interrogation on April 3, that Chalidze had asked Sebreghts to send abroad, through the diplomatic mail, certain of his documents to René Cassin and Speiser and, when that did not work out, that he intended to make microfilms of those documents, and that Chalidze also agreed to receive microfilms from abroad. Sebreghts confirmed his testimony and said that at the first meeting he had received several documents from Chalidze but was afraid to take them with him, since he did not know whether the customs would pass them. Then he tried to send the documents in the diplomatic mail through an acquaintance, Monsieur Corchon. But at the Belgian Embassy he was told that documents from private persons were not accepted for sending through the diplomatic mail. Sebreghts also said that the document that had been found in his money belt had not been received from Chalidze. In telling of our meetings, Sebreghts mentioned that he had come to my home with Volpin. The investigator stated: "Since Chalidze does not mention the names of the persons present at the talks, you should likewise refrain from mentioning names in your testimony."

I expressed my amazement at this interference by the investigator with freedom of testifying, and promised to make a note of it in the examination record, which I did at the end of the confrontation.

From time to time, while the investigator was writing, Sebreghts tried to use a kind of sign language with me. He pointed significantly at the investigator, then at the wall, then to his ear. I waved my hand to let him know it was not important.

Question to me: Do you confirm the testimony of Sebreghts?

Answer: There is much that is confused in the testimony of Sebreghts. Before answering your question, I want to put several questions to Sebreghts.

Referring to the legal procedure for conducting a confrontation, the investigator suggested that I put my questions to Sebreghts at the end of the interview. I noted that the law does not stipulate such a procedure for conducting a confrontation but merely provides that the questions be put with the permission of the investigator. But I had no intention of asking questions without the permission of the investigator. I was prepared to get a reasoned refusal from the investigator when the question was posed.

In the course of subsequent remarks I noted that possibly it was not the law but certain instructions which provided for the possibility of an exchange of questions only at the end of the confrontation. These instructions were of course interesting to me, but they did not bind me to anything. I also noted that I would be satisfied if the investigator, having entered my question in the examination record, refused—as a matter of record, and giving his reasons therefor—to allow putting the question to Sebreghts. Our remarks were of course not translated for Sebreghts, but it was probably of some importance to his morale that I was calm while the investigator became annoyed. And more than once. He reminded me several times that I was not the investigator and was not conducting the confrontation. To this I replied that indeed I was not the investigator, but that today, as a witness, I wanted to sign the examination record.

Finally I was allowed to put my questions to Sebreghts. Here are the questions and the answers to them.

Question from Chalidze to Sebreghts: In our talk I welcomed creative scholarly contacts, but Sebreghts asked me whether the Flemish committee could supply practical help to our committee. How did I answer that general question?

Answer from Sebreghts: I did ask that question, and in answer Chalidze shook his head in the negative. I understood that he did not desire any practical help.

Question from Chalidze to Sebreghts: Did I request the transmittal of documents, or did I agree to give Sebreghts those documents that interested him?

Answer from Sebreghts: Chalidze at no time asked me to send anything abroad. During our talk he showed me some documents, and when he heard that I was afraid to take them, he immediately took them back from me. I wanted to take those documents, but couldn't.

After this there was nothing for me to say. However, for purposes of clarity I wanted to make a handwritten deposition. It went approximately as follows:

There was a good deal of confusion in Sebreghts's previous testimony, but his answers to my questions were accurate and fully cleared up all misunderstandings. I should like to make the following clear.

1. I told Sebreghts that it would be very unpleasant if our articles were published in *Posev*. If, however, any Western committees were interested in our work, in the sphere of human rights, it would be natural for our articles to be published in, for example, René Cassin's *Journal des droits de l'homme*. He interpreted this phrase as a request to transmit my articles to René Cassin. We talked about Speiser as a man who had already visited me and a very respected figure. I don't recall whether I asked that anything be sent to him; but it is hardly likely, since in general I refused any practical assistance.*

* Note upon publication. At this point there is a mistake in my deposition. As I remember now, I asked Sebreghts to send Mr. Speiser my greetings.

2. Actually, in the course of the talk I showed Sebreghts some of the committee's articles, and for a certain time they were in his hands. Needless to say, I would not have objected if he had wanted to take them. But when I heard of his fears regarding getting them through the customs, I immediately took the documents back. Apparently Sebreghts still wanted to take them and looked for ways of sending them, *inter alia* inquiring about the diplomatic mail. But that is his right. As for me, neither my documents nor those of the committee are illegal; and I do not intend to take any interest in where, how, or by whom they are sent.

3. There was in fact some conversation about microfilms. I expressed regret that many UN documents on human rights were unavailable to us. Sebreghts asked if it was convenient for us to read microfilms. I replied that we were interested in the content of the UN documents, and not in the form in which they were prepared. It is possible that he interpreted that conversation as a request to have microfilms sent to us. As for making microfilms, it is possible that Sebreghts drew that conclusion from the fact that when he unexpectedly came to see me on March 26, I was photographing some text by way of a test, having decided to see what kind of reproduction one got with the Minox camera. (As it happened, I got nothing that time.) He may possibly have decided that I was making a microfilm for him; but it was only a test photograph taken by way of practice. I did not give him any microfilms.

Such was my handwritten deposition at the confrontation. When I had finished writing it, the investigator asked Sebreghts why his answers to my questions contradicted his previous testimony. I demanded that my handwritten deposition be translated for Sebreghts before any further questions were put to him. The investigator objected that that was not important, and said that at the end of the confrontation the entire examination record would be translated for Sebreghts. I was amazed and expressed my regret that this departure from the natural course of the confrontation would compel me to enter the appropriate additional notation in the examination record. The investigator then became extremely irritated, and there was further exchange

of remarks. Nonetheless, Sebreghts heard a translation of
my deposition. After this, he was asked about the contradiction in his testimony. He said that he had not lied at the
previous interrogations, but had expressed himself inaccurately; that today at the confrontation he had correctly
answered Chalidze's questions, and that he corroborated
Chalidze's testimony. The latter remark was not entered in
the examination record for the time being. Then it was suggested that Sebreghts ask me some questions.

Question from Sebreghts to Chalidze: I ask Monsieur
Chalidze to tell how he answered my question as to whether
the documents I wanted to take from him were illegal.

Answer from Chalidze: I said that all documents you
saw in my possession were known to the authorities and
contained nothing illegal. I also said that if I gave you a
document, you could tell anyone you wanted to that you
had received that document from me.

Question from Sebreghts to Chalidze: Was there anything illegal in our conversations?

The investigator said that that question had no bearing
on the subject matter of the confrontation. I did not object,
but with the permission of the investigator I confirmed to
Sebreghts, through the interpreter, that there had been nothing illegal in our interview.

The confrontation concluded with my asking Sebreghts
whether he corroborated my testimony. The affirmative
answer was then entered in the examination record.

When the guards had led Sebreghts off—he was more
cheerful by now—I said to the investigator: "Yesterday I
was afraid of slander in the testimony of a frightened foreigner. Today I had the great pleasure of being convinced
that he was an honest fellow and ready to correct the mistakes he made in his testimony."

"You see?" said the investigator. "And you didn't want
to believe his testimony."

To General Volkov, Chief, Investigative Section, KGB

A week has gone by since I wrote you offering my services as a witness in the case of Sebreghts. (In that letter

I mistakenly called him Brecht.) My offer was accepted by you, and I was questioned by an investigator, Major Sevastyanov. Actually, it turned out that I had already been a witness in that case. It was simply that during the search (in the course of which my files and those of the Human Rights Committee were seized) and during the interrogations of March 29 and 30 I was not informed that Case #7 was the Sebreghts case.

During the past week the developments in the investigation in which I have been involved have been strange, to say the least. On April 7 I turned over to the investigator the pasted-up document promised in my letter to you of April 4, 1971, and then transcribed in the examination record the contents of that letter. The subsequent events were amazing.

In the course of three days Major Sevastyanov did not ask me a single question about the illegal activity of Sebreghts, charged with anti-Soviet propaganda under Article 70. Even if the investigator had begun to untangle the detection problem from a far remove and, in concrete questions, had not yet come to the illegal acts of Sebreghts, by law he should have asked me at the beginning of the interrogation what I knew of the circumstances of the case. By "circumstances of the case" the law of course means what bears upon illegal—and, in particular, incriminating —acts. Yet at the beginning of the interrogations I was asked about the circumstances of the interview given to the foreigner but not whether he had engaged in anti-Soviet propaganda or whether he had given me anti-Soviet materials. Actually, Sebreghts did not give me any anti-Soviet materials (no materials at all, for that matter); and apparently the investigator knew that very well. But at the time he had nothing more to ask me about the Sebreghts case.

I was interrogated not about Sebreghts but about myself. Moreover, during the second search, on April 7, photographic equipment which I had possessed long before Sebreghts's arrival was confiscated. I was asked about my actions; and acts were attributed to me which, although not criminal, might have been compromising. This had the result that I demanded that I be presented with an indictment. Fortunately, the misunderstandings were cleared up at a confrontation: it turned out that Sebreghts had expressed himself inaccurately in his testimony, and the investigator had interpreted what he said in a sense unfavorable to me.

But I came away from the meeting with Sebreghts with a distressing impression. I had already stated in the record of the confrontation that I did not believe in the criminality of Sebreghts's actions; and this view remains unchanged. But it is important that Sebreghts be able to organize his defense skillfully, and I can see that this is difficult for him. He does not know Soviet life, and his perception of it is naïve. He does not know Soviet laws; hence he cannot contest the indictment and work out an optimum defense position. Not knowing the laws, and being in a state of despondency (since he is among people whose temperament is alien to him), he may regard individual procedural violations committed by the investigator as corresponding to Soviet law. I do not mean by this that the investigator frequently violates the law. On the contrary, the examination records were correctly prepared, and the interpreter was accurate. But there are always a few lapses in work, and they can hamper the defense. Here is an example. Sebreghts mentioned the name of the person who brought him to me. The investigator, through the interpreter, stated: "Since Chalidze does not mention the names of persons present at the talks, you should likewise refrain from mentioning names." The inadmissibility of such interference with freedom of testimony was obvious to me, and I entered a comment about it in the examination record. But Sebreghts may henceforth think that Soviet law allows this kind of influence by the investigator on the testimony of the accused.

In another instance the investigator, at my insistent demand, corrected a lapse: he had wanted to put further questions to Sebreghts without having first communicated to him, through the interpreter, the information in my handwritten deposition. Sebreghts did not protest against this (nor could he have, owing to his ignorance of the law), although of course such an anomalous procedure for conducting a confrontation limits the accused's possibilities for defending himself. This is not to mention the fact that, not knowing the language, Sebreghts did not understand everything said at the confrontation, since only what was included in the examination record was translated for him. It may be argued that only what is included in the examination record is important. It may be argued that what is said off the record is not important. But we should remember that a person who knows the language used in the investigation hears and takes into account all conversations, even remarks made off the record. Therefore a person who does not know the language is in a relatively disadvantageous position. It is precisely this, and not the question of importance, which is the criterion in the given case. And the spirit of Soviet law requires that a person not be placed in a disadvantageous position because of not knowing a language.

Although the requirements of the law with respect to Sebreghts were in general fulfilled, I still gained a distressing impression of his capacity to organize his own defense. The reasons for this include his ignorance of Soviet laws (he is a law student, but a knowledge of European law may in this case be a hindrance), naïveté in his understanding of Soviet life, and Western prejudices as to the restrictions allegedly imposed on exchange of information. Just imagine! He apparently isn't even aware of his right to refuse to answer the investigator. The foregoing does not mean that the investigator was not impartial, or that he intentionally hindered the defense. But even when the investigation is impartial, the accused may wish to defend himself in a skillful manner.

I trust that the meeting with me at the confrontation improved Sebreghts's morale; but this still does not solve all the problems of his defense. I hereby request that the materials on the case be made available to a Belgian lawyer (chosen by Sebreghts). I also request that Sebreghts be set free on bail during the time of the investigation. I hope that the Flemish Committee for the Defense of Human Rights will be in a position to raise the bail. If not, I believe my reputation among scholars studying the science of human rights is such that other rights organizations will respond to my appeal and contribute the necessary sum.

April 11, 1971

V. Chalidze

"Under a False Mask"*

A student at the Law School of Louvain University, who was to take his final examination for the degree of Doctor of Laws at the end of April, abandoned his businessman daddy, his numerous relatives, and his fiancée Odette, and rushed headlong to Moscow, in order (as he stated at his first interrogation) to familiarize himself "with questions of the functioning of the juridical apparatus" in the USSR.

And if the acquaintanceship was made in an entirely different way from what Hugo Sebreghts had figured, he has only himself to blame—himself and the gentlemen on that "Flemish Committee" who prepared him for his anti-Soviet, subversive activity. For the sake of justice it should be noted that in the end this was the way Hugo Sebreghts evaluated everything that had happened to him in Moscow when, like Jozef Hemschoote, he was charged on the basis of incontrovertible evidence with subversive activity against the USSR.

Hemschoote's master was Roger de Bie. Sebreghts was recruited by a certain Mr. Jacques. Having become convinced during the investigation that he had been fully unmasked and a denial was senseless, the drop-out law student began to weep tears of repentance, to ask forgiveness, to whine that he had been the victim of deceit by Jacques. On his own initiative, Sebreghts wrote in his own hand: "You can easily make a mistake if you constantly get incorrect information." But earlier, in Louvain, after he had agreed to become the emissary for the "Flemish Committee," he had efficiently put the finishing touches on the questions to be elucidated at meetings with "the right peo-

---

* The newspaper *Izvestia* published an article with this title on April 19. The section about Sebreghts is excerpted here.

ple." To make things more conspiratorial, Sebreghts encoded them on the third and eighth pages of a "syllabus" of lectures among terms of commercial law and notarial cases. The instructional questionnaire drawn up by Jacques for Moscow addressees was also camouflaged as a lecture leaflet.

His prudent tutors had provided Sebreghts with everything to make him look like a regular tourist. He even took with him letters from his loving fiancée written in advance, one for every day, in which she admonished him to "refuel himself [!] with a second helping of courage." By day, gulping down tranquilizers (when he was searched a rather impressive supply of drugs was found on him) and looking around him with an eye out for trouble, Sebreghts in his dark glasses wended his way through Moscow, delivering anti-Soviet literature and letters. (Sebreghts had sewed into a wide pocket in his money belt a letter of reply he had received but which Mr. Jacques and Company will never make use of now.)

The time for his departure drew near. The scrupulous Hugo had made a note in his memorandum book reminding himself, when he got home, to order chocolate eggs from the confectioner. In the epistolary opus written by Odette for Sunday, March 28, she expressed the hope that her "little butterfly" was living "in a good hotel room and did not feel lonesome." And he didn't. On that day the "butterfly" went to jail. The same thing had happened before to his friend Luc Quintin, who had also swallowed the bait of the "Flemish Committee," and to other peddlers of anti-Soviet libels.

Once the Belgian bosses realized that the operation involving sending two "tourists" to the Soviet Union had failed ignominiously, a stack of leaflets was rapidly printed up in the name of the "Flemish Committee." I saw one of those leaflets, intended for distribution in the Soviet Union. Our friend Roger de Bie, together with the general secretary of the "committee," Victor Van Brantegem (at one time both these gentlemen were expelled from Moscow for ruffianly anti-Soviet acts) wept great tears over the "illegal" detention of Hemschoote and Sebreghts. Said they: "The young Flemings went to your country as peaceable tourists to become better acquainted with the country and the people."

Enough, gentlemen! As we can see, humor has never been a frequent visitor at Number 58 Grunstadt Street in Antwerp, headquarters of the secretariat of the "Flemish Committee." As the "peaceable tourist" Sebreghts testified at his interrogation, he knew that the "committee" issued special instructions to persons going to the Soviet Union. He was given just such instructions by Jacques. Incidentally, Sebreghts stated he was not convinced that Jacques was the man's real name. Like some kind of Masonic lodge, the "committee" keeps its personnel secret. Its general structure is such that not all members of the organization know one another, and as a rule they call one another by sobriquets.

Jacques also revealed to his protégé something that as a matter of fact is no great secret: the existence at the "Flemish Committee" of direct contacts with the NTS, that hornets' nest of espionage and sabotage directed against the Soviet Union and other socialist countries. It is of course no accident that NTS publications are among the anti-Soviet materials that the scouts of the "committee" try so strenuously to distribute.

What, then, is left of the fig leaves of "fighters for human rights" and "idealists remote from politics" with which these gentlemen—the "philanthropists" of the "Flemish Committee" and similar organizations—try to cover their spiritual nakedness and their moral squalor? One thing remains obvious, and is becoming increasingly clear for world public opinion: the role of the anti-Soviet mouthpieces and centers of subversion, acting in close coordination, constantly exchanging information, and often financed by the same sources that subsidize the activities of Western intelligence services and various radio stations.

It is significant that the "signature" of provocations by organizations like the Belgian "Flemish Committee," the pro-Fascist Italian *Europa Civiltà*, the Scandinavian "*Smogs*," and so on, is one and the same. As agents for their anti-Soviet actions they prefer to recruit young men and women not embarrassed by the laws of morality but usually embarrassed financially and fond of scandalous adventures. Spiritually bankrupt and with no qualms about drugs and sexual perversions, these people are willing recruits for the experienced anti-Soviet types who are specialists in various kinds of sabotage and provocations. It is not so simple to struggle out of their nets. But it is very easy to get caught in them and become pawns in that "cold war" being waged against our country by international imperialist circles.

Bearing in mind that although Hemschoote and Sebreghts were caught red-handed, they gave detailed depositions on the nature of the crimes they had committed and thereby assisted the investigation, the competent Soviet organs, taking their youth into account and proceeding from considerations of humanity, decided not to turn Hemschoote and Sebreghts over to a court but to expel them from the Soviet Union. They have both left the territory of the USSR. The USSR Ministry of Foreign Affairs has made a representation to the Belgian Embassy in Moscow, calling the attention of the Belgian authorities to the inadmissible provocations of the "Flemish Committee."

Every year our country plays host to millions of foreign tourists. Those who come to us with good intentions can always count on the hospitality of Soviet citizens. But for peddlers of libels and anti-Soviet contraband the way to us is barred. Once and for all time.

K. Bryantsev

To the Editor of *Izvestia*

In Monday's issue of your newspaper I read the article by K. Bryantsev on the case of the two Belgians. The fact that the article gives no information about what actually incriminated those young men, and whether any of the charges received more convincing corroboration than the depositions of the accused persons themselves, makes the article unconvincing for those readers who require something besides emotional saturation in order to believe communications. That, however, would not be so bad, since this is the usual style, especially in communications about persons in whom organs of state security have taken an interest.

But there is a mistake in the article which is critical for an understanding of the whole case. It is stated:

Bearing in mind that though Hemschoote and Sebreghts were caught red-handed, they gave detailed depositions on the nature of the crimes they had committed and thereby assisted the investigation, competent Soviet organs taking their youth into account and proceeding from considerations of humanity, decided not to turn Hemschoote and Sebreghts over to a court but to expel them from the Soviet Union.

It is a fact that except for the courts, only the Presidium of the Supreme Soviet has the right, by an act of pardon, to show humanity and take youth into account. Apparently no such act was effected with respect to the Belgians, since in the passage I have quoted it is a question of organs competent to decide the question of bringing a case to trial. Strictly speaking, a court is such an organ; but investigative organs transfer cases to the courts through the procurator's office. And these organs do not have the right to drop a criminal case before it reaches court on any other grounds than those stipulated in the law. The law does not specify considerations of humanity among those grounds. But it does specify (I omit those grounds patently inapplicable to the given case) that a criminal case must be dropped at the stage of preliminary investigation when a corpus delicti is not present in the acts of the accused, or when insufficient evidence has been gathered, provided that all possibilities for gathering evidence have been exhausted.

It is plain that in the present instance the case could have been dropped before trial only if the competent organs had nothing to come to court with—nothing to substantiate the charge.

In mentioning considerations of humanity, the newspaper is helping agencies to justify the institution of criminal proceedings against, and the three weeks' detention of, two people in the absence of a corpus delicti, or in the absence of hopes for finding evidence for the charge. But should this be justified? If the competent agencies have released people who did not commit a crime, or who did not leave evidence sufficient for conviction, it was the right thing to do. It was something these agencies must do according to law.

April 22, 1971

V. Chalidze

To Mr. Roger de Bie, Chairman of the Flemish Committee on Solidarity with Eastern Europe, 58 Rue Grunstadt, Antwerp

In March of this year, being empowered to represent the Moscow Human Rights Committee, I received Mr. H. Sebreghts, who said he was a representative of the Flemish Committee for Defense of Human Rights. I expressed my readiness to have creative contacts with that committee as regards studying the problems of human rights.

Recently, however, I learned from the press (*Izvestia*, April 19, 1971) that Sebreghts apparently represented another committee; namely, the Flemish Committee on Solidarity with Eastern Europe. If such is the case, my statement that I would welcome creative contacts between our committee and the committee represented by Mr. Sebreghts should be considered as having been made as a result of being misled, and hence null.

I am sending this letter to the address given in the newspaper, since the sheet of paper bearing the address which was left with me by Mr. Sebreghts was seized in the course of a search.

Please accept, Mr. Chairman, the expression of my sympathy in connection with the misfortunes which befell the lawful (as I still understand it to be) mission of Mr. Sebreghts.

April 22, 1971

V. Chalidze

To General Volkov, Chief, Investigation Section, KGB

It has come to my attention that the Sebreghts case (Case #7) has been dropped. I consider that the property belonging to me which was seized in the course of the recent searches in connection with that case should now be returned to me.

April 22, 1971

V. Chalidze

To General Volkov, Chief, Investigation Section, KGB

Property belonging to me which was seized in the course of searches, has not yet been returned to me. I have not even received a reply to my letter to you dated April 22, 1971. This is all the more disagreeable to me in that you replied immediately to the letter in which I offered to turn over to the investigators a document I had found.

At the time my property was confiscated, your agents could still give some grounds for it. (For example: "We are taking it because we don't know whether it has a bearing on the case or not. Upon examination, the confiscated property will be returned if it has no bearing on the case.") But now that the case has been dropped, there are not even any quasi-legal grounds for retaining the property. And the law guarantees me the right to recover my property from the illegal possession of another party.

You make it necessary for me to defend my own rights. Unfortunately, this is the most boring task among my activities in the field of defending rights; and I am not sure I shall pay due attention to the defense of my own rights.

But even in defending his own rights, a person is also defending legality. And I remind you that neither the civil laws, nor the laws on criminal proceedings, nor the 1928 summary law on the requisition and confiscation of property (still in force) entitles organs of the KGB to keep my property.

Soviet law, however, has provided other grounds for the alienation of private property without indemnity. Thus from Note 1 to Article 59 of the 1922 Civil Code we learn that a property owner is not entitled to demand the return of property which "was expropriated on the basis of revolutionary law or in general passed into the ownership of the working class prior to May 22, 1922." It is clear that your organization could have used this legal formula to retain property seized in searches before May 22, 1922, but not, so it would seem, up to the present. However, I am an amateur in Soviet jurisprudence in the sense that I can familiarize myself only with published laws. As we know, not every law is published, and *a fortiori* not every instruction. This is not to mention the fact that a telephoned order from a superior is likewise sometimes considered a source of law. Therefore, there may be other legal grounds for my property's "having in general passed into the ownership" of the KGB. Clearly, a legal norm which is not too bad is nonetheless better than illegality. And I am therefore willing, out of respect for the law, if there is such a law (unpublished), to forget about my property claims.

But I am not thinking only of my own interests in requesting the return of my property.

First, it annoys me that many of my friends have lost business correspondence given to me for study. True, for the past half-century a visit from the Chekists has been equated with natural disaster in the sense of extinguishing obligations under civil law. Therefore I hope my friends will not file claims against me. But it is still annoying.

Second, I am worried about the prestige of the Soviet Union as a member of the United Nations. It is sad to think there are Soviet agencies that assume it is feasible to confiscate the Universal Declaration of Human Rights and UN conventions on human rights as anti-Soviet materials.

It is also sad that the authorities considered it feasible to use repression against the Human Rights Committee—to confiscate its files.

May 1, 1971

V. Chalidze

Notes

I received a letter from Leonid Rigerman in New York dated April 19. Here is an excerpt:

The news of the recent search of your apartment was received here with sadness—especially by representatives of organizations for human rights that are sympathetic toward the Soviet Union. They fear that the repressions against people concerned with human rights in the Soviet Union will badly undermine the prestige of these organizations, whose inclination is pro-Soviet.

May 6
Sevastyanov called in the morning. He had just returned from an out-of-town assignment, and called right away so I would not think that my requests were going unanswered. It was his intention to call me in next Monday to discuss the question of my property.
I said it was not a question of discussion but of returning my property.

May 14
They returned the letter (Registered Letter #302, mailed April 23) that I had sent to Roger de Bie at the address given in the newspaper. On the envelope there was a postmark in addition to the Moscow postmarks: "A T . . . , E . . . 29-4, 2000." There was a label, "*Inconnu,*" and a stamp, "*Retour à l'envoyeur.*" Also a notation in Russian: "Not Found."

May 24
I am sick of this business. It is not likely that I will ever get my property back, and it may be a long time before I hear the end of the events set in motion by the visit from Sebreghts. In the meantime I shall publish this selection.

1971
                                                                V. Chalidze

Addendum*

To Valery Nikolayevich Chalidze

The Investigation Section of the Committee of State Security, Council of Ministers USSR, requests you to appear at 1700 hours on November 9, 1971, at (address) to pick up the property belonging to you.

Sevastyanov, Senior Investigator, Investigation Section of the KGB, Council of Ministers USSR.

November 3, 1971

To A. A. Sevastyanov, Investigation Section, KGB

I hereby acknowledge receipt of your letter of November 3, 1971, in which you invite me to come and pick up the property belonging to me.

I was pleased to get your communication, since although I had despaired of recovering what had been seized and did not intend to demand its return, I nonetheless felt the lack of much that you now want to return.

I am ready to receive my property in my apartment; that is, at the place where that property was seized. I shall be at home on November 9 at six o'clock in the evening. If this is inconvenient, we can agree on another day.† Incidentally, it is possible that I should have addressed this invitation not to you but to Dmitry Sergeyevich, who conducted the search, since it is natural that my property should be delivered by one of those persons who was at my home.

November 7, 1971

V. Chalidze

---

* From the *Chronicle of Current Events*, No. 23. This exchange of messages took place early in November 1971.
† They did not come, and I did not get my property back.

Note on Publication

In the summer of 1972 I was called in for interrogation by the KGB "in connection with Case #24." (Apparently this was originally the case having to do with the publication of the *Chronicle of Current Events.*) This last interrogation dealt with the brochure "A Foreigner Came to My Home," which by that time had been published in the West. In a talk with Investigator Fochenkov I did not deny my authorship, although of course I refused to confirm my authorship in the record of the interrogation. I reminded Fochenkov of the principle of the burden of proof, and stated that if the KGB wanted to obtain evidence to the effect that I was the author, the investigators could try to obtain such evidence without my assistance.

Lieutenant Colonel Fochenkov was very displeased with the publication of the brochure. In particular, he showed me the price marked on the cover and said: "Just look. Our enemies are publishing this and selling it. In this way you are helping them to get money."

"Do you really believe anyone will buy that brochure?" I asked.

The question was obviously provocative, and Fochenkov rebuffed the provocation, saying, "No, of course nobody will buy it. But still . . ."

                                                                    V. Chalidze

9

On the Rights of Persons Declared Mentally Ill

Opinion of Member of the Human Rights Committee V. N. Chalidze*

Foreword

"The court must see that the [insane] accused is sent for imprisonment where insane criminals are confined, and where he will remain until instructions come from Her Majesty."[1] This requirement in an old English law reflects the basic tragedy of the fate of the "socially dangerous" mentally ill—the indefinite period of their isolation. Study shows that the indefinite length of the isolation is a consequence of a prejudice, deeply ingrained in both ordinary people and the powers that be, to the effect that the mentally ill are not legally competent. Study also shows that this prejudice has long been the source of suffering for many

* Published in Russian in *Dokumenty Komiteta Prav Cheloveka* (Proceedings of the Moscow Human Rights Committee) by The International League for the Rights of Man, New York, 1972.

people, both those who are in fact seriously ill and those who are too original, too different.

I am discussing the rights of the mentally ill in general, although our attention has been focused by Roy Medvedev's report on a specific aspect of this problem: compulsory hospitalization for political reasons.

In that report, however, this specific aspect is discussed more broadly than is of interest to us from the viewpoint of the science of human rights. In particular, as I see it, we should not devote our attention or analysis to the rapporteur's arguments as to the aims of psychiatric repressions. We are interested in guarantees of the protection of human rights, and we can presume that purposes and perpetrators will be found for the violation of human rights if those rights are inadequately guaranteed. We can thus confine ourselves to that presumption. The question of who perpetrates the violation of rights, and why, is a subject of study for sociologists, politicians, and historians, not our Committee.

But this does not prevent paying greater attention to individual types of violations of rights—in this case to parallel violations of the rights of the mentally ill in general and of a person's right to the freedom of his own convictions and freedom of informational exchange. I shall also speak later on of the rights of political prisoners in psychiatric hospitals.*

There is still another problem in which the Committee cannot meddle: the problem of the correctness of the diagnosis. However much we ourselves, acting in a private capacity, may have been amazed by a diagnosis of the condition of someone known to us personally, and however much we may have doubted the integrity of some particular physician, the Committee as such does not have the right, in view of its stated purposes and in the absence of special knowledge, to contest medical conclusions. This does not mean that we cannot criticize particular medical documents, or the manner of drawing up documents, or the prejudices

---

* For convenience I use the term "prisoners" for persons forcibly confined in a psychiatric hospital by court order. The term "political prisoner" requires further study and clarification.

making for a lack of logic or substantiation in the judgments of persons in any field of specialization, including psychiatrists. Nor does it mean that we are indifferent to the problem of the philosophical and practical definition of the concept of mental health. So far as the latter point is concerned, the extent to which people consider their own opinions and their own knowledge (outside a formal system) to be definitively correct apparently depends upon their style of thought (and their general culture). Therefore it is hard to hope to convince people reared on the traditions of a belief in the possibility of unique correctness in knowledge of the desirability of a relativistic approach to the concept of mental health. But this does not exempt legislators from the obligation to formulate procedures associated with restricting and protecting the rights of the mentally ill without basing themselves on the finality of current views as to the definiteness of the concept of mental health.

The Presumption of Mental Normality

This is nowhere stipulated in the laws. But the legal norms are formulated with the presumption that each person is mentally healthy enough so that even possible illness will not have legal consequences, so long as the contrary is not demonstrated in accordance with established procedure. Such a presumption is customary, and its importance may not be noticed. But if it is not taken into account, substantial violations of rights are possible; e.g., the rights of relatives of persons considered to be suffering from hereditary mental illness.

The belief of a person's associates that he is mentally healthy is important to that person as a kind of guarantee of his contractual capacity and the reasonableness of his behavior, and against any public suspicion of his mental health. That is, not only must the proceedings for declaring a person ill be defined by law, but the right to initiate such a proceeding must belong only to persons and institutions, specified by law, who are obliged to exercise this right in good conscience and only when there are sufficiently substantial grounds.

Raising the Question of Doubt

The initiative in instituting proceedings to ascertain the fact of significant mental illness, and the proceedings proper, are made to depend, by both legislation and practice, on the nature of the legal consequences planned with respect to the given person. In particular (the following paragraphs do not cover all cases when doubt is raised as to mental health; e.g., I have not considered cases of post-mortem examination):

1. AN ACTION INVOLVING INCOMPETENCE.* An action to declare a citizen incompetent may be brought by members of his family, trade unions, and other public organizations, the procurator, an agency of guardianship or wardship, or an institution for psychiatric treatment (Article 258, RSFSR Code of Civil Procedure).

An evaluation of the grounds for bringing such an action is made individually by a judge, after which the judge or the court orders a forensic psychiatric examination.

2. ORDINARY HOSPITALIZATION OF A PERSON WITHOUT HIS CONSENT. The initiative for instituting a proceeding for confining a person in a psychiatric hospital without his consent usually belongs to the relatives of the person, physicians of the general practitioner system, and physicians at psychiatric dispensaries. There are no known normative acts regulating the procedure for taking such an initiative.

3. IMMEDIATE HOSPITALIZATION OF MENTALLY ILL PERSONS CONSTITUTING A PUBLIC DANGER. The 1961 Instructions provide for this kind of hospitalization.[2] According to these instructions, public health agencies have the right, without the consent of the person or his relatives, to hospitalize him "in the presence of a clear danger" from the person to himself or those around him. The instructions do not indicate who is entitled to raise the question of such hospitalization before the public health agencies. From experience it is known that in such cases the initiative is taken by various government agencies, including the police.

* I am not considering limited incompetence here.

4. CASES INVOLVING ABILITY TO WORK. In addition to the person with respect to whom such a case is being studied, the initiative in investigating mental health may be taken by a medical institution.[3] For certain jobs (in particular dangerous ones) and in the case of matriculation at an educational institution, there is a procedure requiring presentation of certification of a state of health; and members of the medical commission providing such certification may initiate a psychiatric investigation. It would appear (although this is not entirely clear) that for special jobs an investigation (with the possibility of subsequent restriction of occupational rights; e.g., the right to hold a certain position) may be made at the initiative of the administration of the establishment.

5. MILITARY EXAMINATION. An investigation of the mental health of a draftee or a military serviceman is initiated, respectively, by the military registration and enlistment office or by the military commander.

6. PRISONERS. An investigation of the mental health of a prisoner (not in the case of a new indictment) is initiated by the administration of the place of imprisonment.

7. SUSPECTS AND ACCUSED PERSONS. The initiative for investigating the mental health of a suspect or accused person is taken by the preliminary investigator, who prepares an order for expert examination if he considers it necessary (Article 184 of the Code of Criminal Procedure). The initiative for such an investigation when it involves substantial restrictions of rights—confinement for in-patient examination if the necessity for this arises in the course of the examination—is also taken by the preliminary investigator, but only with the sanction of the procurator if the subject is not in custody.

An investigation can also be initiated by court order.

A request by interested parties may precede the order from the investigator or the court.

8. WITNESSES, INJURED PARTIES, PLAINTIFFS, AND DEFENDANTS. Investigation of the mental health of a witness, injured party, plaintiff, or defendant in a judicial proceeding is initiated by decision of the court (Article 290 of the Code of Criminal Procedure, Article 51 of the Funda-

mental Principles of Legislation on Public Health,[4] para.
25 of the Instructions on Forensic Psychiatric Examination[5]).

9. RAISING THE QUESTION OF DOUBT IN IDENTIFYING THE
"INSANE." In accordance with the election statutes (see, for
example, the statute on elections to the USSR Supreme
Soviet, Article 14,[6]) persons declared insane under the
procedure prescribed by law are not carried on the lists of
voters. The law establishing this procedure is not known.
According to a methodological letter of the Ministry of
Public Health,[7] the investigation in this case is conducted
at the initiative of a psychoneurological dispensary, or "at
the request" of activists and executive committees.

Liability for Maliciously Raising the Question of Doubt as to Mental Health

Although public doubt as to a person's mental health
does obvious damage to that person, the law makes almost
no provision as to liability for the unfounded or malicious
arousal of public doubt. A civil law defense against such
defamation (according to Article 7 of the Civil Code) is
apparently impossible, since it is natural to consider that
information on a person's illness cannot defame the honor
and dignity of that person.

In those cases where the arousal of doubt has as its aim
the hospitalization of the defamed person, liability for malicious arousal of doubt may ensue as for an attempt at illegal deprivation of freedom. This possibility is not very real,
however, since malicious arousal of doubt does not entail
liability, and in this case the malice can easily be attributed
to error.

The law directly stipulates liability for the malicious
arousal of doubt in only one case: if an action to deprive a
person of his capacity to act has been brought maliciously,
the court makes the person who has brought the action liable for the court costs. This norm applies only to members
of the family of the person against whom the action was
brought, but not to all those entitled to bring such actions.

Ordering Expert Examination and Kinds of Expert Examination

The Fundamental Principles of Legislation on Public Health[8] envisage (Articles 50, 51) only two kinds of expert examination: occupational and forensic.

Organs of investigation and police inquiry, the procurator's office, and the court (or a judge) have recourse to forensic psychiatric examination (para. 4 of the Instructions[9]) when it is necessary to determine the mental health of suspects, witnesses, injured parties, plaintiffs, defendants, or persons against whom an action has been brought to deprive them of their capacity to act (para. 1 of the Instructions[10]).

Forensic psychiatric examinations are made by special commissions or commissions from dispensaries[11] on an out-patient basis, in court, or at the office of the investigator or of the person conducting the police inquiry (and also with the subject not present, and posthumously). The in-patient examination of a suspect or accused person not in custody, and also that of plaintiffs, defendants, and persons against whom an action for deprivation of capacity to act has been brought, may be made (under the Instructions,[12] para. 5) only with the sanction of the procurator's office or by decision of the court. This list does not include the witnesses and injured parties mentioned in para. 1 of the Instructions. The Code of Criminal Procedure (Article 188) envisages the sanction of the procurator only for the in-patient examination of a suspect or accused person not in custody, and does not indicate the procedure for examining a witness or injured party. Since when it is impossible to answer the questions posed by the experts in an out-patient examination, the commission must, in accordance with the Instructions, conclude that it is necessary to confine the subject for in-patient examination, and since Article 79 of the Code of Criminal Procedure stipulates the obligatory examination of a witness or injured party if doubt arises as to his mental state, it must be assumed that in practice it is possible to have cases of the in-patient examination of witnesses and injured parties, although the law does not indicate the procedure for conducting it.* Unlike the Instructions, the law likewise does not indicate the procedure for the examination of a complainant in a criminal case.

In a civil case the procedure for ordering expert examination is provided by law only with respect to persons against whom an action for deprivation of capacity to act has been brought (Article 260 of the RSFSR Code of Civil Procedure). In the event of a clear refusal by the subject to appear, the court in open session, with the participation of the procurator and a psychiatrist, may order the compulsory sending of the subject for examination (the law does not indicate whether on an in-patient or out-patient basis).

The mental state of a witness may also become a subject of interest in a civil case (Article 61 of the RSFSR Code of Civil Procedure), but the law does not indicate the procedure for examining a witness, for for examining a plaintiff or defendant. The law does not empower the court or procurator to deprive a plaintiff or defendant of freedom by means of confinement for in-patient examination. It appears that such powers for the court and procurator are enunciated only in the Instructions of the Ministry of Public Health.[14]†

In the case of persons sentenced to deprivation of freedom who have contracted a chronic mental illness, their examination so that a court can decide whether they should be released from further serving of their sentences is not, strictly speaking, a forensic examination. Both the Code of Criminal Procedure (Article 362) and the Instructions[15] indicate that the decision on the possibility of continued serving of a sentence is made by a "medical commission," not calling this procedure forensic examination.

---

* Professor Karev (p. 232)[13] considers such a possibility. But he does not see a gap in the law here, merely noting that investigating the state of a witness "can also require the use of compulsory measures for confinement in a medical institution."

† I note that the Constitution envisages the power of the court and the procurator only for arrest, and not for other restrictions on the inviolability of the individual.

Occupational psychiatric examination is envisaged in the Fundamental Principles of Legislation on Public Health,[16] and is conducted by commissions organized by psycho-neurological dispensaries and hospitals in accordance with the Statute on Medical-Occupational Commissions of Experts.[17]

Military medical examinations (of draftees and servicemen) are envisaged in the Law on Universal Military Service.[18] Psychiatric military examinations are carried out by dispensaries[19] in accordance with Order No. 110 of the USSR Minister of War dated 20 July 1956.

In unclear and controversial cases, the subjects are hospitalized for examination.

Examinations in connection with deprivation of voting rights are conducted by commissions specially formed by dispensaries.

Establishment of the fact of the mental illness of persons with a view to their hospitalization (at their request, or at the request of their relatives) is effected by physicians from a dispensary by way of treatment without a special expert procedure.

Examinations of the mental state of persons in the case of immediate hospitalization under the Instructions[20] are conducted within twenty-four hours after hospitalization by a commission of three psychiatrists. (Even though the illness may have been ascertained earlier, it is not the basis for such hospitalization.) This same commission establishes the fact of the social danger of the hospitalized person, and whether the diagnosis of his condition corresponds to the criteria in the instructions.

I call attention to specific problems in organizing expert examinations.

1. The legislation presumes the *manifestness* of psychiatric examination in a criminal proceeding. Article 185 affirms the rights of the accused when expert examination is ordered, and Article 184 of the RSFSR Code of Criminal Procedure states: "The order calling for a forensic psychiatric examination, and the conclusion of the experts, are not announced to the accused if his mental state makes this impossible." It is not understandable how the state of a

person can make it impossible to carry out a procedural act consisting in announcing something in the presence of that person. But such an objection is too formal if one takes into account the Soviet tradition in the formulating of legal norms. More important is the fact that the law does not guarantee the necessity of informing the accused of the psychiatric examination, since it does not indicate the procedure which, if carried out, would make the nonannouncement of the examination procedurally legal. True, Article 404 of the RSFSR Code of Criminal Procedure provides that when it is impossible to carry out investigative acts "with the participation of the person who has committed a socially dangerous act" because of his mental state, the investigator prepares a report to this effect. But in the first place, Article 184 concerns an accused person, and Article 404 concerns a person with respect to whom a case is already being prosecuted under a simplified procedure. In the second place, there is probably a difference between a condition of a person which makes it impossible to tell him something, and a condition which makes it impossible for a person to participate in investigative acts. It is also significant that the law does not indicate how and by whom, prior to the examination, the state of the accused is determined and the impossibility of announcing the examination is established.

True, it is of little use to the accused to know that he is being sent for expert examination, or to know of the results of the examination: he has no procedural possibilities for contesting (at any rate, prior to the trial) his being sent for an examination, or for contesting its results. It is not, however, a question of usefulness but of a person's right to know about the acts carried out with respect to him. The law properly presumes that right; but it does not regulate the procedure regarding possible violations of that right.

I also note that the part of Article 184 from which I quoted is so formulated that the possibility of the investigator's referring to it comes up not only when the accused is, in the ordinary sense, out of contact. Whatever the state of the accused, the investigator can decide that by "impossibility" Article 184 means "undesirability," and that warning of the presence of a psychiatrist at the interrogation will prompt the accused to simulate or dissimulate. (So much the worse for the success of the examination, since a proclivity for simulation or dissimulation also characterizes the mental state of the subject.*)

2. So far as I know, the principle of manifestness is not enunciated in norms on other kinds of expert examination. For that matter, it is obvious that in a military or occupational examination its neglect is less likely. It is a different matter when hospitalization is contemplated by relatives or organizations. To prevent a protest or resistance by the person being hospitalized, it is possible to have a kind of preexamination in which the psychiatrist observes the person without having been introduced to him as such.†

In ordinary cases psychiatric doctrine rejects such dissimulation in a meeting with a psychiatrist.‡ But the use of preexaminations would hardly evoke protests from psychiatrists when it is a question of the possible hospitalization of a person for reasons of "social danger."

3. The rights granted to an accused person by Article 185 of the Code of Criminal Procedure in the case of expert examination would be important in the subject's organizing his defense if in practice it were not customary to ignore this article when a psychiatric examination is involved, even if the simplified procedure of Chapter 33 of the Code of Criminal Procedure is not yet being used.

As a practical matter, neither the accused (and persons

---

* I can anticipate psychiatrists' objections to this reasoning (for that matter, see the appendix to the Instructions,[21] the end of the third section). But psychiatrists are not in general agreement on the meaning of an examination (or of a talk with the psychiatrist). This question is really part of the general problem of the use of a falsehood with good intentions; and in medicine this problem is by no means trivial.

† There is an account of such a preexamination in the office of the chairman of a city executive committee prior to hospitalization under the emergency Instructions.[22]

‡ In one handbook the falsehood of introducing the psychiatrist as, say, a friend of the family is rejected because it hampers the initiative of the physician, and in the event of "disclosure" the physician forever loses the trust of the patient.[23]

being prosecuted under the simplified procedure) nor his legal representatives is able, in the preliminary investigation, to influence the choice of experts or put additional questions to an expert. The possibilities for defense counsel are not very great.

4. The Instructions for forensic psychiatric examination stipulate the necessity, in hospitals, of keeping persons undergoing examination separate from the patients. This is an important norm. However, it does not deal exhaustively with present-day requirements as to separate accommodations for accused persons, convicted persons,* and those undergoing expert examination in a civil case. This idea of a separation of categories is also found in international recommendations[24] and to some extent in Soviet law.[25]

5. Unlike the principle of manifestness, the principle which holds that the subject must be present for forensic psychiatric examination has been widely recognized in law and in practice. Examination without the subject's being present is envisaged[27] for exceptional cases. ("When the subject is unavailable for personal testimony; in particular, when he is outside the boundaries of the USSR.") Article 260 of the Code of Civil Procedure stipulates that the subject must be present at the examination in cases when a person's capacity to act is at issue. The Code of Criminal Procedure is not so clear in specifying when the subject must be present.

6. The question of treatment at the time of in-patient examination is important and complex.

The Instructions, para. 22, envisage treatment "in appropriate cases."[28] No other normative (especially legal) provisions on this are known. There is no doubt that the person being examined has a right to receive treatment. But there may be cases where he does not consent to this. Then treatment at the time of forensic examination is compulsory

---

* Morozov states that under an existing statute only convicted persons and accused persons should be kept in examination wards. Plaintiffs and defendants in civil suits should be kept in general wards. No citation is given for this statute.[26]

(in the case of an examination of an accused person conducted prior to a court ruling on compulsory treatment, that ruling being predetermined).

It may seem that the treatment of a mentally ill person without his consent is an ordinary thing. But in this case we are dealing not only with an ordinary violation of rights but with a real danger of changes in the mental state of the subject—changes so substantial that they would complicate a second examination if such were ordered by the investigator or the court. References to a physician's duty to treat his patient are not pertinent here: with respect to the subject, the expert must be exclusively an investigator. A procedure could be provided whereby medical aid is rendered to the subject by physicians not subordinate to the institution conducting the examination. Such a procedure should envisage the possibility of sending the subject for a second examination.

7. The Instructions, para. 22, indicate that in the case of an in-patient examination the necessary methods of investigation are employed. Nothing is said of the agreement of the subject (or at least of his representatives) to the use of complex diagnostic methods on him. But the law stipulates that complex methods of diagnosis can be used only with the consent of patients, and with respect to mentally ill persons (i.e., apparently in cases where the subject had previously been declared mentally ill[29]*), only with the consent of their relatives or guardians.

The Appendix to the Instructions mentions the necessity of examining the spinal fluid of the subject. The law does not indicate what is considered to be a complex method of diagnosis, but there is reason to consider that this should include, for example, the tapping of spinal fluid. (With the most common method—lumbar puncture—traumatization of the substantia medullaris is possible.) Thus the effectuation of a puncture "requires considerable experience and skill." But even with a successful tap, very serious complications are possible. The foregoing provides grounds for

* I am aware of the vagueness of this.

assuming that the expert is restricted by the law in the use of analysis of spinal fluid. However, known norms do not protect the subject from such analysis without his consent.

8. Not only the requirements of the Fundamental Principles of Legislation on Public Health but legal ideas of criminal proceedings may serve as a source of restrictions in the choice of diagnostic methods.

The constitutionally guaranteed right to defense is reflected in criminal procedural legislation by something more than is usually understood by the organization of defense. *Inter alia*, the right to defense is reflected in the law by the recognition of an accused person's right to refuse to testify. Again, an accused person is not liable for giving false testimony. The law allows an accused person to organize his defense using silence and even lies. And it prohibits the use of forcible methods making it difficult for the accused to use such methods of defense. Forcing a person to testify by means of threats or other illegal acts is punishable (Article 179 of the RSFSR Criminal Code). The law does not make special mention of the use of disinhibiting drugs that make a person talkative, although such use is undoubtedly illegal. In the above-mentioned article the law refers only to obtaining testimony, and not other information (i.e., information not procedurally presented in the form of testimony). But it must be presumed that the recognition of the inadmissibility of obtaining any information material to the case by means of using drugs corresponds to the idea of Soviet criminal procedural law.

Yet among the diagnostic methods usually employed is the administration of disinhibiting drugs (for example, sodium amytal with caffeine*) to the patient. The danger that the talkativeness induced by these drugs is always sufficient for the subject to damage his line of defense is not obvious, but it suffices to remember that accused persons

---

* The conclusion in the case of Borisov (report from the Skvortsov-Stepanov Hospital, 1969) testifies to the use of sodium amytal and caffeine in forensic psychiatric examinations. (All the reports of expert examinations I quote from are known to me through their dissemination by samizdat, but I have no reason to consider them substantially distorted.)

not undergoing examination are not subjected to such a procedure. Therefore those who are undergoing examination are in an unequal position relative to the former, even if they experience only the fear that the use of a drug will damage their defense position. I do not mean to say that physicians assume the functions of investigators, listening to the frank remarks of the subject. But the use of this diagnostic method is in no way limited by the conditions of in-patient examination. The examination may be conducted in the investigator's office. Also, the investigator always has the right to be present at an examination (Article 190 of the RSFSR Code of Criminal Procedure). And we should at any rate remember that an expert, like all other citizens, is liable for failure to report certain crimes enumerated in the law. What I have said in this paragraph does not mean that I suspect that disinhibiting drugs have ever helped an investigation. I have no information on this, and I only call attention to the importance of the question.

Diagnosis and Expert Opinion

1. DOUBT IN FAVOR OF THE PATIENT. Such a principle is completely natural for medicine in a civilized society. We have something similar in the complex of ideas on criminal procedural law: I refer to the principle of interpreting doubt in favor of the accused. The principle of doubt certainly prompts the physician, in controversial or unclear cases, to prefer to recognize the presence of mental illness in the subject so as not to leave him without medical care and in special cases so as to help release the patient from criminal liability. This is of course very humane. But there is a good deal to indicate that the application of the principle of doubt sometimes leads to conflicts with the legal interests of the person who has become the object of such humane treatment. It is possible that this conflict is merely a consequence of a different understanding of usefulness, although basic abuses are of course possible, since there is a gap in the system of guarantees of rights.

One difficult question is that of the physician's right to proceed on the basis of his own notions of what is beneficial to the patient, disregarding the patient's aims, aspirations, and rights. It is difficult because upon analysis it turns out that there is no constructive procedure for resolving this conflict in general form.

With regard to expert examination in a criminal proceeding, it is natural to assume that considerations of benefit suggest the appropriateness of the psychiatrist's helping to free the subject from criminal liability, even if the fact of significant mental illness has not been established beyond doubt. And so it has always been. But in recent years several political trials have focused our attention on the fact that such an interpretation of benefit does not correspond to the generally understood aspirations of accused persons. At these trials defense counsel and legal representatives tried to contest expert opinions on the illness of the accused; the accused themselves also tried, but were unable (because of the procedure used in their trials), to contest the opinion of the psychiatrists. There are at least two reasons for this.

One is universal: a person has the right to bear responsibility for what he has done, and he may not want to be deprived of that right. The very fact of the initiation of criminal proceedings, and the consequences thereof, may be considered by the person a chain of events which he himself precipitated, and in which he wants to remain an active participant. Regardless of the possible incomprehensibility of such an approach, it can be fully realized and is being realized; and in itself it is not a consequence of any delirious aspirations. In specific cases in which people are judged for their own convictions or for exchange of information, they do not want the ideas they profess or propagate to be discredited and declared delirious ravings by a court decision.

The other is a product of the specific character of Soviet criminal proceedings. The hearing of a case involving the commission of a socially dangerous act by a person who is mentally ill is conducted under a simplified procedure that does not give the accused* full procedural rights to contest

---

* I arbitrarily use the term "accused" for a person being prosecuted under the procedure envisaged in Chapter 33 of the RSFSR Code of Criminal Procedure.

the charge, and which even (as usually happens) takes place in the absence of the accused.

The conflict between the notions of benefit from the physician's viewpoint and the viewpoint of the subject could be quickly overcome if the physician's motives were not dominated by considerations of so-called social benefit in the formulation known to the physician from circular letters sent out by his superiors, and from the general principles of the social order propagated by the regime (not in the form of laws). A substitution of notions of benefit takes place: sometimes the physician genuinely feels that only whatever does not contravene social benefit, thus understood, is beneficial for the patient.

2. I took the principle of doubt as the point of departure for my discussion of experts' conclusions because, as the psychiatrists themselves admit,* the concept of mental illness cannot always be strictly defined: one cannot draw a clear line between mental health and mental illness. It is also a fact that the activity and behavior of those considered mentally ill often do not require correction for those around them to consider such activity and behavior reasonable and natural.

In conducting an expert examination, psychiatrists are faced not only with the task of determining the fact of the subject's mental illness but with another and very difficult job: to affirm, on the basis of their science, whether the subject could have been aware of his actions, or controlled them, at the time he committed a specific act (RSFSR Criminal Code), or whether the subject understands the significance of his acts or controls them (RSFSR Code of Civil Procedure).

In these instructions to the psychiatric expert the Soviet legislators are very remote from relativism;† they demand a conclusion within the framework of ambiguous logic, despite the vagueness of the very definition of the conditions of nonresponsibility and incapacity.

---

* I do not assert that all psychiatrists understand this.
† The concept of partial responsibility has been discussed in Soviet psychiatric literature but it is not used in law.

It would appear that this barring of relativism entails, quite simply, an expanded interpretation of the concept of mental illness.* If there is no clear line between health and mental illness, and if with respect to any unclear cases one must draw an ambiguous conclusion as to the presence or absence of illness, the same principle of doubt leads to expanding the concept of mental illness. Even if such an expansion is the result of applying the humane principle of "doubt in favor of the patient" and not of a proclivity for abuses of the patient's rights, it would be wise if the psychiatrists, in their humane expansion of the concept of mental illness, would not go so far as to ignore obvious criteria. In particular, the label of significant mental illness should not be applied to a state in which neither the subject's associates nor the subject himself, but only a few psychiatrists, can detect disorders in behavior, thinking, emotions, and perceptions.

One could give many examples of such an expansion of the concept of mental illness. Our rapporteur even notes the opinion that "schizophrenia can also occur without any symptoms" (nonetheless it is customary among Soviet psychiatrists to consider schizophrenia a mental illness). One could also cite many published examples of the fact that different psychiatrists make different diagnoses on the basis of the same case history, and diverge in their opinions as to whether the conditions for nonresponsibility, as stipulated in the law, are present in the patient.† This is quite natural, since psychiatry is an empirical science which is as yet incapable of an adequate level of formalism.

But in the juridical application of this science—i.e., when the conclusions of psychiatrists may entail restrictions on the patient's rights—the contradictory nature of diagnoses and opinions as to the presence of conditions of nonrespon-

---

* Although the experts generally prefer to express themselves vaguely, such reports are still not suitable for a court. For example, according to present-day notions the conclusion in the Yakhimovich case was incorrect: "The condition of the patient must be equated with mental illness." (Riga Republic Psychiatric Hospital, Report #36, June 3, 1969.)

† For example, see the reports on diagnostic seminars.[30]

sibility is the thing that hampers realization of a person's right to equality before the law. As a rule the court does not order additional examination but accepts as evidence the diagnosis and opinion as to responsibility contained in the conclusion of the first expert. Even if additional examinations are ordered, the court invariably (and this is natural behavior) gives preference to those experts with higher rank in the hierarchy of forensic psychiatrists. In actuality preference is given to experts from the Serbsky Institute of Forensic Psychiatry, yet there is reason to assume that the doctrinal notions currently entertained at the Serbsky Institure are not the only ones in psychiatry.

Of course the law does not stipulate that an expert opinion is definitive in the judicial restriction of rights: expert opinion is only one of the pieces of evidence to be evaluated by the court, and it does not have previously established force. It would not be an exaggeration, however, to say that this norm merely provides the court with the illusion that the psychiatric finding is open-ended. As a rule (especially when there are no additional examinations), the court is not able to evaluate the opinion of a psychiatric expert, since special knowledge is required for this—certainly when the opinion does not indicate clear symptoms of a mental disorder. True, the appendix to the Instructions[31] states that the report of the examination must be understandable not only to a physician but to a member of the court; and it even recommends providing a Russian translation of special terms.*

Whatever the difficulties for the court in the critical evaluation of an expert opinion on the mental state of an accused

---

* The recommendation for the use of generally understood language is difficult to implement and often neglected. The nature of this text enables me to refer to a personal impression from the remarks of the expert, Dr. D. R. Lunts, at the trial of Gorbanevskaya.[32] These remarks made a very solid and scientific impression, especially on the people's representatives, because of the abundance of special terms. Gorbanevskaya's condition was characterized by such phrases as "emotional thickening," "the monotony of affective manifestations," "paralogism in judgments," "a proclivity toward philosophism," etc. At the same time, according to Lunts's testimony, Gorbanevskaya did not show clear symptoms.

person, this evaluation can nonetheless be successful when the concept of mental illness has been too much broadened by the expert. The court may then conceive doubts about the grounds for the conclusion and want to order another examination. But this is possible only when the court can form its own notion of the subject's condition. In this case, the importance of a generally understood language, and of the subject's presence in court, is obvious.

3. THE IMPARTIALITY OF THE EXPERTS. An expert may not take part in the proceedings if there are circumstances indicating that, directly or indirectly, he has a personal interest in the case (Articles 67 and 59 of the RSFSR Code of Criminal Procedure). Here I am not discussing trivial cases of interestedness and the difficulties in establishing it. Rather, I am discussing only the possible role of interestedness (and, more broadly, of partiality) in the expert's evaluation of disorders in the behavior, thinking, and emotions of the subject. This is all the more important in that, in the court of the psychiatrist, the patient must present not only those manifestations that might interest investigative and judicial organs but also his feelings, convictions, and principled attitudes toward the world. And here it turns out that, on the average, the psychiatric expert—possessing, like most people, a very limited general philosophical erudition—functions as a decisive and confident judge of the eternal problems and doubts of the human spirit. It turns out that the meaning of many profound problems disappears in the talk with the psychiatrist, because of the criteria of correctness that psychiatrists have gleaned from daily life or from the precepts of their spiritual mentors. I do not even have to discuss the controversial nature of the opinion that hallucinations are evidence of a *disorder* in perception, that indifference to sad news is a consequence of a *disorder* (*inadequacy*) of the emotions, that masochism or sadism must be classified as *perversions of inclinations*. There are sufficient examples of the evaluation of a patient's social ideas as irrational, even when similar ideas have seemed quite reasonable to many people. A consideration of these examples is all the more appropriate here, in that the rapporteur devoted special attention to them.

It is widely known that in the Soviet Union the authorities preach faith in the ideals of communism, in the unique correctness of the official ideology, and in the perfection of the state and social system. If someone begins to preach skepticism or another belief and, as a result of the actions flowing from these convictions, attracts the active attention of the appropriate organs so that, in accordance with the procedure stipulated in Chapter 33 of the RSFSR Code of Criminal Procedure he is brought before psychiatric experts with a view to determining his mental state, the psychiatrists are faced with the ticklish question of evaluating the correctness of the behavior and thinking of this person. Did the subject understand the significance of his acts, and could he control them? This is of course the basic question for the experts. But an evaluation of the correctness of his behavior and thinking according to established practice is still inevitable, especially if his behavior and thinking are ordinary in everything except the incriminating actions and the convictions that prompted him to those actions.

In such a situation, because of a specific belief encouraged by the state, conditions arise under which one may doubt not only the competence but the impartiality of the expert evaluation of correctness of behavior and thinking.

If the expert does not consider the unorthodox behavior and utterances of the subject incorrect, he is behaving in a disloyal manner. Needless to say, he has this right: he is not obliged (although he is accustomed) to evaluate correctness of convictions at all. But people are used to caution; they strive to emphasize their loyalty, and in so doing they go to ridiculous extremes. Thus in a report of the Riga Republic Psychiatric Hospital (in the Yakhimovich case) it is stated that the subject intends to combat "allegedly existing injustice" in our country. It would seem obvious that injustice exists everywhere. It suffices to see a strong child mistreat a weak one, or to read a bulletin of the Supreme Court and learn that even judicial errors can happen. But the experts have preferred to emphasize their own hypertrophied loyalty, and have thus provided grounds for regarding them as lacking in impartiality.

It is widely known that from time to time, in the process

of governing a country, things happen that are naturally considered mistakes. An example is the publication, by a state organ, of a nonoptimum economic decision. From time to time the government leadership itself announces this; and the discussion of past mistakes is sometimes encouraged, and does not always discredit loyalty. The experts of the Serbsky Institute, however, preferred to display circumspection in preparing Report No. 33, on the Yakhimovich case: "Often at night, in his written material, he critically analyzed alleged errors in the governing of the country."

Nor can I detect the impartiality of the experts in a premature categorizing of subjects' acts. Thus even before Yakhimovich's trial an expert from the Riga Psychoneurological Dispensary stated in his report: "The subject began to spread slanderous fabrications defaming the state and social system." "He underestimates his actions, and does not understand their criminal and treasonous nature."

Also improper is the dissatisfaction of experts with the fact that the subject is uncritical toward his illness. It is obvious that the subject must know of his illness before he can take a critical attitude toward it. But prior to the expert examination he may have heard nothing about it from anyone. (Likewise, after the examination he may have some well-founded doubts—like the court that sometimes orders another examination.) But the experts demand a "critical attitude" not only toward one's own condition but toward those around one. Here is an example: "He has an uncritical attitude toward the antigovernment remarks of the mentally ill persons who are receiving compulsory treatment together with him." (The Borisov case, Skvortsov-Stepanov Hospital, 1969.)

The conditions specified in Articles 67 and 59 of the RSFSR Code of Criminal Procedure for challenging and excluding an expert should be considered clearly met if the examination is being conducted to determine the condition of a person charged with committing acts flowing from convictions which might be characterized as manifestations of a bourgeois ideology, vestiges of a private-ownership mentality, religious prejudices, and other vestiges of the past, if the expert is a member of the Communist Party. This is because, under para. 2c of the Rules of the CPSU, a Party member must wage a resolute struggle against the above-listed manifestations; and it is obvious that a resolute struggle in the course of an examination hampers an impartial diagnosis of irrationality in the assertions of the subject.

4. PARTIAL INCOMPETENCE. Article 67 of the RSFSR Code of Criminal Procedure provides for the exclusion of an expert when he is found to be incompetent. This norm (in addition to considerations of professional honor) imposes upon the expert an obligation not to go beyond the limits of his own competence in his conclusions, and this includes the competence of his science.* Thus it is undoubtedly not the business of a psychiatrist (and it is not within the capabilities of psychiatry) to determine the correctness of judgments in the sphere of philosophical views. True, the psychiatrist may have his own philosophical views, and there may be something in the judgments of the subject that he does not respect. Again, a particular school of psychiatry may have its own methodological principles (or even what is called ideological principles), and some of the subject's philosophical or other judgments may contradict the ideological principles of the given school of experts. But a psychiatric expert is not called upon by the court to conduct an ideological examination (Soviet courts do have this kind of examination, too): it is not within his competence. And by probing into philosophical views, he becomes vulnerable to exclusion.

As far as the ideological principles of psychiatry are concerned, they in any case constitute metapsychiatry. One should distinguish between science and metascience, and between a psychiatric expert and (if you will) an expert in metapsychiatry. This is important both as a supplement to the preceding paragraph on impartiality and as a recommendation to experts to detach themselves, in analyzing a subject's judgments, from their confidence in the unique

---

* Obviously, everyone has the right to make judgments about things in which he is inexperienced. Here it is a question of the necessity for being experienced when the judgment entails juridical consequences.

correctness of their own philosophical outlook, even though it is orthodox for the USSR.

The expert must also display a certain caution in evaluating the degree of motivation for acts flowing from convictions unfamiliar to him; in evaluating whether it makes sense to reflect on questions which strike the expert as unimportant;* in evaluating how constructive judgments must be;† and in evaluating the falsity of deductions of mistakes of judgment.‡

Caution on the part of the expert in evaluating the acts of the subject is important. An expert is a human being, and no doubt it is sometimes hard for him to restrain his just indignation (or indignation emphasizing his loyalty) as a citizen upon becoming familiar with the case. However these human manifestations fall outside the competence of the expert as a participant in a judicial proceedings. Not only wise restraint but a respect for the presumption of

---

* "Philosophism is an inclination toward unnecessary argumentation and empty, fruitless philosophizing. Facts not worthy of attention usually constitute the subject of such argumentation."[33] The expert conclusions in the cases of Grigorenko and Gorbanevskaya mention an inclination toward philosophism. It may be assumed that from the viewpoint of the experts, the facts discussed in the remarks of Grigorenko and Gorbanevskaya were not worthy of attention; e.g., the impoverished condition of the Crimean Tatars, and repressions against the Moscow demonstrators of August 1968. However, it is known that many people have a different opinion.

† In one expert report from the Skvortsov-Stepanov Hospital (1969, the Borisov case) we read: "He expressed sharply antigovernment views, but could not formulate a positive program of his own."

‡ "Irrationality means drawing deductions which do not correspond to reality, which arise from a morbid foundation, and which are not subject to correction."[34] "Irrational ideas are false deductions and mistakes of judgment arising from a morbid foundation."[35] I have already noted that the procedure for the administrative defense of rights in the USSR is very imperfect.[35a] From my observations I can judge that some people spend a great deal of time on solicitations—completely understandable to me and many others—in the defense of obvious rights. If the psychiatrist finds in such a person what he calls a "morbid foundation," and if he does not understand the obvious importance of the right being defended by that person, there is a danger that in the examination these solicitations will be evaluated as one form of irrationality—litigiousness.

innocence is required. I have already mentioned the expert's evaluation in the Yakhimovich case (as to the treasonous nature of the subject's acts). Here is an example from an expert report from a Moscow hospital:

She is affected, theatrical, and saccharine. In her emotional expressiveness there are salient elements of habitual affectation. Hypocrisy is strongly pronounced in her entire personality, in which pathetic expressions of the allegedly high religious and moral aims of her behavior and the selfless serving of ideals coexist with shrewdly conceived and profoundly practical antisocial activity: the illegal practice of medicine, and the use of rituals for the purpose of swindling.[36]*

The psychiatric experts will be acting wisely if they prefer to use caution in judging things that are not fully defined, such as correctness in thinking. The diversity of the creative capacities of the human mind is great; and generally speaking, it is terrible to assume that there is correct thinking and incorrect thinking. By way of an observation, the expert can note that the subject does not use the rules of thinking to which the expert himself is accustomed. The problem of interpreting such an observation is not trivial, and depends on the expert's experience and on his own logical acumen. It would not appear that the ways of interpreting such observations are sufficiently uniform. Such words as "paralogism of thinking" in an expert conclusion are virtually meaningless. The expert's attempts more accurately to describe the subject's way of thinking sometimes leads to the construction of new and original terms. Thus one expert conclusion mentions "thinking with emotional logic."[37] But there is no hope that such terminological creativity will make the supposed disorders in thinking any more specific. In any case there is

---

* In this report the subject was declared to be responsible for her actions. Later a commission from the Serbsky Institute found her to be suffering from schizophrenia and nonresponsible. Here I note again the right of a person to equality with others before a court and the law. Uniformity of interpretation is important, since the examination has juridical consequences.

no doubt of the importance, for uniformity in expert evaluations, of having centrally elaborated procedures for studying the properties of a subject's thought process. In
particular, such procedures are described in a Methodological Letter of the Institute of Psychiatry and the Ministry of
Public Health RSFSR (1956).[38]* This letter indicates the
specific nature of the Soviet approach to psychological
experimentation, in particular as regards the use of psychological tests to study a subject's thinking. It states: "One of
the most monstrous perversions of psychological experimentation, based on the fallacious theoretical foundation of
the pseudoscience of pedology, was the method of psychological testing that was condemned by the Central Committee of the All-Russian Communist Party (Bolshevik) . . ."

Among the methods of evaluating correctness of thought,
the methodological letter recommends one that is often
used, the method of classification. The subject's attention is
directed to a set of pictures with representations of living
things, plants, and inanimate objects, and he is told: "Sort
them out by kinds; i.e., in separate piles, so that each pile
contains objects similar to one another."

The interpretation of the results of the testing is specifically as follows: "Any correctly thinking person, even
without an education (including children from approximately the age of seven) . . . will surmise that it is necessary
to put plants with plants, birds with birds, furniture with
furniture, etc."†

---

* One may hope that these recommendations have now been improved,
  but I know of no later documents on the subject. The method described below (classification) has not been discarded.
† One noted mathematical logician was subjected to this test in the
  course of an examination. He sorted the pictures into two piles, on
  the basis of function: into one he put a border guard and a dog, and
  into the other he put all the rest. The experts found this very unsatis-
  factory. Presumably the logician was joking, but such joking seems
  an appropriate response if the subject considers the "scientific methods"
  of the examination laughable. One psychiatrist expressed an opinion
  typical of his colleagues when he said to me, "What normal person
  would joke in such a situation?" Yes, for the experts this means inadequacy of behavior and emotions.

Difficulties

In what I have said about the problems of expert examination I did not intend to defame either psychiatrists or the science of psychiatry. The difficulties of an empirical science which studies such a complex subject are obvious. The difficulties for the specialists in this science in making conclusions for which they bear at least a moral responsibility vis-à-vis individual (usually suffering) people are all the more understandable. True, in public protests there have been specific complaints against psychiatrists in connection with individual cases and whole classes of cases in which one may assume the significance of motives not dictated by science in the behavior of the expert. There are no grounds for disbelieving such disclosures. But it is important to understand that the bad faith of individual experts, if it exists, is possible primarily because of substantial gaps in the system of guarantees of the subject's rights.

Also, the general level of skill in the expert examinations, as well as the degree of uniformity in the conclusions, is directly associated with the level of development of the science. Let us remember the difficulties of a nonacademic nature that have affected many sciences but have seriously hurt psychiatry. Let us remember that recently an official scientific chronicle testified that psychiatry was based on the teachings of Michurin and Lysenko; that psychiatry too had been affected by ideological meddling. (I mentioned above a quotation from a decree of the Central Committee of the All-Russian Communist Party [Bolshevik].) There is no basis for assuming that these difficulties in psychiatry are behind us—not even to the extent that this is true in genetics.

Let us also remember that the healers of human souls are themselves human beings, and that the culture of the average expert is determined by the general level of culture and intellectual freedom in society.

Establishing the Fact of Mental Illness with Juridical Consequences*

1. ORDINARY HOSPITALIZATION WITHOUT THE CONSENT OF THE PATIENT. The procedure is exhausted with the conclusion of the physician (in the matter of beginning treatment or sending the person to the hospital). The juridical consequences of this are such that the patient can be forcibly hospitalized. His right to contest the physician's conclusion or the hospitalization is not recognized, not to mention his right to leave the hospital. In practice, no institution will consider his complaint. Those relatives of the patient who took the initiative with a view to hospitalization can request his release from the hospital; but the physicians have the right to refuse on the grounds of his endangering society. The narrow notion that persons with significant mental illness are not subject to or protected by the law is also shown in other areas from the moment of the experts' conclusion.

2. FORCIBLE HOSPITALIZATION IN ACCORDANCE WITH INSTRUCTIONS.[39] In this case the procedure for establishing the fact of mental illness is also entrusted to physicians who, simultaneously with the examination, establish the fact of social danger and the correctness of confinement. I have discussed these instructions in an article.[40]

3. MILITARY EXAMINATION. It would appear that the experts' conclusion is *per se* sufficient for juridical consequences to ensue.

4. OCCUPATIONAL EXAMINATION. The conclusion of a medical occupational commission of experts is *per se* sufficient for juridical consequences to ensue.

5. IDENTIFICATION OF THE "INSANE." A dispensary commission of experts, with the participation of the chief physician, draws up a report indicating whether the subject is insane. Lists of insane persons, together with the reports on

---

* In this section my discussion is less detailed, since I dare say the following questions have been sufficiently elucidated in the opinion presented by my colleague, expert committee member Volpin.

them, are sent to the appropriate executive committees.[41] Apparently the procedure ends either with this or with the decision of the executive committee to remove the names from the voting lists. One source also mentions court determinations as a basis for removal from voting lists.[42] However, this apparently concerns determinations of incapacity, although the connection between civil incapacity and the right to vote is not clear. The noninclusion of a person on the voting list can be protested by that person or others to the court which is considering the case, with the participation of the declarant, the injured party, and the procurator. Article 233 states that this procedure is possible in cases provided by law. But apart from Articles 233-235 of the Code of Civil Procedure, no other law on this is known.

6. DECLARING A PERSON INCOMPETENT. In this case the fact of mental illness has juridical consequences only if there is a court decision taken in accordance with the procedure of Section 29 of the Code of Civil Procedure. The person against whom the action has been brought is called in for the hearing "if the state of his health permits." The law does not indicate the procedure for ascertaining whether his state of health makes it impossible for him to be called into court. No restrictions on public disclosure are envisaged by the law.

The court reaches a finding of incapacity if, on the basis of an expert opinion, it concludes that the person cannot understand the significance of his actions, or control them.

7. DECLARING A PERSON NONRESPONSIBLE. Nonresponsibility is declared by a decision of the court in accordance with the procedure of Chapter 33 of the Code of Criminal Procedure. The fallaciousness of this procedure, and of practice, deserves special, detailed discussion; and to a certain extent this was done in the opinion presented by Volpin. I would note only that any procedural simplifications weaken the system of guarantees of human rights. The history of Soviet law provides examples of this. It is important to distinguish between proof of the occurrence of a crime and guilt with the presumption of responsibility, and proof of nonresponsibility. Public disclosure is also impor-

tant, along with the introduction of a procedure for ascertaining the impossibility of having an accused person come to a court session because of his health.

The problem of the legislative recognition of partial nonresponsibility merits serious analysis.

8. CONTESTING THE FACT OF MENTAL ILLNESS. Contestation on the part of a person who has been declared mentally ill as the result of an examination is not provided for, and is impossible in practice. An additional examination may sometimes be obtained through the efforts of relatives and a lawyer.* For all practical purposes, it is impossible to arrange for removal of a person's name from the psychiatric records if it has been so entered.

Incompetence

The foregoing shows that with respect to mentally ill persons, both in practice and in the instructions, there is infringement of legal capacity and competence contrary to the law. "No one can be restricted in his legal capacity or competence except in those cases, and under that procedure, prescribed by law." (Article 15, RSFSR Code of Civil Procedure.) As far as the laws are concerned, very often they simply do not take into account the necessity for guaranteeing the rights of mentally ill persons. This too is a violation of the cited norm, since no such restriction on legal capacity or competence is envisaged when it is a question of the procedure prescribed by law.

The judicial deprivation of competence on the basis of a legal procedure is only the nonrecognition by the state of a citizen's capacity, through his own actions, to acquire civil rights and create civil obligations for himself. The court accords to the nonresponsible person those rights and obligations created by his guardian in the name of the nonresponsible person. The meaning of deprivation of compe-

---

* Pisarev gives an example of a lawyer's petition on this (the Grigorenko case, counsel S. V. Kallistratova).[43] I am not discussing here the question of contesting an expert opinion on nonresponsibility. In practice, this problem is no less important.

tence is little understood by the public and the administration. The prejudice as to the legal incapacity of mentally ill persons—the opinion that they have no rights—is even shared by psychiatrists. For example, Professor N. I. Felinskaya states that mentally ill persons dissimulate "in order not to be deprived of their civil rights."[44] Even when the law corresponds more closely to legal principles than do public prejudices and practice, the determination of legal incompetence in the law is in need of adjustments. For example, it is obvious that if a person declared nonresponsible creates a literary work, it is precisely through his own efforts that he acquires author's rights. But the basic shortcoming in the legislation is the fact that gaps in the law permit the flourishing, in practice, of the prejudice as regards legal incapacity. In particular the law should especially guarantee the right of an incompetent person to complain against his guardian, the right to contest the judgment of his incompetence and the right to select his own guardian on a clearer basis than is now the case (Article 126 of the Code of Laws on Marriage, the Family, and Guardianship).

Without going into a discussion of the individual rights of incompetent persons, I note the question of the right to marry and have a sexual life. Soviet law does not recognize the right of incompetent persons to marry. Although there are no legal restrictions on sexual behavior as such there have been cases[45] in which persons were convicted for having sexual relationships with incompetent women, although these women wanted to continue the relationships. It is specifically women who are subjected to this indirect restriction on the right to sexual expression, which means a violation of the principle of equality. The law can of course provide a special procedure for protecting incompetent persons against abuse, but such restrictions on sexual behavior are inadmissible.

Hospitals

Even a person who goes voluntarily to a hospital for treatment cannot expect to be released at his own request.

Requests from relatives* produce about the same results. If the physicians consider the patient "socially dangerous," the refusal to release him involves no other procedure than a reference to the Instructions[46]—so it is stated in an order from the ministries of Public Health and Internal Affairs.[47] Practically, it is impossible to dispute the point with the physicians by means of calling in other physicians chosen by the relatives, not to mention the patient. It is hardly likely than anyone would pay special attention to a patient's complaint about the conditions under which he was being kept in the hospital. Usually a patient's appeal to a procurator or other official is simply not forwarded by the physician, particularly in special hospitals. Letters are censored, and the prejudice as to legal incompetence no doubt prevents those in charge from even remembering the constitutional secrecy of correspondence: the censorship is not concealed. One handbook[48] states: "The irrational ideas expressed in the letters of patients should not become known to the addressees." (This was with respect to ordinary mental hospitals.) In special hospitals even the patient's reading matter is subjected to censorship at the discretion of the physician, without any special procedure.

Victor Fainberg's revelations about the conditions of care in special hospitals,[49] and the widely known letters of Vassily Chernyshev[50] and Vladimir Gershuni[51] make it possible to learn something of the current state of affairs in special hospitals. There are no grounds for disbelieving these authors. It would appear that the protests of Fainberg and Borisov have attracted the attention of the authorities; and there is hope that the results will have an effect beyond their particular cases.

In itself, the fact that their hunger strike caused the authorities to recognize their right to consult with counsel constitutes a very important precedent in the exercise of the obvious right to legal assistance.

There is no need to reiterate what has already become known through these disclosures. I note in particular the inadmissibility of having convicts serve as attendants in

* I also have guardians in mind when I speak of relatives.

special hospitals, where they not only come into contact with the patients but exercise (sometimes on their own initiative, presumably) administrative authority over them. In any case this involves the restraint of patients and, as mentioned in conversations reported by Fainberg, beatings as well. *

Also inadmissible is the fact that in special hospitals, nonmedical personnel—the security guards—come into contact with the patients.

The subordination of the special hospitals to the Ministry of Internal Affairs (see the Instructions[52]) contravenes the idea that nonresponsible persons are exempt from criminal liability. The procedure whereby nonresponsible persons are released from treatment only by court order conflicts with the idea of treatment. There have been instances when courts did not halt compulsory treatment despite the hospital's conclusion that it could be halted. (The Kuznetsov case; see also the reports of P. V. Blinov and Z. G. Us.[53] In such cases no additional examination is ordered.)

It is natural to consider that compulsory treatment in special hospitals should not differ from ordinary treatment in any way except the strengthening of external security and the fact that the patient is being kept in the hospital contrary to his demand and that of his representatives. But practice is too far removed from the implementation of this principle. And the practice of keeping patients in ordinary hospitals is far from the implementation of the open-door doctrine, although of course much has been done in this direction.

Less is known of the practice of keeping patients in psychiatric colonies. The release of a patient from a colony at the request of his relatives is limited by considerations of social danger, the latter being established by a physician without any special procedure.[54]

---

* Although patients in special hospitals are not considered prisoners, it is not superfluous to mention here that in the UN recommendations cited in note 24 there is a prohibition against giving a prisoner administrative authority over other prisoners.

Treatment

1. We know how enthusiastically some psychiatrists greeted the discovery of lobotomy. This operation frees a person from a deeply pathological mental state, bringing him into contact with reality, making him calm, and "returning him to life." But it entails irreversible changes in his volitional and mental capacities. It is also natural to ask psychiatrists to use caution in administering drugs if they can cause substantial irreversible changes in a person's volitional, mental, emotional, and genetic capacities as compared with his condition before the illness. Such caution is all the more necessary in compulsory treatment. Public alarm in connection with the possibility of such irreversible effects on a patient is all the more natural when the subject is a person sent by a court for treatment because of officially disapproved participation in information exchange (e.g., under Articles 70 and 190-1 of the RSFSR Criminal Code) or because of other acts flowing from social and philosophical convictions disapproved by the authorities. In this connection, I should again mention Chernyshev's letter.[55]

2. There should be recognition of the patient's right to be informed of the nature of the treatment being administered to him. The secret administration of drugs is inadmissible.

3. The problem of using lies for psychotherapeutic purposes is special and important for medicine. One example of this is the use of a placebo.*

4. The threat of using, on a disturbed patient, drugs and procedures which it would be natural for him to avoid (electroshock, sulfazyl, etc.) turns out in practice to be a major problem.

5. It is important to recognize the right of a person or his representatives to consult on their own initiative with any physicians they care to.

* One handbook calls for caution in the use of a placebo, since there is a a risk that it will be discovered and that the physician will lose the trust of the patient.[56]

6. The right to refuse certain medical procedures must be recognized, with normative and justified restrictions.

Records of Mental Patients

Psychoneurological dispensaries keep records on mental patients.[57] Records are not kept on persons who come to the dispensary with short-lived neurotic conditions or who do not display symptoms of mental illness. The system of records is described in detail by the Ministry of Public Health.[58] Special records are kept on socially dangerous mental patients.[59]

An Opinion of the Moscow Human Rights Committee Concerning the Problem of Persons Declared Mentally Ill

After studying Chalidze's report and other materials the Moscow Human Rights Committee (then composed of Andrei Sakharov, Andrei Tverdokhebov, Igor Shafarevich, and the author) adopted this statement July 3, 1971:

Having studied

the report of Roy A. Medvedev "Concerning Psychiatric Hospitalization for Political Motives,"
the opinion of expert member Alexander S. Volpin concerning this report,
the opinion of Committee member Valery N. Chalidze "Concerning the Problem of Persons Declared Mentally Ill,"

the Committee deems this preliminary study of the problem sufficient to affirm certain fundamental principles which, in the opinion of the Committee, should be considered by the legislators in improving the system of safeguards for human rights and which should be respected by legal practitioners

with respect to the actions of individuals and organizations taken in relation to persons declared mentally ill,
with respect to the procedure for establishing the fact of mental disability,
as well as with respect to defense and restriction of the rights of persons declared mentally defective or of persons whose mental or volitional state appears to be the cause for restriction of their legal competence or capacity to act even though they are recognized as mentally healthy.

The Committee notes that it is urgent to eliminate serious omissions in and to improve existing legislation concerning procedures for restricting the rights of the persons mentioned and also the scope of such restrictions, so that the rights of an individual, no matter how ill or mentally defective, will not be limited otherwise than by law and only in cases where such restriction is absolutely necessary to protect the individual's basic rights, or the rights of other persons, or the safety of the public. The Committee considers interesting the specific legislative proposals advanced by expert member A. S. Volpin; however, it believes further study of the problem is necessary for the formulation of specific recommendations, in particular with respect to procedures for contesting decisions on legal competence or capacity to act.

The Committee considers important and timely the study of this problem by scholars from different disciplines, as well as broad public discussion of questions concerning the defense of the rights of the persons mentioned above and also of social dangers which are possible consequences of the imperfect state of legislation in this field.

The Committee studied attentively known public statements concerning individual cases related to the problem under discussion. The Committee notes that perception of social dangers is urgent for all mankind and that success in overcoming these dangers depends on the respect of society for human rights and on the quality of legal and, more especially, procedural safeguards; the Committee believes that the elaboration of international recommendations in this field of law is important.

The Committee deems it necessary to continue its study of this problem and hopes to receive recommendations from specialists, in particular jurists and psychiatrists.

I. Basic Principles

1. Restrictions on the rights of persons on the grounds of their mental disability are permissible only when and in so far as: these restrictions are established by law and are absolutely necessary to protect these persons' rights, the rights of others, or the safety of the public; and only when the fact of mental disability has been established by the decision of qualified and impartial specialists according to a legal procedure which permits this decision to be contested, and the necessity for such restrictions on rights has been affirmed by an agency which has been empowered to restrict legal competence and the right to act and which has followed a legal procedure which permits its decision to be contested.

Any other restriction of people's rights because of their mental disability or because of suspicion of their mental disability should be considered impermissible discrimination, including any discrimination based on mental development, personal convictions, religious beliefs, preferred system of ethics, or on genetic or other grounds, although this does not apply to those social, cultural, and economic rights whose realization is acknowledged as possible only if the subject of the right satisfies definite prerequisites fixed by statute or other lawful act.

2. The procedure to contest a determination of mental illness for the purpose of limiting legal competence or the

right to act should, in any event, take account of the vagueness of the terms "mental health" and "mental sufficiency" and also of the deliberately vague terms which have been selected or could be selected by the legislators as criteria for determining when mental illness or feeblemindedness can or must entail juridical consequences. Every stage of this procedure, with the exception only of cases strictly defined by statute, should be designed to provide practical recognition of the procedural competence of the individual who is the subject of the inquiry.

II. Principles of Legislation and Practice

In its evaluation of the soundness of laws and juridical practice and in its effort to improve the system of social safeguards for human rights, the Committee deems the following principles particularly noteworthy.

1. Everyone has the right to be considered mentally healthy and mentally sound as long as lawful procedure has not determined to the contrary. The law should hold individuals or organizations liable for maliciously arousing suspicions concerning the mental health of a person, and recognize the right of the person affected to sue for the damage inflicted by such suspicions if they were aroused maliciously or in violation of the law. The right to raise questions concerning the mental health of a person should not be granted by law to an arbitrary range of individuals and organizations.

2. An organ competent to determine the fact of mental illness or mental deficiency should not have the right to institute proceedings in such a case before: ascertaining that reasonable grounds exist for doubt concerning the health or soundness of a person; examining what legal consequences may be anticipated from a determination of mental disability by the individuals or organizations raising the issue; attempting to determine the extent of personal interest and good faith of these individuals or organizations;

and determining whether these individuals and organizations have the right to initiate the case in anticipation of the legal consequences that will flow from it. With respect to these questions, the competent organ should be obliged to permit the person whose condition is being questioned, and his representative, to set forth their arguments on these questions, and should also be obliged to study their arguments.

3. In cases where the question of the fact of mental illness is not initiated by the subject of the examination in order to acquire a right to some advantage for himself or in order to receive voluntary treatment, then only those agencies are competent to establish the fact of mental illness which: are empowered by law to decide questions concerning the restriction of legal competence and the capacity to act; are protected by law from subordination to the executive power; and are not organs of the executive power. Exceptions to this principle are permissible in law for separate cases involving those special, cultural or economic rights whose realization is acknowledged as possible only if the subject of the right satisfies definite prerequisites fixed by statute or other lawful act, including the right to serve in the armed forces or paramilitary organizations; however, any determination of mental illness resulting from such proceedings must not affect other rights of a person, including the right to refuse participation in this proceeding; and in this case a person must be given an opportunity to waive his claim to that right which requires participation in such a proceeding for its realization.

4. At no stage of a proceeding for determination of the fact of mental illness or mental deficiency of an individual, including the stage of appeal or review, can the burden of proof of mental soundness be placed on the individual or on his representative.

5. The fact of mental illness can be established by a competent agency only after a commission of psychiatric experts has concluded that the individual concerned suf-

fers a degree of mental illness which satisfies those conditions fixed by law as necessary and sufficient for legal consequences to ensue. A person whose mental health is the subject of inquiry, or his representative, has the right in every case to be informed of the results of the examination, to demand the inclusion of specialists of his choice in the expert commission, to challenge the experts selected, to be present at the examination, to pose questions to the experts, and to make statements for inclusion in the protocol of the expert commission. Well-founded suspicion of bias or incompetence must be recognized in every case as reasonable grounds for exclusion of an expert. The agency which sought the examination is obliged to satisfy itself that the experts in their opinions did not exceed the limits of competence of their field of knowledge.

6. Only a law can establish those instances when measures of compulsion may be applied in order to carry out procedures for the determination of mental illness; and the right of a person or his representative, using workable procedures, to contest the legality of use of such measures of compulsion must be recognized.

7. The law must forbid the use of diagnostic methods in the course of examination which are excessively disturbing, dangerous, or prolonged, and also the use of truth serums or other mind-affecting means without consent of the subject.

Treatment during the time of expert examination can be initiated without consent of the subject only in exceptional cases, and a decision to apply treatment can be reached only by means of a special proceeding which permits the proposal to be contested.

8. The law should take into account the vagueness of the terms "mental illness" and "mental deficiency" and also the difficulty of defining precisely those conditions which are necessary and sufficient for juridical consequences of mental illness or mental deficiency to ensue. During contests of the fact of mental illness or mental deficiency, arguments

citing the vagueness of these terms should not be rejected by the agency concerned without studying the relevance of these arguments to the case under study.

9. A proceeding to determine the fact of mental illness or mental deficiency must provide in every case for:

the right of a person to be present during consideration of his case and the obligatory presence of any representative freely chosen by him;

reasonable opportunity for participation of the person concerned or his representative in the hearing of the case;

public disclosure with no greater restrictions than those allowed by law in civil cases even if the determination of the fact of mental illness is conducted in connection with the examination of a criminal case;

the right of a person or his representative to become familiar with all case material concerning determination of the fact of mental illness;

the right of a person to qualified legal counsel;

the right to initiate proceedings for review of a decision.

10. An attempt must be made to separate procedurally a proceeding to determine the fact of mental illness from a proceeding to determine other facts, even when these facts may have been the grounds for raising doubts about mental soundness. In particular, a proceeding which determines an individual not responsible for his actions should be conducted with a reasonable degree of procedural independence from a proceeding to determine whether the individual has committed a criminal act. Also, those safeguards which issue from the presumption of innocence should be stated in law in a manner so that they do not lose their significance in cases when the accused is supposed to be not responsible.

11. Persons who have been declared mentally ill through an established legal procedure enjoy a right to protection of the law from arbitrary restriction of their legal capacity equal to that of other citizens.

12. Only a statute can fix the power of competent agencies to restrict the rights of persons declared mentally ill through established legal procedures, including the carrying out of treatment or hospitalization of such persons without their consent. The law should restrict the rights of such persons as regards involuntary treatment only to the extent absolutely necessary for the protection of the rights of others or for the safety of the public. In all cases the person undergoing involuntary treatment or his representative enjoys the right to a workable procedure to appeal the decision concerning treatment; at every stage of treatment both enjoy the right to seek, through a workable procedure, cessation of treatment, hospitalization, or any other measure of a compulsory nature.

13. Medical institutions should not be recognized as agencies competent to limit the legal capacity of persons undergoing treatment, including the rights of such persons to correspondence, to visits, to creative work, to exchange of information, and to consultation with legal counsel. Only appropriate legal regulations can fix the rights of medical institutions temporarily to restrict certain rights of their patients in order to protect the rights of other persons or the safety of the public in cases not admitting delay.

14. Persons undergoing treatment in medical institutions, including involuntary treatment, enjoy in all cases the right to humane treatment and also the right:

to know the diagnosis of their condition and the nature of any treatment applied;
not to have dangerous diagnostic measures or treatment procedures applied to them without their consent;
not to have applied to them treatment measures, procedures, or surgical operations which can entail irreversible changes in their mental, volitional, emotional, or genetic characteristics;
not to be subject to medical experiments without their consent;
to be free from procedures they consider especially unpleasant,

with the exception of properly specified instances when an exception is necessary for sanitary reasons or for the safety of the public;

to appeal, personally or through a representative, actions of doctors or medical personnel;

to consult doctors who are not subject to the authority of the medical institution where the patient is located;

to be free from compulsory labor even if prescribed for purposes of treatment;

to be free in every case from excessively disturbing contacts with other patients.

15. If a medical institution is specially guarded, patients in this institution should not be subject to forced contact with persons detailed as guards for the whole hospital or its separate departments. Use of convicts as service workers in psychiatric institutions is impermissible if such use will subject patients to enforced contacts with these convicts.

16. Legal restrictions on the rights of persons declared mentally ill or incompetent are permissible only to the extent absolutely necessary for the protection of their rights, for the protection of the rights of others, or for the safety of the public. Such persons should not be subject to restriction of the fundamental civil rights of man, therefore, to any special restriction of their right to marriage or any voluntary sexual activity which does not violate the rights of other persons, although in this regard the law may stipulate special procedures to protect the interests of such persons from abuse.

17. Preventing, against their will, persons declared mentally ill or mentally defective from realizing their inalienable human right of reproduction and also deliberately depriving such persons of their childbearing capacity or fertility, when these actions involve a group of or all such persons, must be viewed by national courts and international tribunals as the crime of genocide; considerations of the eugenic advisa-

bility of such acts must not be regarded by these courts and tribunals as a circumstance removing or lessening responsibility for such acts.

18. The law should recognize the right of association for persons declared mentally ill, including the right to associate with one another, and the law should not restrict their right of association; similarly, the law should not restrict the rights of such persons to free exchange of information, to creative activity, to opinion, to religious freedom, to assembly, and to meetings and demonstrations in any greater measure than these rights are restricted for others.

In particular, one should respect the right of persons declared mentally ill or mentally defective and of their associations to advocate their views on the norms of mental health and full mental development and to achieve by legal means changes in the ideas of society and the state in this regard.

III. Social Questions

The Committee sees serious social danger in a broad interpretation of the concepts "mental illness" and "mental deficiency" while procedures for contesting application of these concepts are far from perfect and when juridical use of these concepts can be an active instrument in restricting rights of individuals or groups. The Committee particularly notes the danger of use of this instrument to limit the right to new ideas by denigrating original or unorthodox scientific, social, political, and philosophical ideas through juridical determination of their authors as mentally ill or incapable of mental creation.

10

The USSR and the Universal Copyright Convention*

Sir:

Presuming your concern that institutions for the international protection of authors' rights should be effective in defending the rights of the authors themselves and not just the rights of the states of the authors' nationality or domicile, and also your concern that these institutions should be beneficial for what is commonly called the advancement of our civilization;

Noting the importance of the Soviet Union's accession to the Universal Copyright Convention;

Taking into account the anxiety of many cultural figures and, in particular, of a number of Moscow intellectuals with respect to possible misinterpretation of the provisions of this Convention;

I wish to call your attention to the significance of the wording of Article 10, paragraph 2 of the Convention: "It is understood, however, that at the time an instrument of

---

* An open letter to the Director General of UNESCO, René Maheu, concerning the USSR's accession to the Universal Copyright Convention.

ratification, acceptance or accession is deposited on behalf of any State, such State must be in a position under its domestic law to give effect to the terms of the Convention."

It is quite interesting to study Soviet legislation from the standpoint of its conformity to provisions of the Convention.

The first reason is the special nature of Soviet law and legal doctrine concerning the protection of civil rights. The Fundamental Principles of Soviet Civil Legislation contains a general norm which can hinder in practice application of the provisions of the Convention; specifically, Article 5 of the Fundamental Principles states: "Civil rights are protected by law with the exception of cases when they are exercised in contradiction to the purpose of these rights in a socialist society during the period of the construction of communism." Despite the existence of a norm establishing the primacy of international law when in conflict with domestic legislation, Article 5 is applied even to cases involving rights stipulated by international convention. I cite for example a dispute of Dr. Boris Zuckermann with the postal administration. In denying Zuckermann's claim to monetary indemnity for loss of international mail by the postal administration, the court decision cited the norm expressed in Article 5 even though the right to receive indemnification in such a case is guaranteed by the Universal Postal Convention.

The second reason is that specific Soviet legislation on authors' rights includes some unusual norms which scarcely correspond to the provisions of the Universal Copyright Convention. For instance, Article 106 of the Fundamental Principles of Civil Legislation provides for "purchase" on a compulsory basis of copyright by the state. There exists a quite real possibility that the state will purchase the copyrights of works which have been written by "dissenting" authors and banned by the domestic censorship, in order to prevent their publication abroad. This will not even burden the state with excessive expense—since the purchase is on a compulsory basis, the state itself will determine the amount of the "fee."

I wish also to call your attention to a terminological defect of the Convention in those sections which discuss "formalities." For instance Article 3 of the Convention provides that a state may require "formalities or other conditions for the acquisition and enjoyment of copyright in respect of works first published in its territory or works of its nationals wherever published."

While it is difficult to predict how onerous for authors will be those formalities which the USSR will establish for copyright protection under the Convention, there is reason to fear an attempt by the state to restrain an author's freedom to disseminate his works. We already know that the new norms for copyright law in the USSR provide: "The procedure by which an author who is a Soviet citizen assigns the right to use his work in the territory of a foreign state is established by legislation of the USSR." Legislation concerning the procedure mentioned has still not been adopted so far as we know, but there is serious apprehension that this legislation will, directly or indirectly, stipulate that an author must receive permission from the state for publication of his works abroad. Is this an objective of the institutions for the international protection of copyright?

Although from the point of view of principle any contradiction between domestic legislation and the spirit and purposes of the Convention is significant, in practice it may turn out to be important what sanctions will be used against an author for attempting to bypass an unlawful prohibition on publication of his works abroad. Under the present liberal arrangements in the USSR, so far as is known, an author is not subject to criminal prosecution for the fact of publication of his works abroad without state permission. Usually in such cases an author encounters difficulties of a professional or administrative nature: exclusion from the Union of Writers, loss of the chance to publish in the USSR, trouble in receiving royalties from abroad. A demand may be made that the author disavow participation in publication abroad, which at times is not difficult for the author, since sometimes the works of Soviet authors are actually published without their consent, and while the Soviet Union is not a member of the Convention, there is no procedure available to the USSR for substantiating the fact of an author's lack of participation.

There exists the danger that in the future the USSR can introduce sanctions more severe than the present ones for publication abroad without the permission of state organs. This fear is based on experience, for it is known that inventors have been subject to criminal punishment for patenting their inventions abroad without the government's permission (see the Decree on Inventions and Technological Improvements, ratified March 5, 1941).

I urge you to foster the study of the dangers which I have noted. At the Twenty-third Congress of the Communist Party of the Soviet Union one delegate expressed the real situation of creative freedom in the USSR in the following words: ". . . in our country everyone who considers himself an artist enjoys the right to create freely, to write freely at his own discretion without the least restriction. But to the same extent, the Party and our state organs enjoy the right to freedom of choice in what to print."

I urge you to encourage the Contracting States of the Convention to study the question, to what degree are they prepared to support the right of the party and state organs of the USSR to select also what is printed abroad?

I urge you also to use your authority for the purposes of providing advisory assistance to the Soviet Union with respect to granting its citizens guarantees protecting their authors' rights against state interference.

Respectfully yours,
V. Chalidze

April 1973

11

The Twenty-fifth Anniversary of the Universal Declaration of Human Rights*

It would be wonderful if, in appraising the twenty-five years of man's history since the adoption of the Universal Declaration of Human Rights, we could speak only of progress in safeguarding human freedom. But history has not brought this about and now we must recall the disappointment of many hopes for securing human rights around the world.

Among the many social problems which have hindered swift progress in this field, there is one which has not received the attention it should. That is the problem of the usage of words.

Judging from the application in practice of international

---

* On December 10-12, 1973, on the twenty-fifth anniversary of the Universal Declaration of Human Rights, a symposium was held in New York under the auspices of the Conference of Non-Governmental Organizations in Consultative Status with the UN. This is the author's speech given there.

legal guarantees for rights, one can see that words often lose their original sense because of an intentional substitution of meaning; the goal behind this substitution often is to alter the meaning of the guarantee which was expressed by the words.

Members of the Moscow Human Rights Committee in their greetings sent to U Thant in 1971 noted that: ". . . the use of force to violate rights is now usually accompanied by a perversion of legal concepts. The longer violence prevails, the more deeply rooted purposely distorted notions of their rights become in the minds of the generation affected."

There are various technical devices for perversion of meaning. Sometimes the international legal instrument itself contains a term so indefinite that it vitiates the guarantee of rights. An example of such a word is "peoples" contained in Article I of both Covenants on human rights. It is not difficult to violate the rights of a national minority group saying that they are not a "people". For example, the Crimean Tatars, deported from their territory under Stalin, consider themselves not simply Tatars but a distinct nationality—Crimean Tatars—and their ethnic distinctness from other Tatars justifies their right to do so. However, in legislative acts of the USSR they are termed: "citizens of Tatar nationality who formerly lived in the Crimea."

Another potentially indefinite term—"mentally retarded" —was included in the Declaration on the Rights of Mentally Retarded Persons; here the lack of precision arises because no procedure is provided for a person to contest the application of this term to himself—fortunately, this problem is not as acute as the problem of the defenselessness of persons declared mentally ill.

In other cases perversion of the meaning of words is a result of the refined logical ingenuity and shrewdness of those who wish to disregard international legal guarantees of human rights. Thus, if an international convention forbids forced labor, workers are subjected to conditions such that they will consider forced labor voluntary. A refusal to volunteer brings difficulties; this possibility exists in the USSR where the urban population is sent to work on farms and if a person does not appear voluntarily, then he may anticipate problems at work or other unpleasantness.

The Russian Tsar Paul I invented a method to subject noblemen to corporal punishment despite the law freeing noblemen from such punishment. He simply deprived those whom he wished to punish of their titles of nobility. A similar method is presently used to safeguard the right of parents to raise their children in conformity with their own moral and religious convictions, a right recognized by an international Convention. A parent who wishes to exercise this right and who does not wish to raise his child in conformity with the moral code of the builders of communism, as Soviet law requires, is simply deprived of his parental rights; this has happened to Baptists who have given their children religious education and most recently to Jews departing for Israel. The word "parent" loses its usual meaning and in practice is replaced by the term "parent by permission of the authorities."

Of course, such perversion of meaning testifies to a certain respect for international legal guarantees. Really, it would be extremely scandalous if in court sentences, for example, they wrote that a person was convicted for signing a petition to the United Nations concerning a violation of human rights. The right of petition to the United Nations is just sufficiently respected that this is not written. Instead, they write, for example: "for dissemination of knowingly false fabrications which defame the Soviet system." But I do not think that this form of respect for the right of petition makes it any easier for those who have been convicted in part for appealing to the UN about the violation of human rights in the USSR. I have in mind Altunyan, Yakir, and Krasin and also those committed on this account to lunatic asylums—Gershuni, Plyushch and Borisov.

In this speech I wish to remind people that the intellectual achievements of our civilization are expressed in, precisely, words. It is difficult to imagine what the beautiful words of the Universal Declaration of Human Rights will come to mean to people of different countries with the passage of time if the perversion of the associated terminology continues in these countries and if this process is not controlled even by public opinion. There is reason to believe that this is a persisting tendency.

This method for justifying evil is convenient and attractive to many; it is sensible at least to study the implications of this danger to civilization.

12

In Defense of
the Crimean Tatars

Letter to Dr. Kurt Waldheim, Secretary General of the United Nations

I should like to call your attention to the fate of the Crimean Tatars (USSR), who until 1944 lived in the Crimea, and were then resettled on the territory of the Uzbek and other Union Republics. To this end I am sending you together with this letter a "Communication on Discrimination against the Crimean Tatars," which I drew up on the basis of facts reflected in Soviet legislation.

I hope that my Communication will be considered in accordance with existing UN procedure for considering private communications on violations of human rights. I further hope that this Communication will be found admissible for such consideration in accordance with the provisional procedure established by Resolution 2 (XXIV), adopted on August 14, 1971, by the Subcommission on Prevention of Discrimination and Protection of Minorities. . . .

So far as I know, the UN documents dealing with the right of petitioning the UN on violations of human rights do not reflect any opinion of the UN or its specialized organizations as to whether petitions to the UN on violations of human rights should, or can, be made public. Profoundly convinced of the desirability of public disclosure in matters pertaining to the defense of human rights, and especially in matters pertaining to the international defense of human rights, I regard this letter, the Communication, and the documents appended thereto as available for publication. In the present instance the publication of these documents is important not only as a matter of principle but also from the practical viewpoint: it may be that when interested and informed persons have read these documents, the United Nations will receive communications from them which may be significant and useful in considering the problem.

In order to facilitate your comprehension of the enclosed documents, I shall conclude this letter with a brief historical note on the Crimean Tatars.

It would appear that the Crimean Tatars are descendants of those who once inhabited a powerful and extensive empire in the south of European Russia. The Crimea had long been the center of that empire; and gradually the Crimean Tatars were concentrated in a part of that peninsula, yielding their northern territories to the expanding Russian Empire. Subsequently the Crimean Khanate ceased to exist, and its territory was annexed to Russia. In accordance with the practice of the Russian Empire in those times, the Crimean Tatars retained their religion (Islam) and, to some extent, their national autonomy.

In the Russian Empire, however, they were aliens and heterodox; and consequently they were subject, from time to time, to experiencing a distrustful attitude toward them on the part of the Russian administration. This distrust was manifested with particular intensity during the Russo-Turkish War in the nineteenth century. According to the *Great Soviet Encyclopedia* (1st ed., 1936), in the autumn of 1854 many Crimean Tatars were resettled from the Black Sea littoral for reasons of security. The author of the article in the *Encyclopedia* writes in this connection:

The emigration of the Tatar working people assumed especially great dimensions in the sixties of the nineteenth century. In the autumn of 1854 the minister of war promulgated an order stating that "the Emperor . . . has commanded that all persons of the Mohammedan faith inhabiting the littoral be resettled to interior provinces." This measure, adopted during the Crimean War for allegedly military reasons, was indispensable to the tsarist government in order to seize the very rich lands of the southern Crimean littoral. The persecution of the Tatars which then began, together with their harassment by the military authorities, because of their supposed espionage, transformed this resettlement into a general exodus. Whole families, and even hordes, emigrated. Hundreds of *auls* [mountain settlements] and villages were emptied of people . . ."

After the establishment of the Soviet regime in Russia, and the formation of the RSFSR, the Autonomous Crimean Soviet Socialist Republic was formed.*

So far as can be judged from Soviet official acts, during the subsequent years the Crimean Tatars followed the same path in the transformation of their way of life as other peoples in the Soviet Union. It must be assumed that the central authority deemed this transformation successful, since the Crimean ASSR (Autonomous Soviet Socialist Republic) was awarded the Order of Lenin. Among other successes in transformation (e.g., the organization of cultural institutions, the development of industry, etc.) I note especially the successes in the collectivization of agriculture, which in the late twenties and early thirties was vigorously implemented throughout the territory of the USSR. According to data for 1933,† in the Crimea "kolkhozes comprised 88 percent of the poor and middle farms." According to data from the *Great Soviet Encyclopedia* (1936), total collectivization of agriculture had been accomplished in the Crimea. I make special note of this, because agriculture

---

* Decree of the All-Union Central Executive Committee and the Council of People's Commissars dated October 18, 1921. Collection of Statutes, 1921, No. 69, Article 556.
† Decree of the All-Union Central Executive Committee dated December 26, 1933.

was the basic occupation of the majority of Crimean Tatars, and because my Communication deals specifically with the rights of kolkhoz members.

During the years of World War II the Crimean Tatars, like other peoples of the USSR, took part in the war against Germany. Detailed data on their role is given in the "Historical Note" appended to the letter of the Crimean Tatars sent to you by the academician Sakharov and other Moscow intellectuals.

After the liberation of the Crimea from German occupation in 1944, the Crimean Tatars—each and every one of them—were resettled from the Crimea to the Uzbek and other Union Republics. From the Preamble to the Ukaz of the Presidium of the USSR Supreme Soviet dated September 5, 1967 (the text of which is given in the first part of my Communication), one can form an idea of the reasons advanced by the authorities as a basis for this measure.

From Professor A. S. Volpin's letter one can form an idea of the conditions obtaining in the areas to which the Crimean Tatars were resettled. Following revocation of the regimen of special settlements (by Ukaz of the Presidium of the USSR Supreme Soviet dated April 28, 1956—unpublished), and until the present day, the Crimean Tatars have demanded with increasing urgency the restoration of their rights to the territory in the Crimea which belongs to them, and restoration of national autonomy. Hundreds of petitions have been sent by the Crimean Tatars to Soviet authorities and to international organizations on the problem of restoring the rights of the Crimean Tatar people; many thousands have signed those petitions. Many Crimean Tatars have been prosecuted for their activities in demanding restoration of the rights of the Crimean Tatar people. The movement of the Crimean Tatars attained great vigor in 1968–69, when their demands were supported by a former major general of the Soviet Army, P. G. Grigorenko, who was arrested in 1969 in Tashkent, where he had gone in order to speak at the trial of a group of Crimean Tatars.

The Crimean Tatars' demands for restoration of their rights were also supported by a Moscow teacher, Ilya Gabai, who was convicted for this activity and served three years in confinement.

Subsequently the demands of the Crimean Tatars were supported by the Moscow Human Rights Committee, which sent to the Presidium of the USSR Supreme Soviet a petition asking that unhindered resettlement of the Crimean Tatars in the Crimea be assured. No answer to this petition was received.

The Crimean Tatars are not only demanding of the authorities that their rights be restored but individual Tatars are actually moving to the Crimea. In the majority of cases, however, they are encountering obstacles set up by the local authorities, who do not issue permits for Crimean Tatars to settle in the Crimea, to purchase homes, or to find employment. These problems are dealt with in detail in the aforementioned letter to you from the Crimean Tatars.

In this brief historical note I have mentioned facts without providing proofs of those facts. This letter is only a covering letter for the enclosed Communication. In the preparation of the letter I was concerned that it (specifically the Communication, and not the covering letter) should be admissible in accordance with the aforementioned Resolution of the Subcommission on Prevention of Discrimination and Protection of Minorities.

In my Communication I speak only of the rights of a part of the Crimean Tatar people. I hope that consideration by the United Nations of other documents on this question, including the aforementioned letter to you from the Crimean Tatars, supported by Sakharov and others, will facilitate a solution of the problem of the Crimean Tatars' return to the Crimea.

Most respectfully,
Valery Chalidze

June 3, 1974

P.S. I have provided English translations of the Russian originals of all documents. My name may be disclosed.

A Communication on Discrimination Against Some Crimean Tatars

On September 5, 1967, the Presidium of the USSR Supreme Soviet promulgated a Ukaz "On Citizens of Tatar Nationality formerly inhabiting the Crimea" (*Gazette of the USSR Supreme Soviet*, 1967, No. 36):

After the liberation of the Crimea from the Fascist occupation in 1944, instances of active collaboration with the German usurpers of a section of the Tatars living in the Crimea were groundlessly leveled at the entire Tatar population of the Crimea. These unfounded charges against all citizens of Tatar nationality who had formerly resided in the Crimea must be withdrawn, all the more so since a new generation has entered the working and political life of society.

The Presidium of the USSR Supreme Soviet has resolved:

1. To revoke the pertinent Resolutions of State organs insofar as they contain unfounded charges against citizens of Tatar nationality who had formerly resided in the Crimea.

2. To note that the Tatars who had previously lived in the Crimea have taken root on the territory of the Uzbek and other Union Republics; that they enjoy all the rights of Soviet citizens, take part in public and political life, elect deputies to the Supreme Soviets and local Soviets of deputies of working people, hold responsible positions in Soviet, economic, and Party organs; that radio broadcasts are produced for them, a newspaper is published in their national language, and other cultural measures are being undertaken.

With the aim of further developing regions with a Tatar population, to instruct the Councils of Ministers of Union Republics to continue rendering aid and assistance to citizens of Tatar nationality in economic and cultural development, taking into account their national interests and traits.

We learn why "citizens of Tatar nationality who had formerly resided in the Crimea" found themselves on the territory of the Uzbek and other Union republics from the

RSFSR Law dated June 25, 1946 (*Izvestia*, June 28, 1946).*

LAW CONCERNING THE ABOLITION OF THE CHECHEN-INGUSH AUTONOMOUS SOVIET SOCIALIST REPUBLIC AND THE CHANGING OF THE CRIMEAN AUTONOMOUS SOVIET SOCIALIST REPUBLIC INTO THE CRIMEAN OBLAST

During the Great Patriotic War, when the peoples of the USSR were heroically defending the honor and independence of the Fatherland in the struggle against the German-Fascist invaders, many Chechens and Crimean Tatars, at the instigation of German agents, joined volunteer units organized by the Germans and, together with German troops, engaged in armed struggle against units of the Red Army; also at the bidding of the Germans they formed diversionary bands for the struggle against Soviet authority in the rear; meanwhile the main mass of the population of the Chechen-Ingush and Crimean ASSRs took no counteraction against these betrayers of the Fatherland.

In connection with this, the Chechens and the Crimean Tatars were resettled in other regions of the USSR, where they were given land, together with the necessary governmental assistance for their economic establishment. On the proposal of the Presidium of the RSFSR Supreme Soviet the Chechen-Ingush ASSR was abolished and the Crimean ASSR was changed into the Crimean oblast by decrees of the Presidium of the USSR Supreme Soviet.

The Supreme Soviet of the Russian Soviet Federative Socialist Republic resolves:

1) To confirm the abolition of the Chechen-Ingush ASSR and the changing of the Crimean ASSR into the Crimean oblast.

2) To make the necessary alterations and additions to Article 14 of the RSFSR Constitution.

Chairman of the Presidium of the RSFSR Supreme Soviet— I. Vlasov

* Previously, on June 30, 1945, the Presidium of the USSR Supreme Soviet had published a Ukaz on the change of the Crimean ASSR into the Crimean oblast.

Secretary of the Presidium of the RSFSR Supreme Soviet
—P. Bakhmurov

Moscow, The Kremlin, June 25, 1946

It is characteristic that in the cited law these citizens are called *Crimean Tatars*—later legislation avoided use of that term.

Although this did not follow from the name of the Crimean ASSR, judging from this Law and other indications, the Crimean ASSR was the national autonomous area of the Crimean Tatars, even though they, like many other peoples with a national autonomous area, did not constitute a majority on the territory of their autonomous republic. Autonomous republics in the USSR are created specifically as national, and not as territorial, autonomous areas. And the basic indication of the nationality which enjoys autonomy by virtue of the founding of the autonomous republic, is the language (in addition to the Russian and republic language—if the latter is not Russian) which is used as an official tongue in that autonomous republic. According to the 1921 Constitution of the Crimean Republic, "Russian and Tatar are recognized" as the official languages of the Crimean Republic. Also testifying to this fact is the Decree of the Crimean Central Executive Committee and Council of People's Commissars on the Tatarization of state organs (*Krasnyy Krym* [Red Crimea], No. 36, February 14, 1922).

It is not known under what normative act the resettlement of the Crimean Tatars was effected. Judging from another case of the deportation of a people—the case of the Volga Germans—one may assume that this act was, and has remained, unpublished: the Ukaz of August 29, 1964,* by which the Presidium of the USSR Supreme Soviet withdrew the "unfounded charges" against the Volga Germans, mentions an Ukaz of the Presidium of the USSR Supreme Soviet dated August 28, 1941, and refers to the "protocol

* See *Sbornik zakonov SSR* (Compilation of Laws of the USSR) (Moscow, 1968), I, 165.

of a session of the Presidium of the USSR Supreme Soviet, 1941, No. 9, p. 256" (but not to any publication where this Ukaz might have appeared).

It is known that certain other peoples, including certain Islamic peoples of the northern Caucasus, were subjected to resettlement like the Crimean Tatars and the Volga Germans. Subsequently, however, their rights to the territory which had historically belonged to them were restored.

Here again the acts in question were not published. However, this generally known fact can be confirmed by the depositions of witnesses, and indirectly by examining changes in the USSR Constitution.

The text of the 1936 USSR Constitution, Article 22, states with respect to the Autonomous Republics and Regions that:

. . . the Russian Soviet Federative Socialist Republic consists of . . . the Tatar, Bashkir, Daghestan, Buryat-Mongolian, Kabardinian-Balkar, Kalmyk, Karelian, Komi, Crimean, Mari, Mordovian, Volga German, North Ossetian, Udmurt, Checheno-Ingush, Chuvash, and Yakut Autonomous Soviet Socialist Republics, and the Adygei, Jewish, Karachai, Oyrot, Khakass, and Cherkess Autonomous Regions.

On February 27, 1947 the Supreme Soviet passed a law amending and supplementing the text of the USSR Constitution. Deputy A. Vyshinsky, in his published report on the amendments to the Constitution, did not mention the fact that certain Autonomous Republics and Regions had disappeared from the list in Article 22.

In its 1947 redaction, Article 22 states in particular:

The Russian Soviet Federative Socialist Republic consists of . . . the Tatar, Bashkirian, Daghestan, Buryat-Mongolian, Kabardinian, Komi, Mari, Mordovian, North Ossetian, Udmurt, Chuvash, and Yakut Autonomous Soviet Socialist Republics, and the Adygei, Jewish, Oyrot, Tuva, Khakass, and Cherkess Autonomous Regions.

The 1968 edition of *Sbornik zakonov SSSR* includes a text of the Constitution in which Article 22 states with respect to the Autonomous Republics:

The Russian Soviet Federative Socialist Republic comprises the Bashkirian, Buryat, Daghestan, Kabardinian-Balkar, Kalmyk, Karelian, Komi, Mari, Mordovian, North Ossetian, Tatar, Tuva, Udmurt, Checheno-Ingush, Chuvash, and Yakut Autonomous Soviet Socialist Republics, and the Adygei, Gorny Altai, Jewish, Karachai-Cherkess, and Khakass Autonomous Regions.

This comparison makes evident: 1) the transformation of the Kabardinian-Balkar ASSR into the Kabardian and then back to the Kabardinian-Balkar confirms the known fact of the resettlement and return of the Balkars; 2) the disappearance from the 1947 text, and the subsequent restoration, of the Kalmyk ASSR and the Chechen-Ingush ASSR confirms a similar conclusion with respect to the Kalmyks and Chechen-Ingushes; 3) the disappearance from the 1947 text of the Karachai Autonomous Region, and the appearance in the present text of the Karachai-Cherkess Autonomous Region (the territory of the Karachai Autonomous Region was transferred to Georgia; however, after the return of the Karachais this territory was transferred back to the RSFSR*); 4) the disappearance of the Crimean ASSR (subsequently, in 1954, the territory of the Crimean ASSR was transferred to the Ukrainian SSR).

I maintain that the involuntary resettlement of certain peoples of the USSR at a time when other peoples were left on their historical territories constitutes discrimination on the basis of nationality. Further, that this discrimination involved restrictions of rights by virtue of the fact that there were violations of the rights of these nationalities to retain their homes, to freedom of movement and choice of domicile, and other rights, including property rights. However, this fact of discrimination does not constitute the subject of the present Communication.

---

* See the Ukaz of the Presidium of the USSR Supreme Soviet dated March 14, 1955, on the transfer of the Klukhorsky Region of the Georgian SSR to the RSFSR, *Sbornik zakonov SSSR*, 1959, p. 58.

I maintain that now, after the territorial rights of certain previously resettled peoples have been restored, discrimination on the basis of nationality is being practiced against the Crimean Tatars in particular, since no measures have been taken to make available to them, for purposes of residence, that territory from which they were resettled. In the Ukaz of 1967 cited *supra*, it was noted that in the opinion of the Presidium of the USSR Supreme Soviet the Crimean Tatars had *taken root* on the territory of the Uzbek SSR. Even if such were the fact, they should nonetheless be *granted the right* to return to the territory in the Crimea which has historically belonged to them. And the opinion of the Presidium of the USSR Supreme Soviet that they have taken root in the Uzbek and other Union Republics should only prevent a new forcible resettlement of the Crimean Tatars.

In lieu of publishing an Act granting the Crimean Tatars the *right* to return to the Crimea (or in lieu of taking measures to aid them in such return), the Presidium of the USSR Supreme Soviet passed a Decree to the effect that "citizens of Tatar nationality who formerly lived in the Crimea, and the members of their families, enjoy, like all citizens of the USSR, the right to live anywhere on the territory of the Soviet Union, in conformity with current legislation on employment and the passport system."*

This means that the Crimean Tatars do not enjoy a *preferential right* to resettle in the Crimea, in contradistinction to those peoples of the Northern Caucasus who were granted a *preferential opportunity* to return to the territory from which they had previously been forcibly resettled. The mention of the legislation on employment and the passport system means that the Crimean Tatars do not have *any greater rights* to resettlement in the Crimea than other citizens of the USSR; i.e., like all other citizens of the USSR, they must receive permission from the local authorities in the form of a residence permit to live in the Crimea. And the residence permit may be refused (as often happens in practice) on the grounds that the applicant does not have regular

* Decree of September 5, 1967, *Sbornik zakonov SSSR*, 1968, I, 167.

employment in the given locality. But regular employment can be obtained only by a person who has a permit to reside in the given locality. I mention this as a generally known fact, and I am prepared to present witnesses to confirm information about this fact. (Acts on the passport system and the procedure for obtaining a residence permit are not published. But it is known that in the USSR, living without a residence permit in localities where this is required—including the Crimean oblast—is criminally punishable under Article 196 of the Ukrainian SSR Criminal Code and the corresponding articles of the criminal codes of other Union Republics.)

It is not difficult to list many rights which are being violated by this discrimination against the Crimean Tatars as compared with persons of other nationalities whose rights were not violated by forcible resettlement or whose rights were restored after forcible resettlement. Analysis shows, however, that for the most part either these violated rights of the Crimean Tatars were not guaranteed by Soviet law (e.g., the right to the restoration of violated national autonomy), or the claims based on them may be regarded as extinguished by statutory limitation (e.g., the right to personal property, including homes, left in the Crimea at the time of forcible resettlement).

Hence in this Communication, by way of substantiating the fact of a discriminatory violation of the rights of the Crimean Tatars, I might have had recourse to the general principles of international law on human rights. But I am reluctant to do this, since many states view these principles as having no binding force—at least in those cases where a critic is trying to apply such principles to their internal problems.

Therefore, in an endeavor to touch only upon violations of a right guaranteed by Soviet law (and, moreover, of such a kind that claims based on it are not extinguished by statutory limitation), I shall speak not of the violation of the rights of all the forcibly resettled Crimean Tatars but only of violation of the rights of a certain part of that people; i.e., those Tatars who were members of kolkhozes (collective farms) and, more specifically, of kolkhozes in which

Crimean Tatars constituted more than one-third of the total membership.

Article 8 of the USSR Constitution states: "The land occupied by the collective farms is made over to them for their free use for an unlimited time, that is, in perpetuity."

Like all other kolkhoz members, the Crimean Tatars who were members of kolkhozes had the right to use this land, together with all other kolkhoz members, *conveyed to them in perpetuity.* And they had the right to the personal use of a *personal plot of land* granted to a kolkhoz household in accordance with the USSR Constitution (Article 7).

In accordance with the Model Charter for an agricultural artel (Decree of the USSR Council of Ministers and the Central Committee of the All-Union Communist Party [Bolshevik] dated February 17, 1935), which was in force in 1944, expulsion from an agricultural artel (kolkhoz) "can be effected *only* [italics added] by resolution of a general meeting of the artel members attended by no less than two-thirds of the total number of artel members." This means that if more than one-third of the members of a kolkhoz were Tatars, they could not, after their resettlement from the Crimea, have been expelled from the membership of the kolkhoz, since it would have been impossible to call a general meeting attended by no less than two-thirds of the kolkhoz members. Consequently, they remained members of those same kolkhozes to which land in the Crimea had been conveyed *in perpetuity.* Consequently, as members of the kolkhoz they have a right to a personal plot on that land, and a right to a dwelling (in accordance with the USSR Constitution, Article 7). Consequently, they have a preferential (as compared to other Soviet citizens) right to settle in the Crimea (or, more accurately, to return to the Crimea), and the nonrecognition of that preferential right by the Presidium of the USSR Supreme Soviet (Ukaz of September 5, 1967) means discrimination against the Crimean Tatars as compared to persons of those nationalities whose preferential right to return to their territories was recognized.

My Communication on the discriminatory violation of the

rights of the Crimean Tatars has to do with only a part of that people. It would be wonderful if the consultative good offices of the UN prompted the Soviet Union to grant all Crimean Tatars the *right* to return to their territory in the Crimea. This would correspond to that principle whose embodiment in the Covenants on human rights the Soviet Union has insistently advocated: "In no case may a people be deprived of its own means of subsistence."

But even if such a general solution of the problem is not reached immediately, I hope that the consultative good offices of the UN would suffice for the Soviet Union to recognize the right of that category of Crimean Tatars of which I have spoken in this Communication to return to the Crimea. Their right to return is guaranteed by Soviet laws, and according to the Constitution the claims based thereupon cannot be extinguished by statutory limitation.

Valery Chalidze

NOTES

Abbreviations

CCE—*A Chronicle of Current Events*, a samizdat journal which has been published in Moscow since 1968, with a hiatus between late 1972 and the spring of 1974. The contents of the first eleven issues were published in somewhat abbreviated and rearranged form in *Uncensored Russia*, edited by Peter Reddaway (London and New York, 1972). Issues number 16 to 27 were translated into English and published by Amnesty International, London.

CHR—*A Chronicle of Human Rights in the USSR*, published by Khronika Press, New York.

M.—Moscow.

OGIZ—State United Publishing Houses.

Sb. zak.—*Sbornik zakonov* (Compilation of Laws).

Sobr. soch.—*Sobraniye sochinenii* (Collected Works).

Sobr. zak.—*Sobraniye zakonov* (Collected Laws).

Sobr. uzak.—*Sobraniye uzakonenii* (Collection of Statutes).

SP—*Social Problems*, a samizdat journal edited by Valery Chalidze in Moscow from 1968 to 1972.

Chapter 1, The Specifics of Soviet Law

1. Lenin, V. I., *Sobr. soch.*, XLIV, 398.

2. See, for example, the Decree on the Courts, Nov. 24, 1917, *Sobr. uzak.*, No. 4, Article 50.

3. *XXII sezd KPSS, Stenograficheskiy otchet* (A Stenographic Report of the 22nd Congress of the CPSU), M., 1962, III, 229.

4. Aleksandrov, N. G. et al., *Teoriya gosudarstva i prava* (Theory of the State and Law), M., 1968, p. 619.

5. Lenin, V. I., *State and Revolution, Sobr. soch.*, 4th ed., XXVI.

6. Decree of the Presidium of the USSR Central Executive Committee, Dec. 1, 1934, "On the Conduct of Cases Involving the Preparation of Execution of Terrorist Acts" (revoked in 1956).

7. Decree of the USSR Central Executive Committee dated Sept. 14, 1937, *Sotsialisticheskaya zakonnost* (Socialist Legality), No. 61, 1937.

8. Decree of the USSR Central Executive Committee and the Council of People's Commissars dated Nov. 5, 1934, *Sobr. uzak.*, 1935, No. 11, p. 84.

9. See, for example, Fundamental Principles of Criminal Procedure, Article 10, *Sb. zak.*, M., 1968, II, 554.

10. See Fundamental Principles of Civil Procedure, Article 47, *Sb. zak.*, II, 542.

11. "Decree on the Red Banner of the Police," *Sistematicheskoye sobraniye zakonov RSFSR* (Systematic Collection of the Laws of the RSFSR). . . , M., 1967, XIV, 406.

12. Constitution of the USSR, Article 126.

13. *Ustav KPSS, XXII sezd KPSS* (Rules of the CPSU: 22nd Congress of the CPSU), M., 1962.

14. Ibid.

15. See, for example, *Izvestia*, No. 146, 1973.

16. Constitution of the RSFSR, 1918, *Sb. zak.* I, 44.

17. Constitution of the USSR Adopted by the Eighth Extraordinary Congress of Soviets of the USSR, Dec. 5, 1936.

18. Fundamental Principles of Civil Procedure, Article 7, *Sb. zak.*, II, 529.

19. Cited in *Ugolovnoye pravo, chast osobennaya* (Criminal Law: Special Part), A. A. Gershenzon and A. A. Pionkovsky, eds., M., 1939.

20. Fundamental Principles of Labor Law, Article 94, *Sb. zak.*, III, 222.

21. Discrimination (Employment and Occupation) Convention, 1958. Ratified by the USSR in 1961.

22. "On Criminal Liability for State Crimes," law of Dec. 25, 1958, *Sb. zak.*, II, 450.

23. *Nauchno-prakticheskiy commentariy ugolovnogo kodeksa RSFSR* (Scientific-Practical Commentary on the RSFSR Criminal Code), ed. V. S. Nikiforov, M., 1963.

24. *Vedomosti Verkhovnogo Soveta SSSR* (Gazette of the USSR Supreme Soviet), No. 52, 1972; cf. also CHR, No. 1.

25. Decree of the USSR Council of Ministers, Sept. 22, 1970, No. 803.

26. *Proceedings of the Moscow Human Rights Committee*, The International League for the Rights of Man, New York, 1972.

27. *The Demonstration in Pushkin Square*, Pavel Litvinov, ed., Gambit, Boston, and Harvill Press, London, 1969.

28. Fundamental Principles of Criminal Legislation, Article 14, *Sb. zak.*, II, 431.

29. *Kurs ugolovnogo prava* (A Course in Criminal Law), N. A. Belyayev and M. D. Shargorodsky, eds., Leningrad, 1968, Part I, p. 536.

30. Fundamental Principles of Civil Legislation, Article 14, *Sb. zak.* II, 360. Report of the Civil Cassational Collegium for 1962, *Sb. razyasn. verkh. suda RSFSR* (Compilation of Interpretations of the RSFSR Supreme Court), M., 1930.

31. Decree of the Central Executive Committee and the Council of People's Commissars "on the Protection of the Property of State Enterprises, Kolkhozes, and Cooperatives . . . ," Aug. 7, 1932, *Sb. zak.*, 1932, No. 62, p. 360.

32. Ukaz of the Presidium of the USSR Supreme Soviet "On Criminal Liability for the Theft of State and Public Property," June 4, 1947, *Vedomosti Verkhovnogo Soveta SSSR*, No. 19, 1947.

33. CHR, No. 1 and 5-6.

34. Lenin, V. I., *Sobr. soch.*, LII, 40.

35. Quoted from Evreinov's book, *Istoriya telesnykh nakazaniy v Rossii* (A History of Corporal Punishment in Russia).

36. Constitution of the USSR, Article 133.

37. "On Criminal Liability for Military Crimes," law of Dec. 25, 1958, Article 28, *Sb. zak.* II, 469.

38. Arkady Belinkov, Letter to the Congress of the International PEN Club, 1968.

39. Constitution of the USSR, Articles 49 and 56.

40. Svetlana Alliluyeva, *Only One Year*, Harper & Row, New York, 1969.

41. From a personal communication to the author.

42. See note 4, p. 620.

43. Fundamental Principles of Health Legislation, Article 3, *Sb. zak.*, III, 117.

44. Constitution of Panama, Article 63.

45. Kuchinsky, V. A., *Lichnost, svoboda, pravo* (The Person, Freedom, Law), M., 1969, p. 72.

46. See note 29, p. 480.

47. "Decree on Comrades' Courts," *Vedomosti Verkhovnogo Soveta SSSR*, 1961, No. 26; 1962, No. 9; 1963, No. 43; 1965, No. 83.

48. "Decree on the Volunteer People's Druzhiny . . . ," *Sistematicheskoye sobraniye zakonov RSFSR* . . . , XIV, 531.

49. CCE, Nos. 8, 9, 11.

50. "On the Responsibility of Agencies and Officials for Disclosing the Names of Worker and Peasant Correspondents after Receiving Letters and Notes of Such Correspondents from Newspaper Editors," Circular of the RSFSR Supreme Court, No. 6, Jan. 3, 1935, *Sb. razyasn. Verkhovnogo Suda*, 1935, p. 212. "On Measures to Combat and Prevent the Criminal Prosecution of Worker Correspondents," Circular of the People's Commissariat of Justice, No. 3, Jan. 6, 1926, *Sb. tsir. NKYu deistv. na 1 maya 1934* (Compilation of Circulars of the People's Commissariat of Justice in Force as of May 1, 1934). See also Circular of the Procurator of the USSR, Dec. 3, 1933, *Za sots. zak.* (For Socialist Legality), 1934; No. 1, Circular of the Procurator of the USSR, June 17, 1935, *Za sots. zak.*, 1935, No. 8.

51. Decree of the Council of People's Commissars, Dec. 8, 1926, *Sobr. uzak.* 1926, No. 88.

52. Circular of the People's Commissariat of Justice No. 81, May 3, 1927, *Sb. tsirk. NKYu deistv. na 1 maya 1934*.

53. Ukaz of the Presidium of the USSR Supreme Soviet, Feb. 15, 1962, *Sb. zak.*, II, 473.

54. See note 27.

55. See the record of the public denunciation in the Gerlin case, in *Politicheskiy dnevnik* (Political Diary), No. 43, p. 361, Alexander Herzen Foundation, Amsterdam, 1972. See also, Yury Aikhenvald, *Po grani ostroy* (Along the Sharp Edge), Echo Press, Munich, 1972.

56. See Yury Aikhenvald, note 55.

57. Lapin, Vladimir, "On the Abolition of the Death Penalty," samizdat, M., 1972.

58. Ukaz "On the Abolition of the Death Penalty," May 25, 1947, *Vedomosti Verkhovnogo Soveta SSSR*, 1947, No. 1.

59. Ukaz of Jan. 12, 1950, *Vedomosti Verkhovnogo Soveta SSSR*, 1956, No. 3.

60. CHR, No. 5-6.

61. *Sb. razyasn. Verkh. suda RSFSR*, M., 1936, p. 55.

62. Verdict of the Tashkent court in the Adelheim case, SP, No. 14, M., 1971.

63. CCE, No. 27.

64. SP, No. 2, 1969.

65. *Belomoro-Baltiyskiy kanal imeni Stalina. Istoriya stroitelstva* (The Stalin White-Sea-to-the-Baltic Canal: The History of a Construction Project), ed. Maxim Gorky and others, OGIZ, 1934, p. 599.

66. Protocol of the Supreme Court, No. 7, May 20, 1930, *Sb. razyasn. Verkh. suda RSFSR*, M., 1936.

67. The Convention on the Non-Applicability of Statutory Limitations to War Crimes and Crimes against Humanity.

Chapter 2, The Soviet Union and International Conventions

1. The basic international conventions on human rights ratified by the Soviet Union are:

The Convention on the Prevention and Punishment of the Crime of Genocide, adopted in 1948 and ratified by the Soviet Union in 1954.

The Discrimination (Employment and Occupation) Convention, adopted in 1958 and ratified by the Soviet Union in 1961.

The Convention against Discrimination in Education, adopted in 1960 and ratified by the Soviet Union in 1962.

The International Convention on the Elimination of All Forms of Racial Discrimination, adopted in 1965 and ratified by the Soviet Union in 1969.

The Slavery Convention (1926) and the Protocol Amending the Slavery Convention (1953) ratified by the Soviet Union in 1956.

The Supplementary Convention on the Abolition of Slavery, the Slave Trade, and Institutions and Practices Similar to Slavery, adopted in 1956 and ratified by the Soviet Union in 1957.

The Convention Concerning Forced or Compulsory Labor, adopted in 1930 and ratified by the Soviet Union in 1956.

The International Covenant on Economic, Social, and Cultural Rights, adopted in 1966 and ratified by the Soviet Union in 1973.

The International Covenant on Civil and Political Rights, adopted in 1966 and ratified by the Soviet Union in 1973.

2. See Boris Zuckermann, Letter to the Editors of *Izvestia*, SP, No. 1; and Alexander Volpin, "Duty or Obligation," SP, No. 8.

3. For information concerning ratifications of human rights conventions, see *Human Rights Journal*, Paris, Vol. V, No. 4, 1972.

4. The General Assembly, A/8991, Jan. 4, 1973.

5. Cf. *Sb. zak.*, Vols. II and III.

6. See note 1.

7. See note 2.

8. CHR, No. 2.

9. Documents in the case of Zuckermann vs. the International Post Office, samizdat, M. See also Zhores Medvedev, *The Medvedev Papers*, St. Martin's Press, New York, 1972.

10. A list of the informational items forbidden to be published in the open press or transmitted via radio or television. Not published in the "open press."

11. See note 1.

12. See note 5.

13. See note 1.

14. SP, No. 5.

15. *Vedomosti Verkhovnogo Soveta SSSR*, 1972, No. 52; CHR, Nos. 1 and 2.

16. *Vedomosti Verkhovnogo Soveta SSSR*, 1955, No. 9.

Chapter 3, The Movement for the Defense of Human Rights in the USSR

1. See Roy Medvedev, *On Socialist Democracy*, Knopf, New York, 1975.

2. *On trial*, Max Hayward, ed., Harper & Row, New York, 1966.

3. Marchenko, Anatoly, *My Testimony*, Dutton, New York, 1969.

4. *The Chronicle of Current Events* has been published in English translation by Amnesty International in London. See also Peter Reddaway, ed., *Uncensored Russia*, McGraw-Hill, New York, 1972.

5. CCE, Nos. 1, 2, 4, 5, 6, 8-16, 18, 19, 21-27; CHR, Nos. 1-4. See also Peter Yakir's memoirs, *A Childhood in Prison*, Coward, McCann & Geoghegan, New York, 1972; Macmillan, London, 1972; and Peter Grigorenko's *Mysli sumasshedshego* (The Thoughts of a Madman), Alexander Herzen Foundation, Amsterdam, 1973.

6. See Natalya Gorbanevskaya, *Red Square at Noon*, Holt, Rinehart and Winston, New York, 1972. For The First Appeal of the Initiative Group, see CCE, No. 8.

7. SP, No. 8, 1970. See also *Proceedings of the Moscow Human Rights Committee*, The International League for the Rights of Man, New York, 1972.

8. Natalya Gorbanevskaya printed Yakobson's letter at the end of her book. See note 6.

9. Decree of the All-Union Central Executive Committee, Jan. 6, 1918, "On the Dissolution of the Constituent Assembly."

10. See note 1.

11. *Vekhi* (Landmarks), M., 1909, p. 143.

Chapter 4, Freedom of Speech, of the Press, of Assembly, and of Association

1. The 1947 Constitution of Japan, Article 19.

2. The law on criminal liability for crimes against the state, Article 26, *Sb. zak.*, Vol. II.

3. Berger, Joseph, *Shipwreck of a Generation*, Harvill Press, London, 1971, pp. 178-179.

4. The Constitution of the USSR, Article 125.

5. See *The Demonstration in Pushkin Square*, Pavel Litvinov, ed., Gambit, Boston, and Harvill Press, London, 1969; and Natalya Gorbanevskaya's *Red Square at Noon*, Holt, Rinehart and Winston, New York, 1972.

6. Mikhaylov, M. P., and V. V. Nazarov, *Ideologicheskaya diversiya—orudiye imperializma* (Ideological Sabotage: A Weapon of Imperialism), M., 1969.

7. *Sessiya VASKhNIL 1948, stenogr. otchet* (A Stenographic Report of the 1948 Session of the V. I. Lenin All-Union Academy of Agricultural Sciences), M., 1948.

8. *XXII sezd KPSS, stenogr. otchet*, M., 1962.

9. *Politicheskiy dnevnik*, No. 33, p. 280, Alexander Herzen Foundation, Amsterdam, 1972.

10. See note 8, III, 121.

11. See Peter Yakir, *A Childhood in Prison*, Coward, McCann & Geoghegan, New York, 1972; Macmillan, London, 1972.

12. *Ustav KPSS, XXII sezd KPSS* (Rules of the CPSU: 22nd Congress of the CPSU), M., 1962, p. 355.

13. Lenin, *Doklad na sedmom sezde RKP(b)* (Report to the Seventh Session of the Russian Communist Party [Bolsheviks]).

14. *Gosudarstvennoye pravo SSSR* (The State Law of the USSR), Prof. S. S. Kravchuk, ed., M., 1967, p. 216.

15. Ibid., p. 222.

16. The RSFSR Civil Code, p. 479.

17. Commentary on the RSFSR Civil Code, E. A. Fleyshits and O. S. Ioffe, eds., M., 1970, p. 708.

18. *XXIII sezd KPSS, stenogr. otchet*, M., 1967.

19. Apparently many norms on this system of permission have not been published. See, for example, the Decree of the Council of People's Commissars dated June 21, 1935, "On the Manufacture and Use of Stamps."

20. Chalidze, Valery, Letter to the Director General of UNESCO (CHR 2); Schwartz, A., "The State of Publishing, Censorship, and Copyright in the Soviet Union," *Publishers Weekly*, Jan. 15, 1973.

21. "Decree on the Main Administration for Literature and Publishing . . . ," Council of People's Commissars RSFSR, June 6, 1931, *Sobr. uzak.*, No. 31, Article 273.

22. Ibid.

23. *Osnovnye direktivy i zakonodatelstvo o pechati* (Basic Directives and Legislation on the Press), compiled by L. G. Fogelvich, OGIZ, 1935, p. 117.

24. *Politicheskiy dnevnik* (Political Diary), No. 9, p. 53, Alexander Herzen Foundation, Amsterdam, 1972.

25. For example, in the book listed in note 23, on the last page: "Glavlit Agent No. B-13909." Books published today bear only a letter and a number: "A-04983" in the book cited in note 14.

26. Medvedev, Zhores, *The Medvedev Papers*, St. Martin's Press, New York, 1972.

27. See note 6, p. 25.

28. Zuckermann, Boris, "Looking at the Law," M., samizdat, 1969.

29. See note 26, p. 455.

30. CCE, No. 9.

31. CCE, No. 26.

32. CHR, No. 1.

33. CCE, No. 27.

34. Ukaz of the Presidium of the RSFSR Supreme Soviet dated April 7, 1960, *Vedemosti Verkhovnogo Soveta RSFSR*, 1960, No. 13.

35. CHR, No. 3; Decree of the Plenum of the USSR Supreme Court, July 3, 1963.

36. Record of Alexander Volpin's testimony before a congressional committee: *Abuse of Psychiatry for Political Repression in the Soviet Union*, Hearing before the Internal Security Subcommittee of the United States Senate, Sept. 26, 1972. U.S. Government Printing Office, Washington, D.C., 1972.

37. CCE, No. 25 (the case of Y. Brind).

38. See CHR, No. 3, p. 65.

39. *Sobraniye postanovleniy pravitelstva SSSR* (Collection of Decrees of the USSR Government), 1972, No. 14.

40. *Vedemosti Verkhovnogo Soveta SSSR*, 1973, No. 30.

41. Fundamental Principles of Legislation on Marriage and the Family, Article 19, *Sb. zak.*, III, 316.

42. Commentary to the Code on Marriage and the Family, M., 1971, p. 92.

43. Cf., for example, "Instructions on the Procedure for Awarding Academic Degrees and Academic Titles," *Byulleten Ministerstva vyschego obrazovaniya* (Bulletin of the Ministry of Higher Education), August, 1972. See also CHR, No. 5-6, on the Fedoseyev case.

Chapter 5, Freedom of Movement

1. Decree on Protecting the National Boundary of the USSR, *Sb. zak.*, I, 659.

2. RSFSR Criminal Code, p. 209.

3. Commentary on the Criminal Code, M., 1971, p. 445.

4. See note 2, p. 198.

5. *XVI sezd VKPB(b), stenogr. otchet* (Stenographic Report of the Sixteenth Congress of the All-Union Communist Party [Bolsheviks]), M., 1931 (Yakovlev's report).

6. CHR, No. 5-6.

7. See CCE, No. 23.

8. CHR, No. 3, p. 22.

9. Fundamental Principles of Civil Legislation, Article 9, *Sb. zak.*, Vol. II.

10. SP, No. 5.

11. Decree on entering the USSR and leaving the USSR, confirmed decree of the USSR Council of Ministers No. 801, Sept., 1970.

12. "On Criminal Liability for State Crimes," law of Dec. 25, 1958, *Sb. zak*, Articles 20 and 21.

13. Ibid., Article 1.

14. See note 11, Article 18.

15. Decree on the Bar of the RSFSR, *Sistematicheskoye sobraniye zakonov RSFSR . . .* , XIV, 811.

16. CCE, Nos. 16-18, 21.

17. See *Harvard Civil Rights–Civil Liberties Law Review,* 1973, Vol. 8, No. 1.

18. See CHR, No. 3.

19. Ibid., p. 35.

20. Fundamental Principles of Criminal Procedure, Article 39, *Sb. zak.*, Vol. II; RSFSR Code of Criminal Procedure, Article 246.

21. Summary Law on the Requisitioning and Confiscation of Property, 1928.

Chapter 6, The Price of Freedom

1. CCE, No. 15.
2. "On the Concept 'Political Prisoner,'" a paper prepared by the author for the Human Rights Committee, SP, No. 15.
3. CCE, No. 23.
4. The law "Concerning Criminal Liability for Crimes against the State," Article 7, RSFSR Criminal Code, Article 70.
5. Lenin, V. I., *Sobr. soch.*, 4th ed., XXXIII, 321.
6. RSFSR Criminal Code, Article 190–1.
7. Ibid., Articles 142, 227.
8. See Natalya Gorbanevskaya, *Red Square at Noon*, Holt, Rinehart and Winston, New York, 1972.
9. CHR, No. 1, p. 41.
10. See CCE, No. 11.
11. CCE, No. 22.
12. See CCE, No. 25.
13. See note 9.
14. SP, No. 7.
15. See *Politicheskiy dnevnik* (Political Diary), p. 361, Alexander Herzen Foundation, Amsterdam, 1972.
16. SP, No. 14.
17. Ibid.
18. See Appendix 5.
19. CHR, No. 1, pp. 9-10.
20. See CHR, No. 2.
21. RSFSR Code of Criminal Procedure, Article 47.
22. Ibid., Article 245.
23. Marchenko, Anatoly, *My Testimony*, Dutton, New York, 1969.
24. *Kazakhstan pravda*, March 14, 1973; CHR, No. 2, p. 55.
25. RSFSR Corrective-Labor Code.
26. Ibid.
27. See, for example, A. Ye. Natashev and N. A. Struchkov, *Osnovy teorii ispravitelno-trudovogo prava* (Fundamental Principles of Corrective-Labor Law), M., 1967, p. 136.
28. Decree of the Presidium of the USSR Supreme Soviet dated July 26, 1966, *Sb. zak.* II, 485.
29. Ukaz of the Presidium of the RSFSR Supreme Soviet dated June 7, 1972.
30. See Fedorov's letter in CHR, No. 2, p. 20.
31. According to data from Peter Reddaway. See his communication to representatives of the press dated Feb. 26, 1973, published by the International Committee for the Defense of Human Rights in the USSR.
32. CCE, No. 2.

33. CCE, No. 24, on Kukui; No. 18, on Burmistrovich.
34. CHR, No. 1, p. 5.
35. See P. G. Grigorenko, *Mysli sumasshedshego* (The Thoughts of a Madman), p. 13, Alexander Herzen Foundation, Amsterdam, 1973.
36. See Alexander Volpin, "An Eternal Handclasp to Peter Grigorenko," M., 1970, samizdat.
37. Fundamental Principles of Health Legislation, Article 36, *Sb. zak.*, Vol. III.
38. RSFSR Code of Criminal Procedure, Sect. 33.
39. See Record of Alexander Volpin's testimony before a congressional committee: *Abuse of Psychiatry for Political Repression in the Soviet Union*, Hearing before the Internal Security Subcommittee of the United States Senate, Sep. 26, 1972, pp. 47-177. U. S. Government Printing Office, Washington, D. C., 1972.
40. Letter from forty-four psychiatrists to the *London Times* (Sept. 16, 1971); see CCE, No. 24. See also a paper by Dr. Perry Ottenberg published in *Psychiatric Opinion*, Feb., 1974; and a report on the work of the Ad Hoc Group of the American Psychiatric Association after studying "Bukovsky's materials," *Psychiatric News*, July 5, 1972.
41. Proceedings of the Moscow Human Rights Committee, The International League for the Rights of Man, New York, 1972.
42. See note 39, p. 136.
43. See note 41, p. 134.
44. See note 39, p. 9.

Chapter 7, The Rights of Minorities

1. Ukaz of the Presidium of the RSFSR Supreme Soviet dated May 4, 1961, "On Stepping Up the Struggle against Persons Avoiding Socially Useful Labor and Leading an Antisocial, Parasitic Life." New version of this ukaz: *Vedomosti Verkhovnogo Soveta RSFSR*, 1970, No. 14, page 225. For a critique of these laws, see A. Tverdokhlebov's report to the Human Rights Committee in 1972, samizdat. See also CCE, No. 26.
2. Decree of the Moscow City Soviet dated Nov. 26, 1969, "On Measures for Reducing the Turnover of Cadres . . ."
3. See, for example, CHR, No. 5-6 on the Zabelyshensky case.
4. See Andrei Amalrik, *Involuntary Journey to Siberia*, Harcourt Brace Jovanovich, New York, 1970.
5. Ukaz of the Presidium of the USSR Supreme Soviet dated July 26, 1940. The proceedings instituted in accordance with this ukaz were handled by a single judge. On this point, see the ukaz of Aug. 10, 1940 (*Vedomosti Verkhovnogo Soveta SSSR*, Aug. 22, 1940).
6. RSFSR Criminal Code, Article 209-1.

7. Ibid., Article 198.

8. Ukaz of the USSR Supreme Soviet, Aug. 21, 1938.

9. *Sovetskoye finansovoye pravo* (Soviet Financial Law), M., 1961, p. 196.

10. Ukaz of Oct. 1, 1971 (*Vedomosti Verkhovnogo Soveta SSSR*, 1971, No. 40).

11. RSFSR Criminal Code, Article 121.

12. *Ugolovnoyo pravo, chast osobennaya* (Criminal Law: Special Part), A. A. Gershonzon and A. A. Pionkovsky, eds., M., 1939, p. 220.

13. Medvedev, Roy, *On Socialist Democracy*, Knopf, New York, 1975.

14. *Raboche-krestyanskiy korrespondent* (The Worker-Peasant Correspondent), 1930, No. 1, p. 44.

15. *Pravda* for March 15, 1960. Quoted in the book *Svoboda sovesti v SSSR* (Freedom of Conscience in the USSR) by F. M. Rudinsky, M., 1961.

16. Shafarevich, I. R., "Legislation on Religion in the Soviet Union: a Report to the Moscow Human Rights Committee" (Russian language), YMCA Press, Paris, 1973.

17. See Ashirov, Nuchman, *Evolyutsiya islama v SSSR* (The Evolution of Islam in the USSR), M., 1972.

18. N. Eshliman and G. Yakunin, "Open Letter to Alexi, Patriarch of All Russia," and "Statement to the Chairman of the USSR Supreme Soviet."

19. Ibid.

20. Talantov, "To the General Procurator of the USSR: a Complaint," city of Kirov, April 26, 1968, samizdat.

21. SP, No. 2, 1969.

22. These innovations are discussed in a letter from a group of priests and laymen to the Ecumenical Council.

23. "On the Liquidation of Relics," signed by Kursky, People's Commissar of Justice, *Sobr. uzak.*, No. 73, Aug. 27, 1920.

24. Rudinsky, F. M., *Svoboda sovesti v SSSR*, p. 55. See also note 16.

25. *XXII sezd KPSS*, III, 121.

26. RSFSR Criminal Code, Article 190-2.

27. Circular of the People's Commissariat of Justice dated Dec. 8, 1923, No. 254. See Gidulyanov, *Otdeleniye tserkvi ot gosudarstva v SSSR* (Separation of Church and State in the USSR).

28. CHR, No. 2, pp. 26-27.

29. CHR, No. 3, p. 44.

30. *Vedomosti Verkhovnogo Soveta SSSR*, 1956, No. 21. (By ukaz of Jan. 19, 1961, the norm on exile was revoked.)

31. CHR, No. 16.

32. See the ukaz on the Crimean Tatars and the Volga Germans, *Sb. zak.* I, 164–167. See also the documents of the Human Rights Committee on the rights of resettled peoples, CHR, No. 5-6.

33. RSFSR Criminal Code, Article 232.

34. *Vedomosti Verkhovnogo Soveta SSSR*, 1972, No. 52; CHR, Nos. 1 and 2.

35. See note 33, Article 235.

36. Ibid., Article 236.

Appendix 9, On the Rights of Persons Declared Mentally Ill

1. Orshansky, I. G. *Sudebnaya psikhopatologiya*. . . (Forensic Psychopathology . . .), St. Petersburg, 1899, p. 153. (Cited here in translation from the Russian.)

2. "Instructions on the Immediate Hospitalization of Mentally Ill Persons Representing a Social Danger," USSR Ministry of Public Health, October 10, 1961. Published in *Praktika sudebnopsikhiatricheskoi ekspertizy* (The Practice of Forensic Psychiatric Examination), G. V. Morozov, ed., Moscow, 1962.

3. "Regulations on Medical-Occupational Commissions of Experts," 1963. Published in *Sistematicheskoye sobraniye zakonov RSFSR* (Systematic Collection of Laws of the RSFSR), Vol. XI, Moscow, 1969.

4. *Osnovy zakonodatelstva Soyuza SSSR i soyuznykh republik o zdravookhranenii* (Fundamental Principles of the USSR and the Union Republics on Public Health), Moscow, 1970.

5. "Instructions on the Conduct of Forensic Psychiatric Examinations in the USSR," USSR Ministry of Public Health, October 27, 1970.

6. "Statute on Elections to the USSR Supreme Soviet," *Sbornik zakonov SSSR* (Collection of Laws of the USSR), Vol. I, Moscow, 1968.

7. "The Organization and Working Methods of Psychoneurological Dispensaries," Methodological Letter of the USSR Ministry of Public Health, 1962.

8. See note 4.

9. See note 5.

10. Ibid.

11. "Regulations for a Psychoneurological Dispensary . . . ," USSR Ministry of Public Health, 1958.

12. See note 5.

13. *Sovetski ugolovnyi protsess* (The Soviet Criminal Trial), ed. D. S. Karev, Moscow, 1968, p. 232.

14. See note 5.

15. See note 5.

16. See note 4.

17. See note 3.

18. "On Universal Military Service," Law of 1967, *Sbornik zakonov SSSR*, Vol. I.

19. See note 11.

20. See note 2.

21. See note 5.

22. Medvedev, Z., and Medvedev, R. *Kto sumasshedshii?*, samizdat, 1971; *A Question of Madness*, Knopf, 1971.

23. *Spravochnik nevropatologa i psikhiatra* (Handbook of the Neuropathologist and Psychiatrist), N. I. Grashenkov and A. V. Snezhnevsky, eds., Moscow, 1968.

24. United Nations Standard Minimum Rules for the Treatment of Prisoners.

25. Statute on Preliminary Custody.

26. *Sudebnaya psikhiatriya* (Forensic Psychiatry), G. V. Morozov and D. R. Lunts, eds., Moscow, 1971.

27. See note 5.

28. Ibid.

29. See note 4.

30. "Materials of a Diagnostic Seminar," Publications of the All-Union Society of Neuropathologists and Psychiatrists.

31. See note 5.

32. "The Gorbanevskaya Trial," samizdat, 1970.

33. See note 26, p. 157.

34. Ibid., p. 159.

35. Banshchikov, V. M., and Nevrozova, T. A. *Psikhiatriya* (Psychiatry), Moscow, 1969. B., p. 35.

35a. Chalidze, V. N. "Important Aspects of the Problem of Human Rights in the USSR," *Obshchestvennye problemy*, No. 8, samizdat, 1970.

36. D. R. Lunts, *Problema nevmenyaemosti . . .* (The Problem of Non-responsibility), Moscow, 1966.

37. See note 26, p. 178.

38. Methodological Letter "On the Experimental Psychological Examination of Patients. . ." Institute of Psychiatry, 1956.

39. See note 2.

40. Chalidze, V. N. *Obshchestvennye problemy*, No. 5, samizdat, 1970.

41. See note 7.

42. *Gosudarstvennoye pravo SSSR* (State Law of the USSR), S. S. Kravchuk, ed., Moscow, 1967.

43. Pisarev. "To the Presidium of the Academy of Medical Sciences," samizdat, 1970 (Appendix).

44. See note 26.

45. See note 42, p. 44.

46. See note 2.

47. Order No. 345/209 of the USSR Ministry of Public Health and the USSR Ministry of Internal Affairs, dated May 15, 1969.

48. See note 23.

49. Fainberg, V. "Letter from the Leningrad Special Psychiatric Hospital." "Notes on a Conversation with a Commission," samizdat, 1971.

50. Chernyshev, "An Appeal to Soviet Society," samizdat, 1971.

51. Gershuni, V. "Letter from a Special Psychiatric Hospital," samizdat, 1971.

52. "Instructions on the Procedure for Compulsory Treatment . . . ," 1967. Published in Morozov's *Praktika . . .* (See note 2).

53. *Problemy sudebnoi psikhiatrii* (Problems of Forensic Psychiatry), G. V. Morozov, ed., Moscow, 1961.

54. "Basic Regulations for the Organization and Operation of Psychiatric Colonies," USSR Ministry of Public Health, 1953.

55. See note 50.

56. See note 23.

57. See note 11.

58. See note 7.

59. See note 47.

INDEX

About the Author

VALERY CHALIDZE was born in Russia in 1938. In addition to being co-founder of the Moscow Human Rights Committee, he prepared and *signed* fifteen issues of the samizdat journal (underground manuscript) entitled *Social Problems*. In November 1972 he came to the United States to lecture at Georgetown University, but because of his very active part in making legal protests in the Soviet Union, he was deprived of his citizenship and refused reentry into Russia. He now lives in New York and lectures at various universities and before law groups. He is editor in chief of *A Chronicle of Human Rights in the USSR,* a bimonthly journal which reports on the human rights movement in the Soviet Union.

About the Translator

GUY DANIELS, a poet and novelist, is also the editor and translator of numerous French and (especially) Russian works of literature and history, including Stendhal's *Racine and Shakespeare, The Complete Plays of Vladimir Mayakovsky, A Lermontov Reader,* and *Russian Comic Fiction.* Mr. Daniels lives in New York City.